Cambridge Studies in French

POETRY AND FABLE

POETRY AND FABLE

*Studies in Mythological Narrative in
Sixteenth-Century France*

ANN MOSS

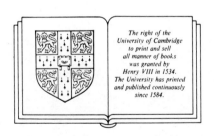

The right of the
University of Cambridge
to print and sell
all manner of books
was granted by
Henry VIII in 1534.
The University has printed
and published continuously
since 1584.

CAMBRIDGE UNIVERSITY PRESS

CAMBRIDGE

LONDON   NEW YORK   NEW ROCHELLE

MELBOURNE   SYDNEY

Published by the Press Syndicate of the University of Cambridge
The Pitt Building, Trumpington Street, Cambridge CB2 1RP
32 East 57th Street, New York, NY 10022, USA
296 Beaconsfield Parade, Middle Park, Melbourne 3206, Australia

First published 1984

Printed in Great Britain at
the University Press, Cambridge

Library of Congress catalogue card number: 83-27286

British Library Cataloguing in Publication Data
Moss, Ann
Poetry and fable. – (Cambridge studies in French)
1. French poetry – 16th century – History and criticism
I. Title
841′.3′09
ISBN 0 521 25889 8

CONTENTS

ILLUSTRATIONS

GENERAL EDITOR'S PREFACE

This series aims at providing a new forum for the discussion of major critical or scholarly topics within the field of French studies. It differs from most similar-seeming ventures in the degree of freedom which contributing authors are allowed and in the range of subjects covered. For the series is not concerned to promote any single area of academic specialization or any single theoretical approach. Authors are invited to address themselves to *problems*, and to argue their solutions in whatever terms seem best able to produce an incisive and cogent account of the matter in hand. The search for such terms will sometimes involve the crossing of boundaries between familiar academic disciplines, or the calling of those boundaries into dispute. Most of the studies will be written especially for the series, although from time to time it will also provide new editions of outstanding works which were previously out of print, or originally published in languages other than English or French.

ACKNOWLEDGEMENTS

I am indebted to the advice and criticism of friends and colleagues who have saved this book from some of its wilder surmises and grosser errors. My most profound debts are to fellow members of the Department of French at Durham University: to Professor Dudley Wilson for the example and encouragement of his devotion to sixteenth-century French literature and his commitment to research; to Jean Braybrook, whose recent thesis entitled 'The Epic Fragment in mid Sixteenth-century French Poetry' (D.Phil., University of Oxford, 1980) made her an exceptionally knowledgeable critic of the second half of the book; and, most of all, to Jennifer Britnell for putting me repeatedly to the test of her sharp and lucid comments, honed on her newly completed definitive study of Jean Bouchet. Professor Ian McFarlane was generous with suggestions and stimulated fruitful lines of inquiry, and Cambridge University Press did me excellent service in providing a most helpful reader.

My gratitude is also due to Durham University for financial help enabling me to visit libraries in London and Paris, and perhaps most crucial of all was the role of Krystyna Stenhouse who typed and retyped my drafts with seemingly inexhaustible good will.

INTRODUCTION

This book is about the way French writers of the sixteenth century read, imitated and adapted classical poetry of a particular kind. Its purpose is to investigate interconnections between modes of reading and modes of literary composition, with particular reference to texts dealing with mythological narrative, that is to say, fables about love and about the pagan gods. Renaissance art was preoccupied with classical fable and made many of its most important statements through it. The reaction of sixteenth-century readers to the mythological narratives they found in ancient authors touched the nerve centre of Renaissance poetry at two vital points. On the one hand, guides to reading pagan myths proposed interpretations for them and so bore upon the relationship of poetic fiction to truth. On the other hand, any close study of the original text of a fable, in the form of critical analysis or even translation, was inevitably bound up with contemporary methods for teaching writers their art by means of the imitation of Greek and Latin models, and literary imitation was basic to the modes of composition practised by later Renaissance poets. Nor are interpretation and imitation separate and distinct categories of literary activity. When a writer reproduces a model text, he reproduces what he has read in the way he has read it.

The work of contemporary French critics, whatever their particular orientation, is proving in general to be an invigorating force in Renaissance studies, precisely because they stress aspects of literary expression which preoccupied sixteenth-century writers. They have rediscovered how useful a tool is the formal rhetoric beloved of their humanist forerunners; they have given us a heightened awareness of the rôle of explicit and implicit textual allusion, which is axiomatic for the sense of works by Renaissance authors, educated as they were to write within, or sometimes against, a received literary tradition; they have taught us to think in terms of decoding texts, with emphasis on the reader's active response, and thus perhaps to put ourselves nearer to the Renaissance reader,

1

whether we envisage him applying systematic codes for exegesis, or using his text as a model for formulating discourse; they have alerted us to the erotic component in aesthetic experience, and so to the transferences between sexual and linguistic themes which are characteristic of late sixteenth-century poetry.[1] My own analysis of specific texts in this book owes much to my somewhat eclectic reading in contemporary criticism. It is my belief, however, that close reading of this sort can not only be illuminating about particular passages of writing, but is perhaps most exciting when it can bring into focus significant changes in the perspective of literature and indeed of man's view of himself and his context for thinking, reflected in the highly self-conscious mode of literary expression. Such shifts are historical phenomena, and my exposition of developments in sixteenth-century reading and writing draws on our knowledge of the history of changing attitudes to Greek and Roman mythology, of classical scholarship and educational practice, and of printing. In these fields, the basic premises for my thinking are provided by the magisterial syntheses of Seznec, Bolgar and Eisenstein, while the impetus to collate the techniques of historical investigation and literary criticism doubtless sprang initially from the brilliant studies made by Curtius in the medieval transformations of classical themes.[2] As I hope to demonstrate, Renaissance literature (and French Renaissance literature as a part of that whole) is a field in which the cross-fertilisation of critical analysis and historical scholarship is likely to be particularly fruitful. The culture derived from Renaissance humanism and its devotion to philology and rhetoric was highly verbal, and this may explain why the reactions obtained by linguistic methods of investigation are especially significant. In the far-fetched fables of the mythological narratives dear to sixteenth-century poets, where questions about the status of fiction are raised in their purest form, we can also hope to read clues pointing to a radical change in Western European perceptions of the relationship of literature to truth.

For the Renaissance, as for the later Middle Ages, the *Metamorphoses* of Ovid was the most important encyclopaedia of fable, a major progenitor of commentary on myths, and the most familiar model for narration. By looking at some sixteenth-century French translations, paraphrases and discussions of the *Metamorphoses* and related texts, I shall attempt to gauge developments in the way classical mythology was read and interpreted in that period.[3] For my analysis of the way fables were written at the time, I shall take examples from the work of Jean Lemaire de Belges, François Habert,

Jean-Antoine de Baïf and Ronsard. These authors, particularly when they draw on material from Ovid or closely associated with him, seem to me to demonstrate with peculiar clarity how the contemporary evolution in modes of reading altered the scope and content of mythological narratives written over a period of about eighty years. I do not intend to offer a complete history of mythological poetry in the sixteenth century nor of influences which shaped its development. I have decided to limit the breadth of this investigation (Italian influences, for example, because they are somewhat nebulous, receive rather less than their due), in order to attend more closely to the detail of my chosen texts and their reverberations. From this precise focusing it becomes clear how enormous, revolutionary even, were the changes both in reading and writing. Moreover, these changes involve other matters of major importance in the history of sixteenth-century literature, matters which are indeed related to the interpretation of classical fable and the transposing of literary models, but which will extend this inquiry more generally. My investigation will therefore embrace not only the direct imitation and citation of classical texts, but also the use poets made of literary allusion and the factors which conditioned it, notably the humanist practice of collecting quotations in commonplace books, and it will attempt some approaches to an aesthetic of sixteenth-century intertextual writing. It will also show that modes of interpreting classical fables were closely related to changing attitudes towards figurative language, and hence to developments in the use of metaphor and other tropes. Finally, there are connections to be made between changes in the writing of mythological narrative and a fundamental shift in the perspective of Renaissance poetry. For Lemaire fable is essentially a moral lesson for the discriminating reader. By the end of our period Baïf and Ronsard are employing Ovidian tales for a radically different purpose, to explore the nature of aesthetic experience and its erotic content.

The interplay between these various currents of thought and literary practice are often very subtle, but they have far-reaching effects. It is in the essays of Montaigne, who stands at the latter end of the chronological period covered by this book, that these currents run deepest and their interactions are most clearly perceived. When Montaigne turns his attention to the area we are about to explore, as he does in the essay *Sur des vers de Virgile* (Book III, number 5), we find him consciously drawing together themes and ideas which developments during the previous eighty years had made the common property of writers working in the last third of the sixteenth century. Without pretending to anything like an exhaustive analysis of Montaigne's essay, I shall use a small section of it as a prologue to the present study. It touches on many of the topics which will concern us and it expresses them and juxtaposes them in such a way as to show how real their interconnections were for the late Renaissance mind.

In his essay, Montaigne explores relationships between sexuality and language. From the verbal constraints exerted by taboo to the most articulate expression of sensual excitement, the essay is as much about language as it is about sexual behaviour. At the core of the essay, as its title suggests, lies the language of classical poetry. When Montaigne turns to himself he finds that it is not in searching his own memory that he recovers most fully the experience of love, but in reading the stylised formulations of poetic fiction, chiefly Virgil's description of Venus in the eighth book of the *Aeneid*:

Mais de ce que je m'y entends, les forces et valeur de ce Dieu [l'Amour] se trouvent plus vives et plus animées en la peinture de la poesie qu'en leur propre essence,

Et versus digitos habet.

Elle represente je ne sçay quel air plus amoureux que l'amour mesme. Venus n'est pas si belle toute nue, et vive, et haletante, comme elle est icy chez Virgile:

Dixerat, et niveis hinc atque hinc diva lacerti
Cunctantem amplexu molli fovet. Ille repente
Accepit solitam flammam, notusque medullas
Intravit calor, et labefacta per ossa cucurrit.
Non secus atque olim tonitru cum rupta corusco
Ignea rima micans percurrit lumine nimbos.
        Ea verba loquutus,
Optatos dedit amplexus, placidumque petivit
Conjugis infusus gremio per membra soporem.   (p. 949)[4]

Montaigne is not only reflecting here the humanists' predilection for ancient poetry and its prestige at the time. He is writing in a very particular way, inserting a quotation into his own composition and generating discourse by a play of interactions between his own thought and the interpolated text. Moreover, he returns to the subject of the literary expression of sexual desire later in the essay with another quotation from a poet, this time from Lucretius (p. 976). The textual layers become more complex, and indeed the essay turns at this point to an explicit discussion of textual allusions, literary imitation, the interference of verbal reminiscences, and questions about originality in written and spoken language. The discussion also focuses on matters of vocabulary and rhetorical figures, again derived

4

from a studied concentration on the words of the quoted passages. And here Montaigne moves towards a close identification of language style with vision:

Cette peinture est conduite non tant par dexterité de la main comme pour avoir l'object plus vifvement empreint en l'ame. Gallus parle simplement, par ce qu'il conçoit simplement. Horace ne se contente point d'une superficielle expression, elle le trahiroit . . . Son esprit crochette et furette tout le magasin des mots et des figures pour se representer; et les luy faut outre l'ordinaire, comme sa conception est outre l'ordinaire. (p. 977)

The particular vision at which Montaigne looks through the language of Virgil and Lucretius is that close association of the erotic with the aesthetic which is characteristic of Renaissance art. Poetry not only transfigures ordinary experience into something more quintessentially true, 'plus amoureux que l'amour mesme'; the image of Venus reflected in the language of literature is also more beautiful than anything reality can offer, 'Venus n'est pas si belle toute nue, et vive, et haletante, comme elle est icy chez Virgile'. Moreover, the poetic language which for Montaigne best exemplifies this transmutation of erotic delight into aesthetic pleasure is precisely the language of mythological narrative poetry. Both his chosen extracts are narrative in kind, both are about the goddess Venus, and both deal not directly in real life but in fable.

In Montaigne's essay the themes which will preoccupy us in this book coalesce to form the matrix for his speculations on the relationship between poetic language and erotic experience. Through close reading of narrative and fable, through quotation and textual allusion, through reflection on the transposition of Latin style to modern writing and the manipulation of rhetorical figures, Montaigne, like his contemporaries Baïf and Ronsard, moves towards the recovery of a vision in which the erotic connotations of aesthetic experience are recognised and reassessed in the new understanding of poetic language which we associate with the Renaissance. But quite what happened to poetry in France in the sixteenth century can only really be appreciated in the light of its previous history and by comparison with the concept of mythological fable which it inherited in its early years from the Middle Ages.

1

THE ALLEGORICAL TRADITION

In 1493, the Parisian printer Antoine Vérard, at the instance of the king, Charles VIII, published a French version of Ovid's *Metamorphoses*, which he entitled *Bible des poetes*. It was virtually a reproduction of an earlier compilation made in Bruges by the printer Colard Mansion and published there in 1484. Vérard's edition, a large volume of which we have copies beautifully illustrated by hand, seems meant for a wealthy and sophisticated vernacular readership. Its popularity over a period of about forty years is indicated by the fact that it was reprinted probably five times, twice by Antoine Vérard and three times by another Parisian printer, Philippe Le Noir, the last edition dating from 1531.

The book is a vernacular paraphrase of the fables of the *Metamorphoses*, but, embarking on the prologue (which paraphrases Mansion's first prologue to his 1484 edition), the reader steps not into Ovid's tangle of tales and turns but into a tidy scheme of explanations and interpretations. For, besides Ovid's stories, the book provides a compendium of ways to read his fables according to well-established methods, seeing that

les saiges et grans clercz . . . d'elles ont tiré allegoricquement, morallement, hystorialement, ou réallement aucunes veritez.   (1531 edn, fol. a ii)

These categories of interpretation are mentioned more than once in the prologue. The terminology of the text which follows is very muddled, as it is in most such texts in the late Middle Ages and early Renaissance, but essentially there are four contexts or 'senses' to be applied to each fable: physical, historical, moral (or tropological), and allegorical in the strict 'spiritual' definition. Each of these senses is on occasion called a morality or an allegorisation. The physical sense identifies the gods with their appropriate planets or with natural phenomena or parts of the human physiology, and it makes the fable represent an enactment of physical laws. Historically, the stories are read as enigmatic accounts of actual historical events (but these

6

'historical events', for example wars waged by kings with the same names as Ovid's gods and heroes, are often themselves patent fictions invented by the interpreter). Morally, the tales demonstrate the triumphs of various virtues and the punishment of numerous vices, and in this sense identifications are frequently made with analogous exemplars of good and evil conduct in late medieval society, kings and prelates, rapacious nobles and dishonest lawyers, pious priests and licentious ladies. In terms of spiritual allegory, the fables are to be read as demonstrations of the relationship between the soul and Christ, especially as it is seen in the narratives of Christ's Incarnation and Crucifixion.

These modes of rationalising pagan fables were not at all novel. They are a codification of practices evolved from late antiquity and were to last in various forms all through the Renaissance period.[1] Our particular text, the *Bible des poetes*, itself illustrates the long history of the allegorisation of Ovid. Colard Mansion, who compiled it, used a late fifteenth-century redaction in prose of a very long fourteenth-century poem, the *Ovide moralisé*. This poem had combined a version of Ovid's fables (and of fables from other sources, including the Judgement of Paris, which will concern us later) with various interpretations roughly falling into the fourfold schema of the *Bible des poetes*.[2] From his prose manuscript Mansion took his 'translation', in fact a paraphrase of the narrative parts of the medieval poem, as well as a certain number of such interpretations as the prose author had retained from the *Ovide moralisé*. To them Mansion added moral and allegorical interpretations from the *Ovidius moralizatus* of Pierre Bersuire (or Berchorius), another fourteenth-century text, in Latin, which itself was not printed until 1509.[3] Apart from a rather small number of what appear to be original interpretations or developments by Mansion himself, the *Bible des poetes* reproduces reading habits current in the fourteenth century, with which the early sixteenth century clearly still felt an affinity. The reader is invited to regard the literal sense of all mythological narratives as 'fable et fiction de poeterie', under which may be discovered expressions of the truth in very clearly defined contexts, physical, historical, moral, and spiritual. It is presumed that he holds these contexts and the meanings they give to his text simultaneously in his mind as he reads, and that he can make immediate equations between these senses and the text, and even, on occasion, between the senses themselves. One may also assume that these reading methods in their turn influenced contemporary writers and became a principle of composition. Before we look more closely at the status of polysemous reading in the early sixteenth century let us see how it operates in the case of one of Ovid's more sensual and erotic narratives, the story of Hermaphroditus and the water nymph Salmacis (*Metamorphoses*, Book IV, lines 285–388), joined together in an embrace which makes them for ever hermaphrodite (Plate 1).

Mansion's narrative of the Salmacis fable copies very closely the prose version of the fourteenth-century French poem. It is scrupulously faithful to the outline of the story as Ovid tells it and omits none of the events of the drama, but it reduces it to plot and dialogue. The exposition of the story is done almost entirely through verbs; and fifteen lines of Ovid (340–55) are summarised in a linear series of successive actions:

Quant Hermofroditus vit qu'elle s'en estoit allée et que seul estoit il se despouilla tout nud et s'en alla baigner en l'eaue de celle fontaine. Et quant Salmacis le veit nud et regarda sa belle et tendre chair qui par l'eaue se jouoit et nouoit elle fut plus eschauffée que devant. Elle se despouilla semblablement toute nue en l'umbre d'ung buisson. Puis s'en vint tout secrettement boutter en la fontaine et embrassa estroictement son amy Hermofroditus.

(1531 edn, fol. xxxviii)

On the other hand, the direct speech of the characters involved is reproduced almost without omission and even slightly expanded. The dialogue occupies a proportionately larger part of the episode as recounted in the *Bible des poetes*, and so now it seems that it is primarily dialogue that sustains the momentum and directs the narrative. What is totally lacking from the medieval version is figurative language and description. The fountain is simply 'belle clere et ferie'; the bodies are naked, but they are not allowed to move nor our eyes to linger (Ovid mentions six separate parts of the body and the vernacular version none); and of Ovid's eleven similes the *Bible des poetes* retains not one. This does not just mean that the French version dispenses with decoration in order to concentrate on the events of the narrative, although that is certainly so. More significantly, the French version cuts out the intricate pattern of cross-references which Ovid establishes through his metaphors and similes, enmeshing his story of sexual ambiguity in images where contraries meet and coalesce, red and white, hard ivory and liquid water, reflections and refractions of light in glass, upward thrust and downward spiral. Ovid deploys such figurative language within the narrative in order to amplify the resonances of the fable, but all the while, however extended its frame of reference becomes, this language keeps to the literal sense of the story and restates the theme of ambivalence. The French version does use the figurative mode and does require us to think metaphorically, but its use of metaphor is quite different. Only after the strictly non-figurative telling of the story do we come to passages interpolated by the editor which make detailed equations between the fable and three of the contexts used in allegorical interpretation. The suggested equations invite us to re-read the story as an extended metaphor or allegory of ideas not immediately apparent in the language of the narrative itself. Metaphor, when employed, as here, as a mode of interpretation, leads us to think in terms of concepts, whereas Ovid dealt primarily in analogies between material things; and it works towards substituting one meaning for another, rather than making variations on the literal sense.

Cestuy enfant Hermofroditus filz de Mercure peult signifier le benoist filz de dieu bel par dessus tous lequel au commencement decreta laisser son propre pays, assavoir paradis, et se transporta en aultre lieu, c'est en terre, à se baigner en la pure et clere eaue . . . Ceste nimphe Salmace peult signifier l'humaine nature lors donnée à oyseuse. Celle fontaine peult signifier la benoiste vierge clere et pure par dessus toutes . . . Finablement quant il luy pleut il descendit en la benoiste vierge Marie fontaine de misericorde. En laquelle ceste nimphe, c'est à dire la nature humaine, se conjoingnit tantost et ainsi furent deux natures divine et humaine mise ensemble.

(1531 edn, fol. xxxviii v°)

Alternatively, in the physical context, the fountain represents the womb with its seven cells, three for male children, three for females and one between for hermaphrodites, 'mais quant est à l'œuvre de nature le membre feminin peult plus que le masculin'. And, from the moral point of view,

Par Salmacis est entendue femme qui met sa cure et entente à elle farder, pigner et parer de joyaux et d'aornements pour abuser les musars et veult user toute sa vie en vanitez et desirs de la chair. Folz et devoyez sont ceulx qui ne les eschievent et fuyent.

(1531 edn, fol. xxxviii v°)

These interpretations of Hermaphroditus and Salmacis are derived directly from the fourteenth-century allegorisations of Ovid, the spiritual sense from Bersuire, and the physical and moral senses from the *Ovide moralisé* by way of the prose redaction.

Overall, the *Bible des poetes* transposes Ovid's text in five ways, in the literal 'translation' and in four allegorical variations. None of the interpretations has a particularly privileged position, and, moreover, there are often patent contradictions between interpretations of a single episode. In the Hermaphroditus story Salmacis may be read either as Christ's human nature or as a woman of easy virtue. Readings of this kind are basically an application of the principle of

1 Salmacis and Hermaphroditus: Ovid, *La Bible des poetes*, Paris, A. Vérard, 1493, fol. xl

2 Venus: Ovid, *La Bible des poetes*, Paris, A. Vérard, *c*. 1507, sig. b i v°

similitude. The reader's mind is exercised in establishing likenesses between elements in the original story (or at one remove from it, in the 'translation') and elements proper to the contexts represented by the four senses. Now the preface to the *Bible des poetes* stresses the usefulness of this mode of reading and suggests that it is a way to accommodate fiction to known truth, the 'facts' of history, science, moral behaviour and religion, 'parquoy tirer verité de fable et poeticque fiction est proffitable' (*Bible des poetes*, 1531 edn, fol. a ii). But there is no hint of any need for interpretations to cohere into a unified, homogeneous explanation of pagan mythology as a whole. In the same way, scriptural exegesis, to which the allegorical interpretation of pagan authors is closely related, stressed the fact that readings of scriptural metaphors differ according to context. A lion, for example, in the Bible may be interpreted either as an allusion to the devil or to Christ, depending on the points of similarity relevant to the context in which the metaphor is made to operate.[4] Reading mythological narrative as extended metaphor or allegory, based on similitudes perceived by the reader, directs attention away from the words of the author (and in the *Bible des poetes* we in fact start from words which have already replaced Ovid's). And it encourages the reader to use his own ingenuity to create for himself a variety of reconstituted texts to superimpose on the original.

Rosamund Tuve, in her book *Allegorical Imagery*, gave an intriguing and convincing analysis of polysemous texts circulating at the end of the fifteenth century and in the first two or three decades of the sixteenth century.[5] She was inclined to think that they supply a côterie interest and do not contribute directly to the mainstream development of French Renaissance literature. It is true that there is not much evidence of a direct influence of the *Bible des poetes* on other authors, in terms of verbal reminiscences of its interpretations. However, I think she did perhaps underestimate the legacy of these texts in terms of the reading habits they developed. The number of re-editions of the *Bible des poetes*, and the fact that they seem to have found a steady market for about fifty years at least, indicate that allegorical interpretation aligned to the four traditional senses provided an important key for decoding mythological texts and offered a blueprint for composing mythological narratives. Nor was the *Bible des poetes* by any means the only text of its type. Molinet's *Roman de la rose moralisé*, published in 1500, 1503, and again in 1521, claims to give the old poem a more modern air, precisely by inserting allegorical interpretations; and Geofroy Tory, a very different writer with predominantly humanist interests, uses the same framework at certain points in his *Champ Fleury* of 1529. The fact that the *Bible des poetes* was printed several times before the Latin work of Bersuire on which it largely draws perhaps indicates that allegorical reading was a more significant factor in vernacular literature than in Latin scholarship, although Bersuire's commentary was printed in France four times between 1509 and 1521, with an introduction by Josse Bade, who usually gave his attention to comparatively recent Italian humanist editions. Certainly the best-known handbook of French vernacular rhetoric in the period, the *Grant et vray art de pleine Rhetorique* of Pierre Fabri, defines poetry as metaphorical language and equates metaphorical language with the 'quatre manieres' of allegorical interpretation as they were used in Biblical exegesis.[6] But allegorical interpretation is far from being a French idiosyncrasy. Probably the strongest authority was given to this mode of reading by the *Genealogia deorum gentilium* of Boccaccio, who provided a vast range of physical, historical and moral explanations and equations for the pagan gods, although he was less inclined than the *Bible des poetes* to make direct analogies with doctrinal Christian belief. For the Salmacis story, typically, he gives the physical interpretation reproduced also in the *Ovide moralisé* and the *Bible des poetes*, but not the spiritual one, nor more unusually the moral one.[7] The Latin text of the *Genealogia* was first printed in Italy in 1472 and in France in 1511, and French translations were published in 1498 by Antoine Vérard and in 1531 by Jean Petit and Philippe Le Noir. So both Vérard and Le Noir were printing the *Bible des poetes* at the same time as the *Genealogia*, which tends to confirm that there was a safe market for allegorical interpretations.

However, the allegorical interpretation inherited from the fourteenth century was not the only mode of reading current in the early years of the sixteenth century, and the way it was opposed and modified by rival methods is part of the history of the reception of Italian humanism in France. One strand in Italian thought seems in many ways to lend support to traditional French reading habits. This is the neo-Platonism represented by such thinkers as Marsilio Ficino and Giovanni Pico della Mirandola and adapted to the elucidation of pagan poetry in the commentaries which Landino made on Virgil. The Italian neo-Platonists apply the categories and the methods of allegorical interpretation to mythological narrative. The sheer ingenuity of their explanations matches that of the French, and they too divert attention from the original words of their texts to reformulations elaborated by their speculations on similitudes. 'Allegory', says Landino, 'is concerned not with what words mean but with what is hidden under a figure of speech.'[8] But there is a major difference in the status they give to the interpretations they make. The neo-Platonists are syncretists who postulate that the mythology of the ancients and the poetry in which it is expressed contain the same essential truths as those revealed by the Christian religion, but in a more obscure tradition and in need of elucidation by those who understand the analogies on which the universe is patterned. This means that the interpretation of poetry can uncover invariable truths, quite different in their status from the *ad hoc* associations made in the *Bible des poetes*. It also means that, whereas the *Bible des poetes* is neutral in its listing of self-contradictory, alternative but equally valid equations, the neo-Platonists initiate discussions about which is the 'correct' reading of a text.[9] Later French poets using mythological material as metaphor often slip, unconsciously, between the neo-Platonist assertion that poets disclose the truth and the more medieval view of secular poetry and mythology as mere figure of speech.

Another strand of Italian humanism was to be more influential in France, not least because it was communicated through the most used school-texts of the time. The late fifteenth-century Italian commentaries which surround the early printed texts of classical poets, such as Raphael Regius's much reproduced commentary on the *Metamorphoses*, promote quite a different form of reading activity. As in the older commentaries, the first stage of reading is paraphrase, but the humanist annotators are preoccupied with the language of their author and the precise functioning of words in their original context. They treat metaphor as a form of linguistic usage, rather than as an agent of interpretation, and mythology as a factor in ancient culture to be documented by accumulating references from other texts. If reading is to incorporate any extension outside the passage to hand, it will be an extension to a specific text which is part of the humanist canon of recognised authorities. The similitudes in the *Bible des poetes* appear as a product of the commentator's own inventiveness; Mansion was only interested in finding likenesses, not in their history or their pedigree, and he makes only occasional references to mythographers like Fulgentius, who is the ultimate source of many of his interpretations. But the humanist mode of reading is carefully controlled and authenticated by the use of textual references. For the Salmacis fable alone, the Regius edition refers to Sextus Pompeius, Ennius, Cicero *De Officiis*, Vitruvius, Juvenal, Horace, and Pliny. All these allusions help to establish the literal meaning of Ovid's words, the only excursus from the text being into what was thought to be well-documented cultural history by way of

14

Vitruvius's account of the civilising of barbarian tribes in the region in which the fable is located, through contact with the 'softer' manners of the Greeks.[10]

No writer of this period was more sophisticated in his response to these different approaches to reading mythological narratives than was Jean Lemaire de Belges. In the next chapter we shall examine in some detail his complex re-creation of the fable of the Judgement of Paris, looking carefully at the modes of language he uses, at the relationships he establishes between his account and other texts, and at his use of allegorical interpretation. The chief divinity of the episode is, of course, Venus herself. Before seeing her through Lemaire's eyes, let us meet her in the guise in which she was presented to Lemaire's contemporaries in the first chapter of the *Bible des poetes*, which translates Bersuire's description of the pagan gods at the beginning of his *Ovidius moralizatus* and provides it with woodcut illustrations (Plate 2):

Venus doit estre painte en la forme d'une tres belle pucelle nue navigant dessus la mer, tenant en sa main une lamine ou plataine d'ardoise aornée et environnée de roses et de fleurs, et dessus des colombz voletans environ elle et si estoit assignée en mariage à Vulcan le dieu du feu qui estoit tres laid et tresdifforme. Devant elle estoient trois jeunes filles nues qui s'appelloyent trois graces desquelles les faces des deux estoient tournees vers elle. Et la tierce luy tournoit le dos. Au plus pres de Venus estoit son filz Cupido empenné de pennes pour voler, mais il estoit aveugle. Et d'ung arc qu'il tenoit tiroit à Apolo une fleche. Pourquoy les dieux furent troublez, l'enfant moult paoureux s'enfuyt mucer de costé sa mere. L'exposition literale à ceste fable si est que toutes ces choses dessusdictes peuvent estre atribuées à la planette qui est dicte Venus, car elle est de femenine complexion. Et si est painte en l'espesse d'une pucelle nue. Elle est chaulde humide: et si est dicte estre mariée à Vulcan qui est le feu: Elle est constituée sur mer affin qu'elle soit congneue estre conjoincte à chaleur at à moysteur. Et pource dit on qu'elle conceupt Cupido le dieu d'amours: c'est à dire la concupiscence de la chair: pour cause que pour sa chaleur et moysteur on dict ceste estoylle esmouvoir la concupiscence de la chair.

Delaissé doncques cest litteralle exposition pouvons moralement entendre par ceste deesse selon Fulgence la vie voluptueuse ou chascune personne voluptueuse et luxurieuse: qui est dicte femme par son inconstance inevitable: on la paingt en navigant en mer pource qu'elle veult tousjours estre en delices: tenant en sa main une ardoyse marine, de laquelle on danse ou chante, car tousjours elle veult estre en lyesses. Pourneant n'est volupté luxurieuse figurée en feminine forme: car elle dure neant ou pou. Elle est nue, car l'homme à peine la peult il celer et ne peult estre qu'elle n'apere, et si veult nager tousjours en la mer c'est à dire en opulence et habondance de delices, s'esjouyr en vaines lyesses. Venus est faincte estre engendrée en mer et c'est pource que luxure est engendrée et causée d'opulantes richesses et delices. A ce propos semble la saincte escripture parler au .xiii. chapitre de ysaie disant Passe ta terre comme ung fleuve de mer: et puis ensuyt: prens ta harpe. Ceste volupté nourrist les colombz c'est à dire les luxurieux: elle ayme les roses ce sont les curiositéz de ce monde: elle produist Cupido son filz c'est à dire la concupiscence de la chair, qui Apolo, c'est à dire les hommes justes navre et tresperce par les sajettes de ses temptations.   (1531 edn, fols. b i v°–b ii)

Venus is said to be 'une tres belle pucelle nue', but her allurements are minimal, her only attribute being the flower-bedecked slate which she had picked up by mistake over the course of centuries.[11] This goddess of love and beauty is in effect neither beautiful nor erotic. What the text solicits is a severely intellectual response akin to puzzle-solving. Venus and her companions are riddles, and it is suggested that the only way to read them is to choose a context for interpretation and to scrutinise the mythical figures and the relationships between them for analogies with it. So, translated as a planet and then as a moral abstraction, Venus disembarks with something less than her antique grace into the world of the French Renaissance.

2

THE THREE GODDESSES: JEAN LEMAIRE DE BELGES

The story

In Chapters 28 to 35 of the first book of his *Illustrations de Gaule et Singularitez de Troye*[1] Jean Lemaire de Belges relates the story of the marriage of Peleus and Thetis and the Judgement of Paris, the moment when, as Homer says, 'the trouble first began and Paris fell into the fatal error of humiliating the two goddesses at their audience in his shepherd's hut by his preference for the third, who offered him the pleasures and the penalties of love'.[2] The *Iliad* makes only this passing reference to the origin of the Trojan War, but in Lemaire's history of the Trojans and their descendants the episode is crucial, it comes at the right chronological moment near the beginning of the work, and its importance is stressed by the length and complexity of its telling. This complexity will be the subject of this chapter, but underlying it runs a basic narrative of events, which in Lemaire's version are as follows.

In Chapter 28, we find a lovelorn Paris away from his Oenone, keeping his sheep in a wooded landscape. There we leave him for the company of the gods and goddesses of the pagan world, who have converged on Mount Pelion in order to celebrate the marriage of Peleus and Thetis. Chapter 29 describes the wedding feast, which is interrupted in the next chapter when Discord, uninvited and unwelcome, throws the famous golden apple inscribed 'to the fairest' in the direction of three goddesses, Juno, Pallas Athene and Venus. All three lay claim to it; Jupiter refuses to judge between them, and on the advice of Ganymede and Mercury, Paris is chosen to award the apple to the goddess he thinks best qualified to receive it. Mercury conducts the goddesses to Paris in his rural retreat. Chapters 31 and 32 present each goddess in turn, first through a detailed description of her dress and adornment and then by means of the long speech by which each seeks to persuade Paris of her superior beauty and power, not forgetting the gifts which will be his in return for the apple. Paris, bemused but unabashed, requests a second view of the goddesses' charms, this time naked, and Chapter 33 describes the undressing of the goddesses and the wonder of all nature at their beauty. Paris bows to the influence of Venus and pronounces in her favour, whereupon Juno and Pallas depart in high dudgeon, leaving Paris to be consoled by Venus and the thought of the new wife, Helen, whom she has promised him. Chapter 34 returns us to the assembly of the gods, where Apollo puts the judgement pronounced by Paris in the context of the history of Troy, doomed to destruction through this fatal choice, yet destined to rise again to glory in the deeds of its future descendants in Western Europe. The harmony of the marriage feast is shattered by discord between the gods, and, on earth too, at the end of Chapter 35, the happiness of Paris and his wife Oenone is troubled by suspicion and fear.

Texts and contexts

Such in outline are the events of the story, although this bald summary bears no resemblance to Lemaire's style of narrative, with its elaborate language and intricate cross-references. In fact the reader's initial approach to the episode is not through story-telling at all, but through Lemaire's prologue to the first book of his *Illustrations*, where certain contexts are suggested for the fable and certain expectations roused in the reader. The prologue presents the matter of the whole work in the form of a commentary on the Judgement of Paris. Paris is introduced as the central figure of the first book of the *Illustrations*, 'duquel la vie nous est principalement deduite en ce volume' (p. 5), and in his encounter with the goddesses lies 'l'esclarcissement de toute l'histoire Troyenne' (p. 4). In so far as Lemaire is writing a history, the judgement scene is given proper prominence as the cause of subsequent events in the chronicle.

But it is also the crucial moment in the moral evolution of Paris, and the goddesses themselves are first presented to us as symbols for a tripartite division of the hero's life into his adolescence and his earlier and later maturity, a schema which in turn is used to explain the organisation of Lemaire's material in his three volumes, 'dediez et intitulez aux seigneuries et hautesses de trois grands Deesses: c'estasavoir, Pallas, Venus, et Juno' (p. 5). The moral interpretation of the fable is then extended outside the book and we are invited to read it as instruction for young princes in general and the future Emperor Charles V in particular. Already Lemaire has set the reader looking for possible equations for his characters and their actions. The precise identifications Lemaire makes in his prologue are not picked up again when we come to the actual episode in the text. Lemaire has not pre-empted our understanding of the fable. But he has made sure that the reader will associate the judgement story very closely with allegorical reading and has alerted him to parallels and plural senses.

Yet another figure connects the prologue with our fable and that is Mercury. Mercury, 'language itself', is the tutelary spirit of the *Illustrations*.[3] As god of eloquence he himself writes the prologue, and we shall see later that Lemaire habitually uses Mercury and his attributes to talk about the operations of language. In the prologue Mercury introduces the main rhetorical modes of the *Illustrations*: first, the mode of clearly stated and authenticated historical fact, the refutation of error on which Lemaire the humanist and historian so prided himself; and, secondly, the essentially figurative mode which deals in similitudes and allegorical interpretation, and grafts complicated patterns of interrelated meanings onto the basic narrative. The two modes are not felt to be mutually exclusive. Indeed, Lemaire affirms that no intelligent sense can be made of either history or fable, unless they are related accurately and unless their full implications are developed in the telling. For this purpose Mercury has encouraged Lemaire to:

redresser, et ressourdre ladite tresnoble histoire, qui presques estoit tombée en decadence, et depravation ruïneuse, comme si elle fust d'estime frivole, et pleine de fabulosité par la coulpe des dessudits mauvais escrivains, qui ne l'ont sceu desveloper, laquelle certes est veritable et fertile, et toute riche de grans mysteres et intelligences poëtiques et philosophales, contenant fructueuse substance souz l'escorce des fables artificielles.   (p. 4)

Mercury makes a specific point of associating his claims to express truth in fiction with his rôle at the judgement of Paris:

veu que à moy (plus que à nul autre) des esprits celestes appartenoit de procurer la restauration d'icelle histoire, attendu, que je fuz (comme chacun scait) ministre presential au jugement des trois Deesses.   (p. 4)

In Chapter 28 the reader begins to move towards Paris's eventual choice of Venus, aware that this episode is going to be a focal point for Lemaire's preoccupations with language and with interpretative reading, as well as with the history of Troy. One of the main ways in which Lemaire keeps the reader alive to the presence of these themes in the narrative is by making intermittent references to other texts. Cross-references to other books and authors and occasional direct quotations from them constitute one of the most immediately obvious characteristics of the *Illustrations*. By way of his literary allusions, Lemaire gives us specific directions for establishing a context for our reading of the Paris episode. At times, he is using them primarily as authorities, to authenticate his history. Such references are common enough in medieval books and occur throughout the *Illustrations*. But they also have a more purely literary purpose. One of Lemaire's earliest productions was probably an anthology of classical and religious texts, carefully arranged so as to create patterns of likenesses and antitheses, in effect a new work in the reader's mind.[4] The same principle of multi-textual composition underlies his account of the marriage of Peleus and Thetis and the Judgement of Paris, to which he attaches a cluster of texts expressing a range of commentary on the fable, from the purely factual to the highly figurative. Some texts are quoted at length, some mentioned more obliquely, but all are identified quite precisely and listed for further reference at the end of the volume. In supplying this bibliographical information Lemaire seems to be suggesting that a complete reading and proper judgement of his work involves an interplay in the reader's mind between his own words and the texts he appends to the narrative. This rather controlled form of literary allusiveness points the reader in very specific directions. Some of the texts are apparently introduced to guarantee the accuracy of the narrative and give it the status of historical truth rather than arbitrarily invented fiction. These are:

(1) Virgil, *Priapeia* (p. 205); the reference is to a short mnemonic poem, *Quae quorum locorum sint numina*, included in some early editions of Virgil's works, for example Venice, 1480 (where the *Priapeia* is unfoliated).

(2) Homer, *Iliad* (p. 228), Book III, lines 39, 46, 54–5, quoted in a Latin verse translation, which, so far, I have failed to find.

(3) Euripides, *Iphigenia* (p. 228), in the translation by Erasmus (Paris: J. Bade, 1506).

(4) Pius II, *Descriptio Asiae* or *Cosmographia* (p. 260), printed at Venice in 1477, and in an edition by G. Tory at Paris in 1509.

(5) Dictys Cretensis, *Ephemeris belli troiani* (pp. 270, 271), of which several editions were printed before 1500.

For the basic content and disposition of the narrative of the Judgement of Paris, 'la structure literale', Lemaire claims to have followed to some extent:

> Apuleius, *De Asino aureo* (p. 272), almost certainly the edition with the commentary by Philippus Beroaldus (Bologna, 1500) which he had mentioned previously (p. 120).

But embedded in his text are the senses of traditional allegorical interpretation, as we have already met them in the *Bible des poetes*, and again our explorations within these contexts are directed by specific references as follows:

for the historical sense:

> Dictys Cretensis, *Ephemeris* (p. 271).

for the physical sense:

(1) Fulgentius, *Enarrationes allegoricae fabularum* (p. 271), doubtless the edition by J. B. Pius (Milan, 1498) listed at the end of Book II of the *Illustrations*.

(2) Julius Firmicus Maternus, *Matheseos libri VIII* (p. 273), published at Venice in 1497.

for the moral sense:

> Fulgentius, *Enarrationes* (p. 272).

for the spiritual or allegorical sense:

> Clement of Rome, *Recognitiones Petri Apostoli* (pp. 273–5); the only available printed edition was by Lefèvre d'Etaples, published with his *Paradysus Heraclidis* (Paris: J. Petit, 1504).

Rather more pervasive throughout these chapters of the *Illustrations* are references to incidents from Ovid's *Metamorphoses* and the *Heroides*, and reminiscences of Boccaccio's *Genealogia deorum gentilium*, which plays a much larger part in Lemaire's description of his gods and goddesses than his actual references (pp. 205, 270) would let us guess. To the texts mentioned we must add the commentaries to which he alludes either here or elsewhere in the *Illustrations*. These form yet another layer in the complex infrastructure of Lemaire's narrative, and the commentaries make further references to other texts. Lemaire doubtless picked up the passage in Firmicus Maternus (p. 273) from the commentary by J. B. Pius on Fulgentius (1498 edition, fol. e ii + 2v°); and the actual plot of the story as Lemaire tells it seems to me to conform most nearly to the summary given by Ubertinus Clericus in his commentary on the *Heroides* (Lyons: J. de Vingle for E. Gueynard, 1503, fols. i v°–ii), a commentary which Lemaire definitely used in his first volume (pp. 133, 198). The ramification of texts and commentaries grows round the original fable very much as commentaries encircle the text of an early humanist edition, and invites a similar mode of cross-reading. The texts to which Lemaire makes explicit reference and which he lists in his bibliography are printed texts. Like the humanist commentators, he is exploiting the fact that the printing-press has made it comparatively easy for the individual reader to juxtapose a number of texts and make cross-references. Of course, the reader may choose not to follow up these allusions, but in that case he delimits the meaning of the narrative, which is fully realised only by reference from text to text. Lemaire has seen potential here both for increasing and for orientating the range of response his work may solicit from the intelligent and well-informed reader.

Once we have been alerted to Lemaire's multi-textuality, it is inevitable that we should look for traces of texts other than those he names. Apart from the episode in Apuleius's *Golden Ass*, the most famous versions of Lemaire's material available in ancient literature are Catullus's poem on the marriage of Peleus and Thetis (no. LXIV), and Lucian's dialogue on the Judgement of Paris. Lemaire does not refer specifically to Catullus, but there had been several Italian editions of his poems since 1472 and Lemaire was certainly acquainted with some of his work.[5] If he does owe anything to Catullus, it would be the overall design of the work, as we shall see later. Pius refers to Lucian in his Fulgentius commentary, as does Beroaldus in his notes on Apuleius, and both quote him in Greek, but there does not seem to have been a printed Latin translation of the relevant dialogue before the publication of the *Illustrations*. Nevertheless, the Greek text was available and interest had been aroused by Erasmus's translation of selected dialogues (Paris, 1506).[6]

Catullus and Lucian are possible further factors in the formal structure of Lemaire's narrative, and in the quality of his overall vision of the pagan gods, if not in the detail of its expression. These authors may have only very ghostly echoes, but there are much more substantial ghosts than these. There is a group of texts Lemaire does not mention at all, and which are indeed conspicuous by their absence. The story of the Judgement was far more widespread in medieval literature than in classical versions. Lemaire must have met it in at least one example of each of its two most influential medieval forms:

(1)   Benoît de Sainte-Maur, *Le Roman de Troie*, lines 3845–921 (ed. L. Constans (Paris, 1904), I, pp. 196–200), and its derivatives, notably Guido de Columnis, *Historia destructionis Troiae* (ed. N. E. Griffin (Cambridge, Mass., 1936), pp. 61–3). The latter was printed seven times between 1477 and 1494. Lemaire mentions it deprecatingly (p. 127). It was from this source that most early woodcuts of the scene derive, perpetrating the errors that so scandalised Lemaire in 'peintures et tapisseries modernes . . . faites apres le patron desdites corrompues histoires' (p. 4). Such woodcuts had been most widely disseminated in the 1490s in printed editions of Raoul Le Fèvre's *Recueil des hystoires troyennes*, where, as in Columnis, the goddesses appear naked to the sleeping Paris in a dream. There is also an

3   The Judgement of Paris: Lucas Cranach, 1508

important woodcut by Cranach, dated 1508, which belongs to the same tradition and forms the model for several subsequent pictures by the same artist (Plate 3).

(2) *Ovide moralisé*, Book XI, lines 1242–2533 (ed. C. de Boer and J. T. M. van't Sant, 5 vols. (Amsterdam, 1915–38), IV, pp. 147–78), and texts based on this, for example:

(i) Guillaume de Machaut, *La Fonteinne amoureuse*, lines 1633–2144 (*Œuvres*, ed. E. Hoepffner, 3 vols. (Paris, 1908–21), III, pp. 201–19)

(ii) Christine de Pisan, *Le Livre du chemin de long estude*, lines 6144–92 (ed. R. Püschel (Berlin 1887, reprinted Geneva, 1974), pp. 260–2)

(iii) *La Bible des poetes.*

To affect to disregard these texts indicates a deliberate intention on Lemaire's part. He is dissociating himself from previous vernacular literature and placing his telling of the fables very firmly in the context of ancient literature, Boccaccio's *Genealogia*, and contemporary humanist (primarily Italian) scholarship. Nevertheless, the interpretative schemes associated with the *Ovide moralisé* linger tenaciously in his text, validated, as we have noted, by references to Dictys, Fulgentius, Firmicus Maternus, and Clement of Rome. Lemaire defines his vision partly by opposing and ignoring the medieval tradition, but partly, as we shall see, by rehabilitating it in his own style, marking out common ground between the tradition and his acknowledged authorities.

One other version of the Judgement remains, with particular relevance to the rôle of Venus in Lemaire's exposition. In volume two of the *Illustrations* Lemaire refers twice to the epistles of Marsilio Ficino,[7] and Ficino discusses the Judgement of Paris in a letter dated 1490.[8] This text, in which Venus emerges as the pleasure principle underlying all human endeavour, brings into play the possible influence of Italian neo-Platonist thinking on Lemaire's treatment of the goddess of love and beauty. The Venus chosen by Paris has only the most slender of Italian connections[9] and Lemaire will not put her in a fully developed Italian context until the *Concorde des deux langages*, published in 1513. But already in 1511 his ambivalent, seductive and dangerous goddess is associated with a particular aesthetic and a particular language. A choice of moral and aesthetic values is being offered and Lemaire deploys all the resources of a sophisticated rhetorical tradition to put these opposing values in terms of different language codes. It is to Lemaire's use of language, and especially his use of its figurative and allegorical modes, that we shall now turn.

Men and gods

Lemaire's narrative in Chapters 28 to 35 moves between two spatial contexts, the world of men and the world of gods, with a conjunction of the two in the scene of Paris's choice. The fable itself suggests this structure. In their earlier literary forms the stories of the marriage of Peleus and Thetis and the Judgement of Paris were in fact two separate episodes, not related by any very well-known author before the second-century mythographer Hyginus, from whom the account in the *Ovide moralisé* tradition ultimately derives.[10] Lucian and Apuleius do not mention the marriage of Peleus and Thetis, and Catullus does not mention the apple or Paris. Nevertheless, Catullus does extend the dimensions of his poem by including within it the story of the desertion of Ariadne, and ending with the prophetic song of the Fates foretelling the doom of Achilles and the war of Troy. There are no verbal reminiscences of Catullus in Lemaire, but there are notable parallels in the structure of the two accounts. Both revolve on a contrast between the felicity of the marriage feast in heaven and desertion and betrayal of human love on earth. Both cloud a bright vision of celestial harmony, to end their narrative with the tragedy of human history and the theme of paradise lost. Lemaire may have found a pattern in Catullus for the grand scale on which he elaborates his material, while the antithesis on which Catullus's poem is built would have reinforced his instinct for a basically spatial ordering of the narrative, with clearly defined places for divine and human action. This diagrammatic principle of narrative exposition, planned on a series of successive locations, underlies virtually all the serious allegorical literature of the period. It will reappear in a much clearer way in the separate temples of Venus and Minerva in Lemaire's *Concorde des deux langages*. Here, as there, two different visions disclose themselves in two different places and in two different languages.

The human world is the world of pastoral. Paris is a shepherd and is clearly placed in a pastoral context, in terms of both place and language. The moral parameter of this world is identified by Lemaire's cross-reference to Terence which stands at the beginning of his description of the pastoral paradise where we find Paris (p. 200). This is the realistic mode of comedy, the mode of ordinary domestic life. Paris is consistently associated with nature, with trees, vegetation and birds. His food, in contrast with the urbane luxury of the marriage feast of the gods, is frugal and natural, 'un peu de pain avec des dattes, et des franches meures, qu'il avoit cueilli souz les arbres prochains' (p. 227). Even his faculty of judgement has taken him no further than the evidence of nature, a point we must infer from the anecdote about a rustic competition of which Paris had been judge (pp. 224–5). In the complete version of this episode (as told for example by Bersuire) the bull to whom Paris gave a prize for strength was really Mars in disguise. Paris trusts the evidence of his senses, without discerning the truth beneath appearances.

Lemaire does not merely describe the elements of this pastoral vision of man's natural state. It is encapsulated in a particular language. Ancient and medieval rhetoric both made a distinction between high, middle, and low styles, and medieval theorists in particular, basing their definitions on Virgil's three works, the *Aeneid*, the *Georgics*, and the *Eclogues*, had identified pastoral with the low style.[11] This does not necessarily imply either vulgarity or plainness, at least to the medieval mind. Lemaire deliberately keeps a consistently elevated level of diction by using aureate or Latinical vocabulary as a common factor throughout his narrative, and we find it in the pastoral passages, for example 'Le doux vent Favonius . . . faisoit cresper doucettement et figurer multiformement la partie superficielle des nobles undes de Scamander' (p. 202). But the low style is essentially linear, it tends to preclude metaphorical expression and figures of thought, and it is marked by frequent use of diminutives.[12] The language through which we see Paris in his natural habitat is precisely the language of this low style:

Si s'en alloit souventesfois à tout sa panetiere et sa houlette, sa harpe et ses flageoletz et musettes, menant paitre ses berbisettes, et ses chevres, et ses gras bœufz et toreaux en la valee prochaine. (p. 200)

When we return to the human dimension after a long visit to the gods, the language reverts accordingly:

Et tout alentour du berger ses chevres broutans les branchettes des arbres, ses berbisettes et ses toreaux paissans l'herbe menue, espesse et drue. (p. 227)

All the description of the *locus amoenus* in which Paris is located is coded in this style. It can be amplified and elaborated, but only in certain ways. The mode of amplification proper to it is through accumulation of words, more particularly of nouns, for example in the long lists of trees and birds on pages 202 and 203. Within such lists further ornamentation is possible, although confined to the sound of the words, through patterns of alliteration, assonance, rhyme and rhythm, for example:

estourneaux, merles, mauvis, jays, loriotz, masenges, nonnettes, pies, picz
vers, pinçons, pyvoines, passerons, serins, tarins, verdiers, calandres, lynot-
tes, aloettes, et autres de diverses especes. (p. 202) (Note the alphabetical
progression, as well as the alliteration and assonance.)

Il chantoit sur sa harpe harmonieuse. (p. 202) (assonance, and a standard
rhythmical pattern for the end of a phrase, the *cursus planus*; Lemaire
frequently uses the rhythmical patterns established in elaborate medieval
Latin prose)

But although this language can produce endlessly interlocking
patterns of sound, it does not transcend its function as an agent for
naming particulars in the external world and arranging them into
categories. Moreover, these categories are taxonomic classes, where
trees, birds and so on are grouped according to purely physical
likenesses, and they never cross boundaries of sense in the way that
metaphor does. It is a literal language, not a figurative one (apart
from figures of sound), and the world we see through it is purely
physical, a material world of objects in space. This is not the language
of the gods, as we shall see shortly. How far it differs is stressed by the
description of human music (p. 228), which Lemaire puts in pointed
contrast to the music of the gods (pp. 218–20). The language through
which we hear Paris's pastoral notes is prosaic and factual, not the
language of music at all, but the language of historical minutiae.
Lemaire quotes Homer, Euripides, and the example of David in the
Old Testament in order to confirm that Paris knew how to play
musical instruments, 'parquoy il suffit qu'il appere, que non feinte-
ment nous luy avons atribué la science du jeu de la harpe. Qu'il
sceust aussi jouer des flutes et musettes pastorales.'[13] He says nothing
about the music Paris played.

Lemaire's literal vision of nature owes nothing to the language of
classical poetry, but at the beginning of this section of his narrative,
true to his multi-textual mode of composition, he insinuates another
text into the reader's consciousness. Paris's valley literally is
'Mesaulon', but it is like Tempe, 'dont Ovide fait vne belle
description en son volume de Metamorphose' (p. 201). While the
language of nature in Lemaire's pastoral is entirely neutral, recurring
reminders of this other text, the *Metamorphoses* (and on one
occasion, the *Heroides*), hint at darker, sadder things, the tale of
Philomela (p. 202), and Paris's eventual desertion of Oenone (p. 202;
the quotation is from *Heroides* v, lines 21–32, where Oenone
reproaches Paris for his infidelity). The references to Ovid become
more insistent at the end of the story, when we return to the natural,
human world of Paris and Oenone, now under threat of disinte-

4   The Judgement of Paris: engraving of a picture by Luca Penni after a design
by Raphael, 1543–5

gration. Oenone's language is full of the shifting forms of Ovid's
unstable universe, Actaeon, Niobe, Arachne, Antigone, Semele (pp.
277–8). These allusions fill the pastoral paradise with dark forebodings, but note that the fables are to be understood in a literal sense, or
at most as examples of impious behaviour. There is no allegorical
interpretation. Indeed, Oenone does not know 'en quel sens interpreter la vision de Paris' (p. 276), and the list of metamorphoses
emphasises her puzzled state of mind, but does not help her to
understanding. A literal reading of Ovid belongs to the same stylistic
register and reproduces the same vision as the low style of pastoral.

Shortly after the beginning of Chapter 28 we move from the place
of men to the place of gods, and from one mode of language to
another. The transition is marked by a periphrasis, whose literal sense
(the astrological conjunction of the Sun and Aries) is also a
synecdoche (it is a way of saying 'it was spring'):

Un jour donques entre les autres que la laine du mouton à la toison d'or,
Prince des douze signes, resplendissoit par les rais du soleil vernal . . .

(p. 203)

28

The language of pastoral modulates into an essentially figurative code, in which speech is ornamented in such a way that the literal sense of words is altered, or transcended, or integrated into a complex of other meanings. In the rhetorical terminology familiar to antiquity and to the Middle Ages this form of ornamentation is called a trope. Tropes include metaphor, metonymy, allegory, simile, synecdoche, hyperbole, all of which involve a transference of sense and all of which work on the conceptual level. Even when, soon after the transition, Lemaire drops the level of style to the middle range of expression in order to denote a sequence of events, as he does to explain the circumstances of the marriage of Peleus and Thetis, he decorates the names of his characters with epithets, such as their full title and pedigree (p. 203). When the narrative resumes, the entry of Mercury (p. 204) signals the moment when Lemaire moves from merely decorative tropes to the mode of allegorical interpretation and its multiple senses, tropical language in its most fully developed form, which will be the language properly associated with the gods of Lemaire's fable. The literal description of Mercury is overlaid with 'signifiances':[14]

[Mercure] affubla sa riche capeline, que les poëtes nomment Galere, laquelle est garnie de belles plumes, en signifiance que l'homme eloquent est armé de deffence et de diligence, contre tous ennemis: Puis chaussa ses talonnieres de fin or, garnies de belles esles, qui luy servent à voler parmy l'air, en denotant la grand velocité de la parole, qui va legerement en diverses regions loingtaines.   (p. 204)

Lemaire insists much more than most of his sources on the identification of Mercury with language, an identification already established in the prologue. The fact that he makes this immediate association between allegorical interpretation and language draws our attention beyond his particular equations of meaning and focuses it on the mode of allegorical discourse itself. And twice in this passage he reminds us that the language he is using to describe Mercury is the language poets use.

The gods and goddesses proceeding to the wedding feast are described in ornate and vivid terms, the reader moving back and forth between the richly realised scene and the physical senses embodied in the gods, who represent aspects of the natural order of the universe, Vulcan fire, Diana the moon, Apollo the sun, and so on. It is physical interpretation which dominates at this point, later to be confirmed and further extended by the texts referred to in Chapter 35, the *Enarrationes allegoricae* of Fulgentius and Clement's *Recognitiones*. But the text most obviously incorporated into the narrative itself is

Boccaccio's *Genealogia deorum gentilium* (to which Lemaire refers specifically on p. 205). It is from Boccaccio's encyclopaedia of allegorical interpretations that Lemaire takes many, but not all, of his explanations of the gods and their attributes. On the other hand, the narrative exposition, the procession of gods journeying to Mount Pelion and the order of the feast itself, is an amplification of the rather brief and literal account in *Ovide moralisé*, Book XL, lines 1242–98 (ed. de Boer, IV, pp. 147–9).[15] The way Lemaire uses the *Ovide moralisé* is significant. In the older text the most memorable moment of the feast prior to Discord's apple is a licentious episode involving Venus and Priapus. Lemaire omits this entirely, giving Priapus a rôle at the feast, but a subordinate one (pp. 208, 216), and in fact transmogrifying the little god into a text, the *Priapeia* attributed to Virgil (p. 205). Lemaire dissociates himself quite specifically from the ribald, sub-articulate gestures which signal the presence of Venus at the feast in the *Ovide moralisé*. But he does retain the anthropomorphic scenario and describes the banquet in Chapter 29 in terms of aristocratic ceremonial. The gods perform human offices of cooking and serving in a highly decorous and ritualised fashion, and Lemaire even integrates into his description the language code previously associated with man's purely natural and literal view of the universe, the code of accumulative lists of nouns, most obvious in the two lists of flowers used as decoration (p. 215). It is in the concept of order, manifested here as social hierarchy, urbanity and aesthetic decorum, that the worlds of men and gods coincide. However, the language of the scene remains essentially metaphorical. Read in the literal sense it delights the eye, but read in the fullest sense the gods must be understood conceptually as tropes. They are metonymies, and Flora, Mulciber, Ceres and Bacchus are signs for the flowers, fire, bread and wine they signify. Even so, the individual 'signifiances' are less important than the process of allegorical reading itself which by following tropes and analogies reaches beyond particulars to coherent patterns of meaning. Nowhere does Lemaire juxtapose different language codes more clearly than at the end of this chapter, when he describes the three types of music played at the feast. First, we hear the non-intellectual music of libidinous sexuality, played by the Sirens and associated with hell and sea-monsters, a music composed merely of sound patterns, which in the end dulls the mind and which the gods reject:

Les quatre Siraines . . . se presenterent sur le beau bout, ayans visages de pucelle, esles au bras, pour facilement voler d'un lieu à l'autre, le corps feminin jusques au nombril, auquel est situé toute leur libidinosité, les queües de poissons comme bestes lubriques et legerement coulans, et les piedz de

coq, à tout lesquelz elles grattent par tout pour trouver pasture. Ces quatre meretrices et monstres marins . . . prononçoient si doux accords et prolations de diapason, triple, diatesseron et autres figures de musique, que à la melodie non accoustumée, plusieurs s'oublierent et s'endormirent à table.
(pp. 218–19)

Secondly, the gods turn their ears to the song of Pan, god of shepherds, whose music is the dancing rhythms of the natural universe. But it is set to the language of pastoral, the code of uninterpreted nature, 'la confusion des choses', ultimately reflecting nothing but itself, like Ovid's Echo (even the allusion to the *Metamorphoses* fable recalls the world of Paris and Oenone):

Pan est le Dieu des pastoureaux d'Arcadie, qui signifie, le tout universel . . . et tenoit en sa main une houlette pastorale, servant au regime et substentacle de nature naturée. Lors souffla Pan en sa chalemelle de sept buseaux accordez selon l'harmonie des sept Planettes, et feit danser Eglé et Galatée les belles Naiades, avec les plaisans Satyres, Pans, Egypans, et Tityres qui faisoient merveilles de saillir, de trepper, et de se demener. Si renforça la douce noise par retentissement des prochaines valees, esquelles la Nymphe Echo jadis amoureuse de Narcissus, respondoit tousjours au dernier verbe selon sa nature . . . (pp. 219–20)

Third come the songs of Apollo and the Muses, which alone have intelligible words, the conceptual language of history and science and, highest of all, of poetry:

Polymnia la neuvieme, et la derniere, meslée de plusieurs sciences, accentua maints chants Royaux, balades, serventois, lays et virelays, aornez de couleurs rhetoricales. Lesquelles choses pleurent singulierement au Roy Iupiter, et aux autres Dieux. (p. 220)

Words and pictures

After Discord has disturbed the feast, Mercury, Juno, Pallas and Venus fly down to the world of geographical space (p. 227) and find Paris in his pastoral setting. The 'structure literale' of the judgement scene derives from Apuleius, *De Asino aureo*, Book x, Chapters 30–4, where the episode is a theatrical performance in mime. Apuleius describes the goddesses and their followers solely in terms of their costumes, their superficial appearance which immediately strikes the eye, although the spectator knows it to be merely a theatrical illusion. No one speaks on Apuleius's stage; all communication is through purely physical signs, through gesture and dance. It is a 'literal' structure indeed, onto which Lemaire grafts language and a complex of allegorical senses.

Like Apuleius, Lemaire introduces each of his three goddesses with a description of 'les riches habillements dont elle estoit parée' (p. 230). But these rich clothes are veils of metaphor and allegory, fabulous mantles which appear to conceal, but in fact reveal conceptual truths to whoever can read plural senses. We are still in the allegorical mode of the description of the feast in heaven, and Lemaire's method of composition here is the same: vivid and elaborate description, interlaced with detailed allegorical equations often taken from Boccaccio, but often, I think, original, and all illuminated retrospectively by a reference in Chapter 35 to a text (Fulgentius again) which gives an overall interpretation of the three goddesses. Fulgentius explains Juno as the active life, which pursues material riches and power; Minerva as the contemplative life devoted to wisdom, justice and truth; and Venus as the life of pleasure, seeking only sensual things, which corrupt and decay.[16] These interpretations direct our reading of Lemaire's account of his goddesses' attire, giving added meaning, for example, to his initial association of Venus with spring and sunset, beautiful but transient moments of time proper to Venus and her star:

Sa cotte interieure estoit d'un verd gay comme l'herbette, du temps vernal: La houppelande de dessus estoit de couleur jaune et dorée, brochée à estincelles d'argent, entrechangée d'un bleu celeste par si agreable representation, que ce sembloit une nuée vespertine, enflambée de la resplendeur du Soleil occidental.   (p. 241)

The veil which Venus wears is thin and reveals nothing so clearly as her body:

Et estoient tous ses aornemens de si deliée filure, que quand le doux vent Subsolanus ventillant pressoit iceux habits contre ses precieux membres, il faisoit foy entiere de la rotondité d'iceux, et de la solidité de sa noble corpulence.   (p. 241)

Lemaire's words at this point are close to those of Apuleius, and recall his purely literal vision; what allegorical interpretation reveals is the superficiality and physicality of this seductive goddess. Her ornaments also suggest her ambivalence, like the cestos or girdle of chastity she may or may not wear (Lemaire's emphasis on this parallels Boccaccio's) and the posy of roses 'lesquelles luy sont dediées tant pour leur beauté singuliere, comme pource qu'elles poingnent en cueillant' (p. 242), which we find in both Fulgentius and Boccaccio.[17]

The language in which Lemaire clothes his goddesses is the language of tropes, but Paris, as we have seen, cannot read this language. To communicate with him the goddesses use another mode, the mode of rhetorical persuasion.[18] In giving his goddesses speech Lemaire is departing from Apuleius and returning to the *Ovide moralisé*, where each goddess talks at length. But in the *Ovide moralisé* they quarrel among themselves and address themselves to Jupiter as well as Paris. Lemaire sharpens the focus, and reserves their spoken words as the medium by which the goddesses reveal themselves to men. And whereas in the *Ovide moralisé* they talk in statements, in Lemaire their language is very oblique, none more so than that of Venus. For she especially is goddess of 'faconde', 'blandices', 'secrettes collocutions' (p. 242), 'dulciloqua maxime' as Boccaccio calls her. The verbal forms in which Lemaire's goddesses express themselves are exact correlatives of the styles of life they represent. Juno talks in active verbs, Pallas in abstractions, demonstrations and complicated extended metaphors, but Venus uses flattery, insinuation, 'eloquence artificielle' and 'paroles delicates' (p. 249). Her speech is decorated with figures of diction, alliteration, assonance, and rhyme. She defines herself in this language: 'Venus venuste, en beauté principale, Princesse d'amours amoureuse, à toutes gens gentille et gracieuse, pleine de urbanité traitable sans aucun traict de plaintive orphanité, et de penible offension' (p. 244), and the patterns of sounds in this sentence are almost bewildering in their complexity. But these are only figures of sound, not tropes which mediate between sense and concept. Indeed, Venus deflects Paris from 'valeurs intrinseques', and restricts him to a literal interpretation of the issue at hand and to the evidence of his 'beaux yeux corporelz' (p. 245). She appeals directly to the judgement not of his mind, but of his physical senses, especially sight, his 'regard corporel' (p. 246). Yet this goddess too talks the language of tropes, picking up the metaphor of the well-guided ship launched by Juno (p. 234) and developed with elaborate decorum by Pallas (pp. 238–9). But the map Venus offers for the voyage is her own peculiar 'carte de tendre', a map for a ship of fools perhaps, based not on the rational arguments and logical analogies of Pallas, but on the exigencies of 'volupté corporelle', 'doctrine naturelle, et la propre inclination de ton sens' (pp. 246–8). She can outdo Pallas with sea metaphors, for the sea is her natural environment, 'attendu que de la mer je suis extraite'; she is born of the waves, her planet is star of the sea, and she talks with first-hand knowledge of marine monsters, pirates and Sirens (pp. 247–8). To anyone who can read polysemously of course the dangerous implications of Venus are clear, reinforced by echoes of the Sirens' song we have heard previously (pp. 218–19), as well as by the references to Boccaccio and Fulgentius, who both stress the perils of Venus's sea, signifying as it does 'the life of unhappy lovers, full of bitterness, tossed by storms, and frequently shipwrecked'.[19] The ambivalence basic to Venus shapes sound and sense in her speech, where 'mellifluence' turns to 'male influence', 'douceur' to 'douleur', 'honneur' to 'horreur', 'luisance' to 'nuisance' (p. 248). 'Rhetoriques couleurs' indeed, but 'retorquées en douleurs' (p. 249) for whoever looks no further than the literal sense and does not use the perspicacity of his intellect to read the plural senses of metaphor.

Lemaire makes a distinction between language in itself and the reaction to it of reader or listener. Language in itself, be it literal or allegorical in sense, is morally neutral, and this is made explicit, before ever we see the effect of Venus's speech on Paris, by the intervention of Mercury, whom Lemaire associates so closely with language and whose planet, he now insists, is 'neutre et indifferente, bonne avec les benivoles, mauvaise avec les malivoles' (p. 249). Lemaire seems to anticipate the qualms of the next generation of humanists about rhetoric's moral ambivalence (Erasmus in the *De Lingua* and Rabelais in the *Tiers Livre*), but he puts the issue very precisely in terms of the response of the reader/listener, in this case Paris and the choices he makes. His first choice is to put aside the fabulous allegorical mantles of the goddesses in order to see them naked. Venus disrobes with the symbolic gesture of removing the belt which bound her to chastity (p. 252). As we undress the goddesses, we move from the language of allegory to the literal language of lists. The clothes of the goddesses as they discard them become mere objects, 'coiffes, guimpes, atours, couronne, chapeau, salade, et autres accoustrements de teste', and so on (p. 253), and the goddesses themselves step delicately into the world of pastoral and its diminutive vision, 'de peur que l'herbette poingnante n'offensast leurs plantes tendres et doucettes' (p. 253). The last vestige of metaphorical language left to them is a simile:

Lors elles se presenterent toutes trois sur le beau bout, telles que l'aube du jour blanche et clere, coulourée de splendeur vermeille se monstre à l'œil du pelerin qui beaucoup l'ha desirée.   (p. 253)

Loosely tropical and properly a figure of thought, but material in content, simile here has a transitional function, stressing external colour, the perception and desire of the senses, and with the minimum of conceptual overtones. With it we move to the third manifestation of the deities: after the language of trope and rhetoric, the language of aesthetic vision.[20]

All nature crowds to see the naked goddesses, and the scene

described on pages 253 to 254 is exquisitely beautiful. But the language remains within the confines of the literal sense and the pastoral code, anthropomorphic but not allegorical. What the reader sees is presented in the form of a list, an enumeration of nymphs and natural phenomena which in their turn are sensitive only to physical appearance:

Les Nymphes des fontaines revestues de mousse et cresson, jetterent leurs tresses mouillées hors du parfond de leurs sourses. Les Dryades gentiles, parmy les crevasses des escorces de leurs arbres florissans meirent hors leurs belles faces . . . Les Vents retirerent leurs haleines, et n'osoient à peine souspirer de peur de les grever. Les fueillettes espesses et drues qui faisoient umbrage aux Deesses ne se remouvoient tant soit peu, à fin de ne faire bruit. Les ruisselets argentins decourans au long des herbages contindrent leurs douces noises. Et brief, toute chose terrestre feit silence, et se tint en grand paix et admiration pendant l'ostentation des corps divins, lesquelz avoient desja tout embaumé l'air circonvoisin de leur flairante redolence divine et ambrosienne. (pp. 253–4)

It is a purely aesthetic vision, without any sense of what the goddesses signify. Simplicity and innocence seem its hallmarks. In terms of the registers established by the three kinds of music played at the feast of the gods, this is the natural music of Pan, innocent of the 'libidinosité' of the Sirens as it is of the intellectual concepts of the Muses. Venus, who alone of the goddesses, according to the mythographers, is most truly herself when naked, decorates herself with natural roses, pruned of any allegorical extensions, their thorns hidden 'à fin que les branchettes espineuses ne violassent sa chair tendrette' (p. 255); and the narrative proceeds with an enumeration of the parts of her body (pp. 255–6) as they appear to the 'rude sensualité' of Paris. This is sheer physical beauty, described very much in the manner of a Pléiade poet listing the 'beautez qu'il voudroit en s'amie'. But Lemaire, as later Ronsard will do more subtly, reveals the sexual fascination which lies so close to aesthetic response. In the eyes of the human beholder, the beautiful and the erotic are compounded:

les yeux estincelans, et les prunelles errantes et vagabondes, alentour de l'image Venerique, denotoient assez son appetit sensuel estre cateillé d'un desir non chaste, et tout enflambé de luxure excessive. (pp. 256–7)

After Paris gives the apple to Venus, the reactions of Juno and Pallas bring us back to allegorical interpretation and metaphor, making the clearest moral distinctions in order to define exactly what choice Paris has made:

O homme brutal, beste transformée . . . N'as tu eu honte de preferer la vie voluptueuse et inutile, à la vie active et contemplative? [a direct recall of

Fulgentius's three lives] N'as tu eu vergongne de postposer la perdurable à la transitoire? de laisser le grain pour la paille, la seve pour l'escorce, le fruit pour les fueilles, et le gain pour la perte? (p. 258)

Moreover, the rancour of the two defeated goddesses exactly follows the narrative of the *Ovide moralisé* and this strong textual reminder of the allegorical tradition underlines the moral senses to be read in the episode. Nevertheless, although Lemaire leaves us in no real doubt about the error of the judgement Paris has just made, the aesthetic based on sensual delight and associated with Venus is conveyed so alluringly that the reader is almost as captivated as Paris. In contrast, metaphorical language, which is the only access to conceptual truth, comes harshly at this point from the lips of a singularly unattractive Juno, speaking 'd'une voix aigre, sonoreuse et abrupte' (p. 258). This ambiguity will be even more fully realised in the *Concorde des deux langages*, where only a careful reading of the whole text reveals the corruption within Venus's temple of art and beauty, and where the vanity of its speciously ornamented but seductive language is fully understood only by comparison with the more substantial riches hidden in the more austere style associated with Minerva.

There is certainly nothing like Lemaire's rendering of sheer aesthetic delight in the *Ovide moralisé*. This vision belongs to quite another sensibility, and we are more likely to find it in Renaissance Italy than in medieval France. The Italian neo-Platonists also use allegorical interpretation to explain the Judgement of Paris, and Ficino, like Lemaire, borrows the definition of the three lives from Fulgentius. But he hesitates to refuse Venus. Ficino's wise prince, Lorenzo de Medici, gives all three goddesses equal place, recognising the motivating force of beauty and pleasure in the lives of the senses, of action, and of reason.[21] Generally speaking, neo-Platonism identified beauty and love with goodness, thus making possible a celestial Venus, without any of the ambivalence of Lemaire's goddess. But for the medieval scholastics goodness and beauty belonged to separate faculties (the appetitive and cognitive respectively) and were essentially discrete experiences.[22] Lemaire stands at the meeting point of these two philosophies, which he represents in contrasting language codes, the literal language of sense experience for beauty, and the language of tropes for truth and moral choice. In the end, both here and in the even sharper analysis of the *Concorde des deux langages*, he opts for the more medieval view of art as truth of concept, expressed in the allegorisation of the things of the senses. He is deeply sensitive to the aesthetic which associates the beautiful with the good, but he suspects its limitations and its erotic undercurrents. Ultimately he rejects it, and with it, perhaps, mimetic art altogether. It is exciting proof of the vitality of pagan fable that Lemaire should have seen mythological narrative as the form in which to express one of the crucial issues of his age.

Conclusions

Lemaire devotes the first half of Chapter 35 to concluding allegorisations of the fable of Peleus and Thetis and the Judgement of Paris. The traditional schema of historical, physical and moral interpretation, 'raisons . . . philosophales, morales et historiales', is here more explicitly brought into play than earlier in the narrative (pp. 270–2); and Lemaire refers to particular texts for his explanations, notably Fulgentius, Firmicus Maternus, and Clement of Rome. Not only is the reader asked to read multi-textually, aware all the time of parallel accounts and interpretations, he is also being asked to read retroactively. When he comes to Lemaire's final allusions and analyses in Chapter 35, he will remember the foregoing narrative, and modify and extend his understanding of it in the light of the concepts just introduced. Lemaire puts forward two sets of ideas in particular which illuminate his text retroactively. We have already noticed the first of these, when we connected Lemaire's description of the three goddesses with Fulgentius's interpretation of Juno, Pallas and Venus as the lives of action, contemplation and pleasure. A more detailed analysis of their three speeches to Paris would show how carefully they express and illustrate those concepts. In the second place, Lemaire spends some time on an astrological explanation of the action, presented as his own original interpretation, 'ce que je imagine' (p. 272), and then grounded in a text by Julius Firmicus Maternus (p. 273), who describes at length the influence of the planets on personality types and in particular the miserable effects of the impure love which is often the gift of Venus. Venus was in the ascendant at the birth of Paris, and so the conjunction of his stars 'l'enclinoit à choses amoureuses et veneriennes' (p. 272). This requires us to give more weight to those passages in the narrative where the gods are described in terms of their planetary characteristics, particularly to the star of Venus, who alone of the three goddesses has a planet (pp. 242, 247). It also raises the fundamental question of the rôle of free will in the choice Paris has made. Already Venus has suggested to Paris that her influence is irresistible (p. 247), and already Mercury has stated the contrary, that 'en toy gist liberal et plenier arbitrage' (p. 249). Lemaire's astrological speculations put the dilemma even more clearly, balanced as they are against affirmations of free will, as in the passage only a few lines further on, where, following both Fulgentius and Boccaccio, Lemaire explains Jupiter's delegation of the judgement to Paris, 'pource que Dieu laisse faire le cours aux destinées, et ne veult tollir à l'homme son franc arbitre' (p. 272).[23] This carefully non-committal juxtaposition of the claims of astrological determinism and of belief in free will is even echoed in the quotation from Clement:

Et peult on gouster et apprendre . . . comment le monde est gouverné par chacune situation des estoilles. Mais toutesvoyes tout homme ha sa liberté, quant à cela: et n'est point tenu de taster de ladite science, s'il ne luy plaist.
(p. 274)

Lemaire, through his allegorical interpretation of Paris's choice of Venus, and through his textual cross-references, has opened up speculation on a fundamental theological problem, and at the same time allowed the ambivalence inherent in the myth to keep the question open-ended. This is a much more sophisticated vision of possible analogies between pagan insight and Christian truth than is offered in the summary equations of the *Bible des poetes*, which were to prove incompatible with the humanists' critical sense. Lemaire does not make explicit identifications of his characters with Christian figures and concepts, but he keeps the notion of a spiritual level of interpretation very much alive. He does, I think, hint at a specifically Christian extension of his fable by referring to the question of free will, especially after he has awoken the reader to its theological implications by concluding his discussion with a religious text, Clement's *Recognitiones*. In this light, a retroactive reading of Lemaire's narrative is likely to pick up insistent parallels between Paris's choice and Adam's. Both lived in married bliss in a natural paradise; and Discord is described as a 'criminelle serpente' (p. 221), hides in a tree (p. 222), brings about confusion with an apple, and 'le grain de sa malheureuse semence demoura et fructifia si fertilement, que le goust en dure encores par tous les siecles' (p. 222). Nothing in Lemaire's text draws the reader's attention directly to these parallels, unlike the clear indications given by the spiritual interpretation appended to the *Ovide moralisé*, which refers tersely but quite explicitly to the story of the Garden of Eden.[24] Lemaire's system of signs, although it maps the same territory, is much more complex and more cryptic, and more closely integrated into the narrative.

The more we explore the text, the clearer it becomes that Lemaire's method of composition and the response he invites from the reader depend on polysemous interpretation. The mythological narrative is a nexus of meanings, which the 'ingeniosité' of the reader must draw out. This definition of the relationship of the reader to the text is ratified by the spiritual authority of St Peter in the *Recognitiones*,

> S. Pierre ... dit, que certainement les hommes ingenieux recueillent beaucoup de semblances de verité, par les choses qu'ilz lisent. (p. 275)[25]

Lemaire emphasises the phrase by repeating it in Latin. It states that allegorical interpretation reaches through similitudes to truth (the equations are 'verisimilitudines'); and the ideal reader is intelligently alert to these similitudes. It is not quite clear whether Lemaire would concede that the reader has infinite licence to look for likenesses and build interpretations on them. Certainly many of Lemaire's own interpretations interpolated in the narrative are not to be found in Boccaccio and are, I think, the product of his own ingenuity, perhaps designed to stimulate the reader to creative reading. On the other hand, he uses his parallel texts as controls, defining to some extent the areas in which profitable significances are to be sought. The final text is a carefully co-ordinated whole, a meticulously wrought complex of correlatives and cross-references which concentrates the reader's attention on certain themes and discourages arbitrary associations and self-contradictory interpretations. Lemaire has mined the rich potential of ancient fable, and used Paris's confrontation with Venus to contrast different aesthetics and to explore the ambivalent attractions of physical beauty, the moral commitments available to man, and the paradoxes surrounding his freedom of choice. The serious implications which the interpreting reader unfolds in Lemaire's work, combined with the coherence he discovers in its structure, are what constitute its 'truth'.[26] And Lemaire registers this 'truth' in extremely sophisticated language. It is not the language of the classical and late-classical texts which he takes as his authorities for technical details and from which he derives suggestions for the organisation of his material and its interpretation. They are used as repositories of myth, but not yet as models for its expression. He uses to some small extent the language of modern humanist commentaries on these texts, which fill the margin of nearly every edition of Lemaire's source-books with long lists of synonyms, cognate words, and words of similar sound. Their language is perhaps a link between contemporary vernacular style and humanist ideals of elegant expression based on classical usage. Rather, Lemaire's use of language belongs almost wholly to the complex tradition of medieval rhetoric, and mirrors patterns of speech and language codes found in late medieval Latin, not in classical poetry. Yet, it is by applying the distinctions and classifications of medieval rhetoric to mythological narrative that Lemaire is able to define poetic language as he understands it. Writing in prose, he avoids any simple identification of poetry with rhyme, which is a merely verbal figure. Deploying all the figures of speech known to rhetoric, he differentiates the truly poetic language of the gods, the language of tropes, metaphor and allegory, from the prosaic language of the literal sense, however elaborate its verbal figures and however beautiful the objects it presents to the imagination. For Lemaire, as for Boccaccio, the essence of poetry, pure poetry, 'mera poesis' is to be found in the most fully developed of tropes and the one best able to carry conceptual content: fiction, allegorically interpreted.[27] In his Judgement of Paris, Lemaire has written a fiction which at one and the same time interprets an existing fable and itself demands to be read allegorically, 'esquelles choses qui bien y voudra viser, on peult cueillir assez de fruít allegorique et moral souz couleurs poëtiques' (p. 231).

3

ALLEGORICAL INTERPRETATION IN A TIME OF CHANGE: FROM THE BIBLE TO OLYMPUS

Twenty years after Lemaire's Judgement of Paris we reach a crucial date in the history of French translations of Ovid and evidence of a definite change in the way mythological narratives were read. In 1532 the *Bible des poetes* was completely revised and reissued by Denys de Harsy for Romain Morin at Lyons under a new title, *Le Grand Olympe des Histoires poëtiques du prince de poesie Ovide en sa Metamorphose*. This revision clearly marks a fundamental and lasting change in taste, for the *Grand Olympe* totally replaced the *Bible des poetes*, which was never printed again, whereas the new version was reprinted at least thirteen times up to 1586. The anonymous editor of the *Grand Olympe* provided three very short prefaces to the three volumes into which he divided his *Metamorphoses*, and there we find evidence of the change in attitudes towards literary texts which prompted his revision. Ovid's poem, he says, is worthy to be read in French 'selon le naturel du livre sans allegories' (fol. a i v°).[1] The poem is now felt to be a self-sufficient entity, onto which the allegorical interpretations of the *Bible des poetes* have been 'unnaturally' grafted from an alien stock. Reading means a process of responding directly to the author's words as they stand, and involves some notion of respecting the autonomy of the text, which does not allow it to be reconstituted and reformulated to fit superimposed contexts. At the same time, the editor does not deny that the allegorical interpretation of mythology is valid. It is, he says, a legitimate exercise, but a separate exercise from that of reading a poem. Therefore he envisages a separate translation of Fulgentius, whom he considers the best example of how to explain and rationalise the fables of the ancients. But the translator of Ovid should translate what Ovid wrote in the sense he wrote it, 'et par ainsi à chascun autheur sa louange sera gardée' (fol. a i v°). On the other hand, 'garder le naturel du livre' does not necessarily exclude polysemous reading, for plural readings are still taken to be the essence of poetry:

41

Poesie mere de subtille et joyeuse invention soubz une couverte de Fable elegante a si vrayement exprimé la doctrine moralle et humaine, que si l'entendement du liseur n'est du tout effacé par ignorance il en tirera honestes enseignemens et maniere de bien vivre. (fol. AA i v°)

The moral sense at least is inherent in the text. It is a 'philosophie latente' to be recovered afresh at each reading, but not formulated explicitly and interpolated in the narrative, which is 'assez d'elle mesmes allegorisant' (fol. AA i v°), that is to say it contains within itself adequate clues as to what it may signify.

The rather summary remarks in the prefaces need to be seen in the context of the *Grand Olympe* as a whole. It basically consists of the text of the *Bible des poetes* with all the interpretations removed, so that it reads as one long narrative like the original *Metamorphoses*. But apart from some minimal rewriting, mostly at the beginning of Book I, there is no attempt to translate Ovid literally. The editor's sense of the 'naturel' of his author does not take him back to the Latin text. He is content with the narrative portion of the *Bible des poetes*, which, as we have seen, is a prose paraphrase of a fourteenth-century verse paraphrase of the *Metamorphoses*. This may give the substance of the fables more or less, but is a very different kind of text from the *Metamorphoses* as far as style and language are concerned. The Salmacis fable in the *Olympe*, for example, is exactly the same as in the *Bible des poetes*, apart from some very minor modernisations of vocabulary. So what we have in the 1532 version are the characters and plots of Ovid's tales, told in language which deliberately avoids figurative expressions and now shorn of the allegorical extensions provided by the *Bible des poetes*. It is a plain narrative style which relies very much on dialogue and from which metaphor in any of its forms is almost entirely absent. Yet this linear mode of exposition is still expected to conceal a plurality of meanings, especially if it involves itself with mythology; it is expected to be a 'philosophie latente . . . soubz une couverte de Fable elegante'. It is even possible that the new appreciation of the 'naturel du livre' may encourage the reader to look for an even greater proliferation of meanings now that the controls formerly exercised by the recognised allegorical 'senses' have been removed. This is a question with clear implications for authors writing at this time of change.[2]

Several factors had converged to discredit explicit allegorical interpretation and so to alter the way mythological narrative was envisaged. Between the fourteenth century and the early years of the sixteenth century the Church had tolerated and even promoted the practice of appropriating pagan poems by recasting them as moral and spiritual allegories. Bersuire's Latin compilation, on which the *Bible des poetes* had drawn, was still being advertised in its sixteenth-century editions as a reference work for preachers looking for interesting parallels with which to expand their sermons, and we know that it was so used. But in the early years of the century the easy assimilation of profane texts into sacred contexts was under attack by critics from all shades of religious opinion. Orthodox Catholics like Clichtoveus in France recalled St Thomas Aquinas's injunction against applying to profane literature modes of reading which he claimed were exclusive to writings inspired by the Holy Ghost. Moderates like Erasmus made a mockery of spiritual interpretations; Luther and the Reformers reviled them. By 1559 allegorical and tropological interpretations of the *Metamorphoses* were on the *Index*. Those who criticised allegorical interpretation from a religious point of view were primarily concerned with spiritual interpretation, and their attacks sprang to some extent from a growing sensitivity to a fundamental distinction between the sacred and the profane, which was embarrassed by the sort of equation which turns Hermaphroditus into the Son of God.

The most significant factor effecting this change of attitude to allegorical interpretation was the influence of humanist scholarship and the critical criteria it developed in readers of classical literature. These are already evident in the humanist commentaries mentioned in Chapter 1. They all promote a strong sense of anachronism, which resists any attempt to impose on a text a meaning at variance with its known historical context. This disallows spiritual allegories, while remaining rather ambivalent about physical interpretation, and it radically alters the sort of moral sense which can be derived from mythological poems. Medieval tropological interpretation made detailed, point-by-point equations between the original narrative and its moral implications, tending to substitute contemporary moral and social values, and even elements from the contemporary social scene, for the figures in the poem. So the moral interpretation of the Judgement of Paris in the *Bible des poetes* runs as follows:

A cestuy jugement peuvent estre plusieurs juges de nostre present temps acomparez qui s'abusent et se layssent aveugler par les falaces, deceptions et vaines promesses avec transitoires delictz des coulpables et ayans tort. Tellement que par leurs blandissementz ils obtiennent la pomme d'or. Dont par apres le royaulme, la contrée ou la cité où telz jugementz se font en sont par la permission du droicturier juge subvertis, demolis, abatus. Et les habitantz, et mesmes ceulx qui de cestuy faulx jugement ne sont coulpables le comparent, et faitz en sont profuges mendians et amenez à mendicité perpetuelle comme nous avons veu depuis nagueres.   (fol. cxix)

But the humanist sense of historical decorum forbids any attempt to translate the poem in this way. It is to be read on its own terms, in its own historical context, 'au naturel' as the editor of the *Grand Olympe* has it, and its moral inferences are transmitted not by tropes but by means of another rhetorical idiom much favoured by the humanists, as *exempla*. To read a fable as an *exemplum*, an example of moral behaviour, is to leave aside precise identifications and analogues for an overall view, a very generalised sense of the fable's moral import, which may impinge very little on our response to details in its telling. When Erasmus claims that 'under all the inventions of the poets there does lie a hidden meaning' he goes on to list in the briefest terms the moral interpretations that can be deduced when fables are read as *exempla*:

It is quite obvious . . . that the tale of Icarus falling into the sea warns that no one should rise higher than his lot in life allows, and the story of Phaëthon that no one should undertake to perform a task that is beyond his powers. Salmoneus cast headlong into hell teaches us not to emulate what lies far beyond our fortunes, and Marsyas flayed alive teaches us not to try conclusions with those more powerful than ourselves . . . The labours of Hercules tell us that immortal renown is won by effort and by helping others; the wish of Midas that the greedy and insatiable are suffocated by their own wealth.[3]

The suggested meaning is isolated from the narrative to form an *exemplum*, which Erasmus envisages will be used as a form of rhetorical proof in some other sphere of discourse. The original mythological narrative to a large extent retains its autonomy. Tropological allegory, on the other hand, was a fully elaborated figure of thought, to be applied systematically in any reading of the fable. It is Erasmus's approach which seems to coincide with that adopted by the editor of the *Grand Olympe*, who insists that the *Metamorphoses* be read 'selon le naturel du livre sans allegories', and who believes, as does Erasmus, that the intelligent reader will have no difficulty in drawing from it 'honestes enseignemens et maniere de bien vivre', although he is given no explicit interpretation.

The shift from trope to *exemplum* has connections, I think, with another change produced by the humanist critical spirit. This concerns similitudes in general, and we have already seen that allegorical interpretation depends on similitudes. In Chapters VIII and IX of *Gargantua*, which appeared only about two years after the first edition of the *Olympe*, Rabelais is dealing with the interpretation of colours, and he extends his argument widely to touch on what are and what are not valid likenesses between things and concepts. True likenesses are to be discovered only by a thorough understanding of things, 'la vertu, proprieté et nature des choses', reached by natural reason or derived from accredited authorities. What Rabelais condemns are arbitrary similitudes invented by the reader or based on mere verbal likenesses. Now medieval allegorical interpretation, as we have seen, made no claim to invariable truth, but worked through *ad hoc* juxtapositions and parallels, and very often through verbal reminiscences. Rabelais's criticism demotes it to the level of an ingenious but trivial game, and one which is positively offensive to the humanists' deeply serious interest in natural analogies between things and concepts, as well as to their sense of historical anachronism.[4] The humanists by no means deny the validity of tropes or the capacity of serious literature to transmit plural meanings. However, their critical analysis of the similitudes on which polysemous reading was based does perhaps underlie the much more diffident and hesitant approach to figurative modes which one can sense in a good deal of writing in the 1530s and the early 1540s. It is not irrelevant to Rabelais's equivocations about allegorical meaning in the prologue to *Gargantua*. And as far as French verse is concerned it is an age of plain speaking, an age which on the whole avoids metaphorical complexities in longer poems. At its most typical the poetry of this period is a sophisticated imitation of ordinary speech. The favourite forms, verse-letter and dramatic monologue, invite the reader to a conversation or a discussion. This is the enormously influential idiom of Marot's mature poems, but it is also the manner of the poems connected with the *Querelle des amyes*, and of many minor talents. The preference for a rhetoric of persuasive argument rather than extended metaphor is also evident in poems transmitting neo-Platonic ideas, which are a significant factor in the literature of the period, ideas for which the Italians earlier had found allegorical mythology to be the most pertinent form of expression. Antoine Héroët in his *Androgyne*, probably written in 1536, follows Ficino's use of myth and interpretation fairly closely, but in his more original *Parfaicte Amye* of 1542 the mythological element is greatly underplayed, virtually reduced to a single passage at the end of the second book, where the Queen of the Blessed Isles (whom Héroët had found in Bembo's *Asolani*) is presented as an enigma to rest with the reader, without any specific guide to interpretation.[5] We have noted a parallel development in the pruning away of allegorical extensions from the *Bible des poetes* and it is even to be detected in the history of Latin editions of the *Metamorphoses*, which precisely at this moment change from large fully annotated volumes to small plain texts. Moreover, Marot's translation of Book I of the *Metamorphoses*, which perhaps dates from 1531 and was printed in 1534, adheres scrupulously to the original and makes no forays into extraneous interpretation.

More precise indications of how attitudes had changed about mythological narrative and about poetic language in general may be gleaned from the chief curiosity of the *Grand Olympe*. As far as the story of the marriage of Peleus and Thetis, the *Grand Olympe* had been following the narrative sections of the *Bible des poetes*, with very little alteration. But at this point, and for the next twenty-six pages (vol. III, fols. 9–22v°), the old text is replaced with something much more exciting, none other than the episode of the Golden Apple and the Judgement of Paris lifted from Lemaire's *Illustrations*. The plagiarism is not acknowledged and the sudden slip into Lemaire's elaborate style takes the reader completely by surprise. Even more surprising perhaps is that the passage is not reproduced in its entirety. It has been carefully and systematically trimmed, presumably to accommodate it to the prevailing taste. A brief look at where the omissions were made may be quite informative about the literary climate of the 1530s.

To begin with, we have nothing of Lemaire's description of Paris in his pastoral paradise or of the gods in heaven, and so the careful distinction between language codes is completely lost. The marriage of Peleus and Thetis occurs in the *Grand Olympe* as a link passage between the text of the *Bible des poetes* and Lemaire's description of the intrusion of Discord, and it is reduced to two prosaic sentences:

Juppiter pour decorer la festivité matrimonialle de son nepveu Peleus et de la belle Thetis, si voulut en personne trouver avec toute l'université des dieux et déesses invitez par son herault Mercure, lesquelz furent en grand nombre et bel arroy. Et fut le festin exquis et sumptueux et grandement celebré par Hymeneus et Genius.   (vol. III, fol. 9)

This is a very plain narrative style, with nothing of either the poetry of Lemaire's grand manner or the low comedy of the *Bible des poetes*. The preparation of the Golden Apple, the dissension between the goddesses, Jupiter's reluctance to judge between them, and the intervention of Ganymede and Mercury are related exactly as in the *Illustrations* (pp. 221–5). This is a mainly narrative section in Lemaire, with very little comment or interpretation. It does include, without expansion at this point, the references to the fatal effects of the apple and to Jupiter's refusal to use his foresight to determine the issue between the goddesses, both of which will retrospectively acquire profound meaning in Lemaire's account. The *Grand Olympe* keeps these passages, with their as yet latent significances (which it does not uncover further), but it omits Lemaire's physical interpretation of Ganymede as the stellar sign Aquarius (p. 223). The descent of the goddesses into the pastoral world of Paris is omitted, as is any talk of music (pp. 226–9). The speeches of the goddesses are reproduced almost exactly, except for a few of Lemaire's more extreme examples of aureate language and, more significantly, the traditional etymologies of Juno and Minerva, which were based solely on verbal similitudes, without any historical or philological justification for them (pp. 233–40). Another notable omission is Venus's astrological explanation of herself (p. 247). But whereas the *Grand Olympe* seems well content to reproduce at length Lemaire's exercises in persuasive rhetoric, the same is not true of the description of the goddesses which precede their speeches. Here the new book has retained all the material description of their attire, but has systematically cut out practically all Lemaire's explanations of their adornments and of their companions, by which he had added metaphorical extensions to the literal sense. So Venus keeps her coloured skirts, for which Lemaire had given no explicit interpretation, but her girdle is only a girdle with appropriate pictures:

Sa ceincture (dont elle estoit ceincte) appellée Ceston estoit de grand pris, en laquelle avoit divinement esmaillé la déesse Nature: les figures d'amytié, desir, faconde, soubriz: plusieurs signes d'amours et secretes collocutions.

(vol. III, fol. 15vº)

While these pictures hint at allegorical personification they do not give the moral sense which Lemaire had worked into this passage, immediately after drawing attention to the special poetical language whose function is not only to name Venus's girdle univocally but to generate plural senses. From this language, largely by means of verbal likenesses ('ceston', 'inceste'), Lemaire derived his interpretation:

Sa precieuse ceinture dont elle estoit ceinte, s'appelle Ceston par les nobles poëtes. Et la luy donna et forgea jadis dame Nature mesmes, à fin que la trop vagabonde lasciveté de Venus, fust cohibée et restreinte par propre vergongne, et aussi par l'autorité des loix conjugales. Et en icelle avoit divinement esmaillé ladite Deesse Nature, les figures d'amitié, desir, faconde, blandices, plusieurs signes d'amours et secrettes collocutions. Laquelle ceinture icelle Deesse Venus ne porte jamais, sinon aux noces chastes, honnestes et legitimes. Et à ceste cause toute autre convention qui se fait de femme à homme, est appellée inceste, quand Venus n'y ha point sa ceinture Ceston. (p. 242)

In the *Grand Olympe* the jewel which adorns the head of Venus is not related to her planet, and her posy is made up merely of 'blanches roses et vermeilles rendant souesve odeur', with no aura of beauty or of danger (vol. III, fol. 15v°). The effect of this careful deleting of allegorical interpretation is very clear at the end of the description of Venus:

Grand Olympe

Son filz Cupido à tout son arc d'ivoire et ses flesches dorées et Volupté sa fille estoient avec elle. Et derriere elle à sa queue estoient ses troys graces toutes nues. C'estassavoir Pasithea, Egialle, et Euphrosine. Apres les graces pouvoit on voir consequemment les deux femmes de chambre, et servantes de Venus, lesquelles tenoient le chariot de la déesse tiré par les Cygnes et par blanches Coulumbes. (vol. III, fols. 15v°–16)

Lemaire

Son filz Cupido à tout son arc d'yvoire, et ses sajettes dorées, et Volupté sa fille, estoient avec elle: car jamais Venus n'est sans amours et sans plaisance. Et derriere elle, à sa queüe, estoient ses trois Graces, appellées Charites, toutes nues. C'estasavoir Pasithea, Egyale, et Euphrosyne. La premiere attrayant, la seconde entretenant, et la tierce retenant fermement les amans en amours: et sont filles de Jupiter et de la Nymphe Autonoë, ou selon aucuns, de Venus mesmes. Elles estoient ainsi nues, pour denoter qu'en captant la grace et benivolence d'aucune personne, on ne doit point estre feint ne couvert. Apres les Graces pouvoit on voir consequemment les deux femmes de chambre, et pedisseques de Venus, dont l'une se nommoit Accoustumance, et l'autre Tristesse, comme met Apuleius, De asino aureo. Le curre ou chariot de la Deesse estoit aupres d'elle, pour designer le cours et velocité de sa sphere et planette. Et les cygnes estoient dediez à son service, en signifiance de la blancheur et netteté des dames: et aussi pource que c'est un oyseau doucement chantant. Et les coulons aussi estoient souz sa tutelle et sauvegarde, pource qu'ilz sont luxurieux et fecondes à procreer leurs pigeons. (pp. 242–3)

The *Grand Olympe* evokes a picture, a composition of human, animal, and material objects, which requires only a visual response, and is worded in exactly the same idiom as the description of the naked goddesses later on in Lemaire which the *Grand Olympe* reproduces in its entirety. The only other major omission from Lemaire's Judgement of Paris narrative is the passage where Lemaire describes the wonder of nature at the naked beauty of the goddesses (pp. 253–4), precisely the moment where Lemaire seems to us to anticipate the poetic language and vision of the Pléiade. The *Grand Olympe* reduces Lemaire's prose-poem to the literal sense, but it fails to respond to the aesthetic of physical beauty which Lemaire glimpsed in his naked goddesses and consciously rejected. And Juno's reference to Paris's choice of 'la vie voluptueuse et inutile' and his rejection of 'la vie active et contemplative' (p. 258) is almost all that remains of Lemaire's allegorical interpretations, just enough perhaps to give the reader a clue as to how to understand and apply the fable, in its most general terms, as an *exemplum*. As the victorious Venus turns to speak to Paris the *Grand Olympe* reverts to the language of the *Bible des poetes*. None of Lemaire's references to other texts are retained, either at the end of the fable or in the body of the narrative. This is the fable 'au naturel', stripped of metaphor and taken out of Lemaire's carefully arranged contexts. Our next step is to see how Venus and her fable are transformed in the poetic mode which seems to emerge in the 1530s.[6]

4

THE THREE GODDESSES:
FRANÇOIS HABERT

Narrative exercises

Mythological narrative does not, by and large, engage the attention of the best poets writing in France between the mid 1530s and the late 1540s. There is evidence, as I have suggested, that this period saw very radical changes in the way existing narratives in the genre were read, and these may have produced as their corollary a certain hesitancy about how to use this particular mode of expression. Jean Bouchet, living in the provinces and already well established, is relatively unaffected. In fact he uses mythology with increasing assurance, but as late as his *Triomphe du treschrestien Roy* of 1549 he is still looking at it through the interpretations of Boccaccio's *Genealogia*. Marot, much more in touch with the developing literary scene in Latin as well as French, is certainly responsive to the poetry of the *Metamorphoses* and his translation of the first two books (published in 1534 and 1543) is bright, accurate and sensitive to the language of the original. It reproduces it strictly 'selon le naturel du livre', transmitting the literal sense only. However, it seems an exercise very distinct and separate from the lines his own mature poetry pursues, which rarely lead him into the vicinity of Ovid's fabulous world. Other poets, Guillaume Bouchetel, Jacques Colin, Louis des Masures, possibly inspired by Marot, produce workaday literal versions of individual stories. Of the major talents, Marguerite de Navarre and Scève briefly experiment with the mode of mythological allegory, both of them imitating in part the *Salices* of Sannazaro, Marguerite in 1543 with the *Fable du Faux Cuyder* and Scève with his *Saulsaye* in 1547. By reason of the genres into which these authors translate the *Salices* (homily and eclogue), neither of their poems is very germane to our theme of mythological narrative. Moreover, the curious coincidence in their choice of the same neo-Latin model, in spite of the enormously rich resources of material in the genre in ancient poetry, is perhaps indicative of that unease we have noted. To see how mythological narrative could be written at this period we shall have to turn to a poet whose gifts fall far short of Lemaire's, to François Habert. Second-rate he may be, fuzzy and prolix in his use of language, but François Habert is an excellent example of an author writing regularly over a period vital to developments in literary history (in his case from about 1541 to 1561) and writing so consistently in response to the prevailing taste that his work can provide a reliable gauge of changes in the literary climate of the time. Habert is particularly relevant to us because throughout his career he remained faithful to his favourite ancient poet, Ovid, and the majority of his poems are versions of the *Metamorphoses*, the *Heroides*, or their derivatives.[1]

Habert's first collection of poems appeared in two volumes in 1541, the *Jeunesse du Banny de Liesse* (his poetic pseudonym) and a *Suite du Banny de Liesse*, both published at Paris by Denis Janot. The same printer had reprinted the *Grand Olympe* in 1539 in a rather superior edition with numerous woodcuts, mostly from his basic stock of illustrations originally made for other books. He also used some of them for this collection of Habert's poems. The first part of the *Jeunesse* contains two long poems modelled on Ovidian tales, *La fable de Piramus et Thisbe et de leurs amours infortunees* (fols. 91vo–104vo) and *La fable du beau Narcissus amoureux de sa beaulté, dont il mourut* (fol. 105 to the end). Both these poems are announced as 'traductions' by Habert, but 'amplifiées de son invention' (fol. 89). In the case of the Narcissus poem this amplification is fairly minimal. The poem is in fact a verse rendering of the fable as told in the *Grand Olympe*, with only occasional sideways glances at the *Metamorphoses*. There is no trace of the interpretations which the *Bible des poetes* had appended to the tale (and which the *Grand Olympe* as usual had omitted).[2] The additions to the Pyramus tale are more substantial and show that Habert already had an interest in reworking mythological narrative. Again it is the *Grand Olympe* that Habert follows rather than the *Metamorphoses*, but he creates a framework for his story that is not in either source. In both the *Metamorphoses* and the *Grand Olympe* the story of Pyramus and Thisbe is a story told in exclusively human terms. Habert adds an introduction and a conclusion which attempt to translate it into a story where gods intervene in human affairs. His Thisbe is wooed first by Mars and then by Cupid, and when she refuses them they concert together to wreak vengeance, Mars by giving Pyramus the fatal sword, Cupid by causing Pyramus and Thisbe to fall in love. The purpose of this introduction seems more decorative than anything. Habert makes most play of the irony whereby Mars the conqueror is vanquished by Thisbe, and Cupid, who governs the hearts of men and gods, has lost his own to her. This is a very commonplace sort of compliment to pay a classical beauty, certainly not a figure that mediates between the literal sense of the story and its conceptual significance. And we cannot make much of the divine motivation which Habert gives his plot. Although later in the fable he does refer to what Cupid and Mars have done, it is also made clear that the love between Pyramus and Thisbe antedates Cupid's rejection and has a purely natural origin, and the subsequent events really owe nothing to the gods who are supposed to have set them in train. Habert's attempt to add a divine dimension to the story may lack conviction, but he is obviously interested in the possibilities. At the end of his fable it is Pan and the nymphs who bury the lovers, whereas in both the *Metamorphoses* and the *Grand Olympe* it is the parents who perform the rite. This ornamentation slackens the narrative structure, but it is clear from the other ways in which Habert expands on the *Grand Olympe* that it is not primarily narration which interests him. He puts much more stress than even the *Grand Olympe* on dialogue. The speeches of Pyramus and Thisbe (not to mention Mars and Cupid) are by far the most important element in his telling of the story. And there are moments when he inclines to improve on his original by additions, indicating at least an embryonic sense of that proliferation of material and variety of expression advocated by Erasmus in his influential *De Copia*. Habert's language is much more dilated than that of the *Grand Olympe*, his speeches more full of imprecations and ejaculations, and not only does the mulberry tree change its colour at the end, but the marble tomb where the lovers meet turns from white to black, and the nearby stream ceases to flow. Habert's Narcissus and Pyramus and Thisbe poems are presented 'selon le naturel', as the *Grand Olympe* has it, without interpolated explanations. But Habert does give them each a 'sens moral' in four lines at the end of each poem. Neither of these epilogues is derived from the *Bible des poetes*. They are very summary conclusions to the fables, nothing more than indications of how they might be used as moral *exempla*, with a suggestion, reminiscent of the *Grand Olympe*, that the moral sense is implicit in the text and hardly needs drawing out for the reader:

> Aymer est bon, voire bien ardemment
> Par mariage, ou ce que Dieu commende,
> Mais Piramus et Tisbe follement
> En ont usé, nul est qui ne l'entende.

The feast of the gods

In the *Suite du Banny de Liesse* we come to a poem which concerns us much more directly, *Le iugement des troys Déesses, Juno, Pallas, et Venus, par Paris prononcé, juge delegué par les Dieux, par amplification du Banny de Lyesse* (fols. 3–38). It is a much longer, much more important-looking poem than the two we have just discussed, with subtitles and numerous illustrations (although they were not made for this poem). The narrative runs from the banquet of the gods up to Paris's desertion of Oenone. The latter part (fols. 31v°–38) is closely modelled on Ovid's Oenone epistle in the *Heroides*, but the precise sources of the preceding narrative are not quite so easily identified. It certainly belongs to the tradition of the *Ovide moralisé* rather than Guido de Columnis, but it does not derive from the *Ovide moralisé* itself. Habert could have used the *Bible des poetes*, or Lemaire in the *Illustrations*, or Lemaire as he appears in the *Grand Olympe*, or all three. He is composing now at a greater distance from his sources; he is more selective, more bold with his amplifications, and quite possibly more eclectic.

Habert's poem introduces the reader to the world of the gods at a feast which is clearly the same feast as that described by the *Bible des poetes* and by Lemaire, but it has now lost all connection with Peleus and Thetis and their marriage. Habert provides no heavenly counterpart to the human relationship of Paris and Oenone, and indeed there is no longer any clear sense of division, of parallelism or of antithesis between the world of gods and the world of men. Essentially they inhabit the same world and have the same pleasures and the same appetites:

> Advint ung jour que descendus des cieulx
> Sur Pelion le mont delicieulx
> Alloient jouer les Dieux en ce prins temps,
> Ou les espritz des humains sont contens.   (fol. 4v°)

The description of the feast in Habert concentrates on two features: music and dancing, and eating and drinking. His heaven is full of music. Venus, Juno and Pallas all dance to the music of Amphion and Mercury. But there is no distinction at all between different kinds of music, no indication that it means anything more in the poem than grace and sensual delight, or at most amicable concord:

> Lors Orpheus a prins son instrument
> Et met au vent une doulce chanson
> Dont on n'avoit encor ouy le son,

Mercure, adonc le son finy, s'advance
Et d'entonner sa musette commence
Avec Pallas, qui mesure tenoit,
Et pour accord Mercure entretenoit,
Et Amphion chantoit d'aultre costé
Avec Venus déesse de beaulté,
Laquelle alors sa doulce voix mesure,
Pour avec luy tenir bonne mesure,
En ce soulas sur ce mont plantureux
Prenoient les dieux le deduict amoureux.   (fol. 6v°)

Lemaire's description of the music heard by the gods had already disappeared from the *Grand Olympe*. The prominence Habert gives to it may be his own invention, or it may be a more classically correct and decorous amplification of the 'trompes, tambours, cors, vielles et cimbales' of the *Bible des poetes* (fol. cxvi), but his purely literal description of it is all of a piece with the very human way his gods enjoy the physical pleasures of eating and drinking. In Lemaire we do not see what they eat: 'le raconter excederoit pouvoir humain' (p. 218). In Habert's poem on the contrary, Pallas, Juno and Venus are most vividly realised at the beginning, not in their appearance, but in what they eat and its physical effects:

En ce convy Venus rien ne voulut
Menger sinon du lievre qu'elle esleut,
Pour maintenir beaulté continuelle
Sept jours durans, et grace naturelle,
Juno donnoit d'une chaulde tortue
(Qui les amans reffroydis esvertue)
A Juppiter le grand Dieu son espoux . . .
Pallas estoit bien sobre en sa pasture,
Et beuvoit peu ensuivant sa nature,
Pour eviter que sa grande doctrine
Par trop menger ne tombast en ruine.   (fol. 6–6v°)

At Habert's feast the human and physical is not perfected and transfigured in a world of gods and transcendent concepts. Here it is the gods who have descended to the human plane, nowhere more clearly than in their predilection for the 'vins du beau Pays de France', in preference to the customary nectar (fol. 6).

Habert does not use special language codes to discriminate between the vision of gods and men. The style of these opening pages is a plain, middle style, somewhere between the elevated, decorated and metaphorical language of Lemaire and the grotesque buffoonery of the *Bible des poetes* (Habert sobers down Bacchus and drops

Priapus altogether). There are no metaphors at all, the language of the feast is in no sense tropical, and unlike the *Bible des poetes* and Lemaire, Habert invites no allegorical abstractions to mingle with his gods and alert us to other dimensions of meaning. The only way Habert distinguishes his gods from humans at this point is by stating, quite prosaically, what part of the physical universe they govern: Flora 'qui des fleurs est déesse'; Jupiter 'dominateur du ciel et de la terre' (fol. 4v°); Bacchus

> Auquel adonc par divine entreprise
> Porter flaccons la charge fut commise. (fol. 5)

Even then it is their physical appearance of which we are made most aware, rather than the concept they represent. Habert's definition of the different spheres of influence of his three main goddesses comes some time after we have met them familiarly at table together:

> Juno avoit le tiltre de richesses,
> Et de beaulté copieuse et nayve
> Venus avoit le nom par grace vive,
> La tierce estoit Pallas qui de scavoir
> Tresexcellent, avoit divin povoir,
> Chaste et pudique aymant literature
> Et decorée aussi de l'armature. (fol. 7)

This very meagre exposition of the goddesses moves the poem on to the judgement made between them, and Habert is faced with the question of how to introduce distinctions based on abstract concepts into his, so far, very literal narrative. He grasps the issue fairly firmly, addressing his apple not to the fairest, but to the most worthy, 'celle des troys qui aura par droicture plus merité' (fol. 8). Implicit here is a shift away from the aesthetic criterion which had raised such important issues for Lemaire. Even so, the preliminaries for the judgement scene, as Habert describes them, are not at all edifying. The goddesses wrangle as they did in the *Bible des poetes* and even quarrel about which of the gods should judge them, each accusing the others of choosing the god who will favour them – all of which has little or nothing to do with the concepts the gods represent. This episode may have had its germ in Lemaire (p. 223; this passage is included in the *Grand Olympe*), but in developing Lemaire's sugges- tion of family bickering and making it the sole cause of the action at this point in the narrative, Habert avoids the issue of divine foreknowledge and free will which Lemaire gradually allows the fable to open up.

Speeches and ideas

Jupiter intervenes to appoint Paris to judge the case, and sends the goddesses off to earth. Once Habert starts to incorporate concepts into his narration he tends to simplify it, cutting off possible ramifications in order to expose the root of the matter: the choice offered to Paris. Mercury and the significances Lemaire had given him in the *Illustrations* disappear. So does any sense of earth as a visibly distinct and separate place from heaven. Like the version of Lemaire which had appeared in the *Grand Olympe*, and like the *Bible des poetes* before that, Habert gives no description of the Vale of Ida where Paris is to be found. The action of the story has no background and is not spatially organised in a visual sense. What does distinguish the Judgement part of Habert's poem from the banquet is the very rigorous tripartite structure he introduces to organise the interview between Paris and the goddesses. This structure is already to be found in their consecutive speeches in the *Bible des poetes*, and Lemaire had emphasised it by adding his parallel descriptions of the three goddesses, dressed and undressed. Habert, as we shall see, develops it even further by building in yet another tripartite division of persons and speeches. Throughout this section of the poem, Habert simplifies description and stresses structure.

Before each of the goddesses takes her turn to speak, Habert gives a brief account of her appearance, and it is here that the contrast with Lemaire is particularly marked. He seems to have taken nothing from Lemaire, except, perhaps, the pattern of description followed by direct speech. Habert's goddesses are most clearly distinguished by colour: white and green for Pallas, black and gold for Juno, and purple for Venus, complemented by her golden hair and white skin. Apart from these colours, the description is minimal and imprecise, and our visual impression of the goddesses is slight. The colours are not related to any concept, except in the case of Pallas, whose white silk gown signifies 'arrogance abbatue' and who carries a white lily,

> Se demonstrant de Paix conservatrice
> Ainsi qu'elle est des lettres amatrice.   (fol. 9v°)

But these significances create more mystery than they explain – where did Pallas get her lily, and why does it mean what Habert says it means? Are we intended to make a connection between the virtues of Pallas and the royal lilies of France? These ladies belong to no classical or even medieval tradition. In their appearance they are wholly Habert's invention, and it is a curiously enigmatic appearance. But it is just the case that French writing at this period, while chary of most forms of tropical language, makes an exception for enigma. Enigma has special attractions for satirical writers like Rabelais, because it gives them both camouflage and latitude, but we find it frequently in other modes of writing besides satire. Mythological and other strange figures appear pregnant with meaning, and yet the similitudes and related tropes which formerly carried the reader from sign to concept are missing or very obscure. We have touched already on contemporary misgivings about the traditional modes of allegorical explanation. Here we have Habert declining to interpolate similitudes, interpretations or cross-references into his descriptions, and at the same time feeling free to change the familiar images of his goddesses. The effect of the enigmas thus produced is immediately to stimulate enquiry in the reader and engage him on a solution. It is a response not dissimilar to that invited by the type of enigma much favoured in contemporary humanist circles: the emblem. Habert's goddesses are not emblems in any strict sense, but it is in their speech that his pictures will reveal their meaning.

Before we follow Habert further we must have a closer look at this new transformation of Venus:

> Adonc Venus se presente à Paris
> Le saluant d'ung gracieux soubzris
> De pourpre estoit faict son habillement
> Par elle mesme ouvré divinement
> Ayant esleu la façon italique
> Qui decoroit sa grace venerique,
> Ceincte elle estoit de ceston sa ceincture
> Qu'elle portoit de diverse paincture,
> Pour convertir, voire l'inimitié
> D'ung cueur de marbre, et luy mouvoir pitié,
> Ses blondz cheveulx jusqu'en terre espandus
> Eussent les Dieux à son amour rendus,
> Son doulx regard, sa belle contenance
> Eussent tout heur peu mettre en oubliance,
> Son nez bien faict, sa bouche mesurée
> Eussent l'amour de Phoebus attirée,
> Par son maintien, par son port asseuré
> Ung cueur mourant eust à vie aspiré,
> Ses deux tetins sembloient boulles d'ivoire,
> Son estomach plus blanc que cristal, voire
> Que n'est la neige alors qu'elle est recente.   (fol. 14v°)

With Lemaire in mind, we might be tempted to relate this Italianised Venus to the Venus of his *Concorde des deux langages*, where the goddess appeared as the epitome of Florentine elegance. However, by the time Habert was writing, the association of alluring fashion with things Italian had become a commonplace. More significant perhaps is her girdle. The figures with which Lemaire had decorated it are reduced to the simplified 'diverse paincture'. There is no recall of Lemaire's interpretation of the cestos, and indeed this had already disappeared from the *Grand Olympe*. But what is added by Habert is the power of these pictures to move, the emotional effect they have on the observer. And his account of Venus is all in this vein. Habert states that she is beautiful, but, apart from the merest gesture made by the conventional colour similes in the last three lines, he does not attempt to give the reader an aesthetic experience through his description of her (and we must remember that the *Grand Olympe* had failed to find a place for the most aesthetically exciting passages in Lemaire, as well as for his interpretations). The idea of her beauty is communicated in verbs expressing the emotional attraction she exerts on the beholder, and they are conjugated in the conditional tense, indicating an inevitable and universal response to her presence, but stressing that hypothetical response rather than her visible presence. It is here, in the reaction solicited by the goddesses and in their powers of persuasion, that Habert defines the meaning he gives them. The reader's response does not involve either the heightened aesthetic awareness we found in Lemaire nor the ingenuity Lemaire demanded for decoding his tropes and similitudes. Habert's goddesses make their appeal through their rhetoric. They explicate themselves in what Habert makes them say, but in the kind of arguments they use to persuade rather than in figurative language.

Pallas proclaims herself to Paris as goddess of knowledge, the means of truth, and as goddess of verbal expression, in rhetoric and poetry. Her speech is an exact correlative of what she says she represents. She rationalises, connecting together in good order logical arguments and expositions, and including some of the modes of interpretation by which abstract truth is revealed in metaphor. Pallas alone of the goddesses uses allegorical equation, when she explains that the battles her adepts win are battles against wickedness:

> On me dict Déesse de Science
> Et de bataille, et soubz ma sapience
> Sont fortunez tous ceulx qui veullent vivre
> Soubz ma doctrine, en mon scavoir poursuyvre,
> Ceste bataille il fault interpreter,
> Pour au conflict les vices surmonter. (fols. 10v°–11)

Habert is making quite careful connections between his descriptions of his goddesses and the language he gives them, for it was only in the case of Pallas that he supplied any interpretation of their attire. Juno, on the other hand, 'la déesse opulente', proceeds by denigrating the claims of her rivals from what she regards as her position of material strength. Hers is a type of rhetoric which insinuates into the hearer a sense of superiority, a complicity in worldly cynicism, for which irony is the proper mode:

> Car confessons que charité soit morte[;]
> A l'avarice ung chascun se comporte[,]
> Possession temporelle surmonte
> Tout le scavoir, duquel on ne tient compte.   (fol. 13v°)

Venus's speech lacks both the logical organisation and the rhetorical force which Habert had given to Pallas and Juno. Her mode of persuasion is much more insidious. She softens her audience by constant reminders of how easily she sways hearts and bends wills. She claims no knowledge. Although she gives a correct etymology for her name, she can get no further than its literal sense:

> Et si par moy confesser il convient
> Que de la mer mon origine vient,
> Et que mon nom Aphros on interprete,
> Qui est escume en raison manifeste,
> Ce neantmoins ma beaulté supernelle,
> Ne peult tollir ma louenge aeternelle.   (fol. 15v°)

Her apparently loosely connected exposition of her power reflects what she claims for it: that it is arbitrary and irrational, that men surrender to charm and beauty involuntarily and irresistibly:

> Et où me plaist mes graces distribue,
> Où il me plaist je fais cueurs approcher,
> Voire plus durs feussent ilz qu'ung rocher.   (fol. 16°)

It is not through understanding metaphor that Paris and the reader may evaluate the claims of Habert's goddesses but primarily through responding to different rhetorics of persuasion and making comparisons between them.

The next development in Habert's poem takes us right away from Lemaire and from the *Bible des poetes*. It does not occur to this Paris to ask the goddesses to undress. This suggests a deliberate choice on Habert's part, a refusal to turn our eyes to the purely aesthetic possibilities of the fable, with all their erotic connotations. Instead he turns his Paris for help (and our ears for more speeches) towards three personages who arrive on the scene and whose names are Raison,

Honneur Mondain, and Lubricité. Personifications of abstract concepts are common enough in certain types of poetry in the earlier years of the sixteenth century, and particularly in the drama of the second quarter, but this is the first time we have met them sharing the stage with figures from mythology (except as very subordinate characters in the train of certain deities at the feast as described by Lemaire and the *Bible des poetes*).[3] Their advent and the speeches they address in turn to Paris are a further elaboration of the tripartite design of Habert's poem, and point to his interest in a strongly structured exposition of material, for which he had found prototypes in his models and which he now reinforces. His allegorical abstractions are clearly labelled and clearly linked, Raison with Pallas, Honneur Mondain with Juno, and Lubricité with Venus. Their names define them, and by association they in turn define and clarify the moral status of each goddess. However, the personifications are not to be equated with Pallas, Juno and Venus. They exist as separate characters in the drama and cannot replace the goddesses, as figures from the moral and allegorical senses could be made to replace characters in Ovid's fables in the *Bible des poetes*. Nor do they impel us to a retroactive reading of the speeches we have already heard from the goddesses, although the reader is free to use them in this way. In fact, the speeches assigned to the allegorical abstractions are used to amplify as much as to explain the themes Habert has already introduced. They expand what the goddesses have already said, with an extended range of reference, including within the purview of each goddess related fields which their own rather simplified speeches had not explored. Habert is attempting to include in his mythological narrative topics which Lemaire had drawn in by trope and interpretation. But Habert, as we have seen, is chary of using metaphor and similitude as means of translating things and literal propositions into concepts. Moreover, he declines to intrude into his own narrative with suggestions for interpretation. He does in fact imply a very different notion of authorial 'voice' and function. There are sections headed 'l'aucteur' in the poem, and they are all pure narration of events, linking the speeches and keeping to a plain style and literal sense. Given Habert's refusal to extend his range of significance by metaphor or interpolation, his introduction of personified abstractions is an interesting attempt to solve the problem he sets himself in explicating his fable. However, what interests Habert is perhaps not so much how to invest his narrative with non-literal meanings as how to extend the range of his rhetorical debate. This is precisely what his abstractions do, reducing Pallas, Juno, and Venus, when they refer to them, to bald metonymies, and stopping the narrative in order to orate.

Lubricité alone of the personifications is given a physical presence. She is a sort of caricature of the Venus we have already met, put in a clear moral perspective. She is similarly alluring, but in a more impudent manner, her breasts plainly 'descouvers', 'son entretien à tout œil hazardé'; and, whereas Venus charmed the gods, and her skin was compared, in one of Habert's rare similes, to the pure, natural white of ivory, crystal, and snow, Lubricité's appeal is to 'ung amant lourd, voire rude et amer', and she is painted (fol. 24v°). The parallels are clearly deliberate. The hints of beauty in Habert's description of Venus are not transferred to Lubricité, but the close relationship between the attractions of the goddess and deforming lust, although not stated explicitly, are plainly there to be recognised by the reader. In a similar manner, Habert makes Lubricité's speech exaggerate what Venus has already said and turn it into a more coherent, unambiguously expressed philosophy of life, to be set against those of Raison and Honneur Mondain in this trial of rhetorics. It was knowledge, says Lubricité, that disturbed the bliss of paradise:

> Quand on scaict bien que c'est heureuse vie
> Si on ne prent de rien scavoir envye,
> Car si Adan aulcun scavoir n'eust sceu
> De paradis terrestre n'eust yssu.   (fol. 26v°)

Venus and Lubricité represent submission to the natural cycle, with a hint of astrological determinism, in contrast to Raison, who instructs nature. It is Lubricité who can ensure worldly success in ways more secret and more telling than Honneur Mondain, reversing social roles and changing men's natures:

> Inciter puis ung cueur plus dur que marbre
> Et l'emouvoir comme fueilles en l'arbre[;]
> Ce grand povoir de Venus je retiens
> Et en ce monde heureuse je me tiens.   (fol. 27)

So Habert incorporates in Lubricité something very like the moral sense which Lemaire and the *Bible des poetes* had given to Venus, but in the form of an excursus from the fable proper and using the language of rhetorical proof rather than the poetic veil of allegorical similitudes. In order to make his choice Habert's Paris appears to need the translations with which the personified abstractions provide him. It would seem that the mythological figures on their own remain enigmas, suggesting solutions, but rather obscurely and certainly unsystematically. Habert has to move into another mode of discourse

61

altogether to derive from his narrative unequivocal statements about moral behaviour.

When making his choice Paris is swayed by the rhetoric of Raison, Honneur Mondain, and Lubricité in equal measure. It is Helen who finally determines him. Habert thus avoids issues raised by rhetoric's power to deceive, deflecting our attention instead to the extraordinary pastiche of judicial language with which Paris is made to decide the case and with which Habert concludes his transposition of mythological fable into forensic oratory. The enigmatic Venus disappears. In Lemaire and the *Bible des poetes* she lingered awhile to encourage and advise Paris. Habert returns her to her proper sphere, to a heaven totally empty of moral and allegorical senses:

> Qui en lyesse et soulas s'est rengée
> En son illustre, et divin jardinet
> Ou Adonis entra ce matinet
> Pour veoir s'amye, aussi pour reposer
> Sur la verdure apres le doulx baiser,
> Auquel Venus, de luy fort asseurée,
> Luy presenta ceste pomme dorée.   (fol. 31)

Habert is not prepared to entrust her with a moral significance. Only the moral abstraction, Lubricité, can convey this without fear of ambiguities:

> Lubricité ne passa les cypres
> De ce beau lieu, pour estre tousjours pres
> De son Paris, et pour le frequenter.   (fol. 31)

References and commonplaces

It is not only the demise of traditional allegorical interpretation that has made it difficult to control the reading of mythological poetry. There is also the question of textual contexts. Lemaire's allusions to other texts during his exposition of the story and in his conclusion had made available a proliferation of ways to read his Judgement of Paris. But those very allusions, because they were so specific, had also established certain perimeters and functioned as directions and constraints on the reader's way into the work. By Habert's time, the *Metamorphoses*, in Latin and in French, has been divested both of its traditional categories of allegorical interpretation and of its context of cross-references, and the plain text 'selon le naturel du livre' lies open to the licence of the reader (or writer), to do with it as he will.

Habert, in fact, seems dimly conscious of the usefulness of putting his poem into a context of literary references. He never inserts them into the text, and although there is plenty of evidence from the arrangement of the poem that he was following Lemaire (most probably the abridged version in the *Grand Olympe*) and very possibly the *Bible des poetes* as well, he seems to make a deliberate point of so altering their vocabulary and terms of expression that it is impossible to find any verbal recall of his base texts. He links himself into a tradition by using what is recognisably the same structural model, but, as with many of his contemporaries, his actual language asserts a difference. He composes 'oultre l'invention De tous Autheurs' (fol. 3v°). However, although he does not use textual allusion as a system of composition or interpretation, Habert does refer sporadically to other texts in the margin of his poem, if to no very clear purpose, and these texts are all from Latin literature, either classical or contemporary. There is the occasional Latin version of an adage quoted in the poem, the 'sine cerere et Baccho friget Venus' of fol. 14. A reference to Polydore Virgil's encyclopaedia of inventors confirms that Venus was the founder of prostitution (fol. 21). Two well-known lines from Ovid (*Tristia*, I, ix, lines 5–6) are quoted in Latin and French (fol. 23v°). And Lubricité invokes Cornelius Agrippa to prove that ignorance is bliss (fol. 26v°; Habert published a translation of passages from Agrippa in the same year as the poems of the Banny de Liesse).

In Habert's poem, these sorts of quotations are confined to the speeches, and indeed all the oratorical handbooks of the time recommend quotation as a means of reinforcing one's argument, as a variety of rhetorical proof. However, Habert's marginal references also point to the commonplace book, and in this way they resemble the marginal annotations made to many French editions of Latin poems published after the 1530s. The commonplace book was probably the most important instrument in the humanist programme of education which so profoundly influenced the intellectual formation of writers in France from the 1530s on. All the major humanists who wrote on the theory of education, Erasmus, Vives, Melanchthon, and the Jesuits after them, insisted that the student should keep two, three, or even four notebooks, in which he was to list vocabulary, elegant turns of phrase, examples of rhetorical figures, and passages illustrating important concepts, in particular moral values.[4] These notebooks or commonplace books were divided by headings and subheadings, and the pupil was expected to extrapolate all his reading to fit into appropriate sections. He was helped in his task by the editions he or his teacher used, which, in the 1530s, began to stud their margins with pointers to commonplaces in their text and occasional references to passages where other authors had treated the same topic. The conscientious student would have to hand an ever-growing supply both of material and of forms of expression, out of which he would construct his own compositions. The commonplace book thus influenced both reading and writing. By the 1530s it had become so much the norm in educational practice that printers supplying the school market, like Robert Estienne at Paris, were producing ready-made printed versions, with extracts from a great variety of classical authors. The printing industry, as we have noted before in the case of Lemaire's bibliographies, sometimes has an important rôle in promoting reading habits and is always crucial in reinforcing them.

Habert's marginal quotations, unsystematic and trite though they are, are perhaps best understood in the light of the modes of reading being developed by the commonplace book, although they represent a very primitive stage of that development. His notes, like his own style, make no reference to models of linguistic expression. But they do point out some ideas common to his own poem and to other texts. The primary purpose of these allusions is not now to plot the reading of one particular narrative, adding layers of sense to the basic matter. They do not bring in reformulations and interpretations of the core material from a diversity of texts. Instead they work outward from the poem, opening it up to a series of relationships with a number of general themes, which are not necessarily closely connected to each other. We are invited to read the poem as a loose nexus of instances of these themes, possibly fragmenting it in the process. All this is very much in embryo in Habert's margins, but there is already a discernible shift in the way cross-references to other texts are being made to work in a new poem.

Haphazard as he is with his allusions for most of his narrative, Habert fills his margins with much more conviction when he comes to the end of his poem. Into its last pages (fols. 34–7v°) he inserts a translation of Ovid's Oenone epistle (*Heroides*, v), which he calls an imitation, and a fair number of the Latin lines are quoted in the margin. For the first time Habert follows Ovid's style of expression closely, but not to narrate or describe. The verse-letters of the *Heroides* give him a pattern for the kind of writing which clearly interests him most: the monologue, exemplifying a particular mode of persuasion, modulated through various forms of rhetorical argument, and using language as a means of demonstration and debate, not as trope and metaphor. Habert speaks with the voice of his time. It is no accident that it is only during the 1530s and 1540s that the popularity of Ovid's *Metamorphoses*, as shown by the frequency of editions in Latin and in French, is challenged by his *Heroides*.

Pagan error and Christian truth

Habert did not bid farewell to his three goddesses in 1541. He returned to them with a worrying insistence which possibly betokens some anxiety about how to read, and consequently how to write, mythological poetry. The nearest he comes to a critical examination of theories of interpretation is in his *Exposition morale de la Fable des 'rois Deesses, Venus, Iuno, et Pallas*, an appendix to his *Deploration noetique de feu M. Antoine du Prat* (Lyons: Jean de Tournes, 1545, pp. 41–53). This poem argues a rational explanation of why the ancients made Venus goddess of beauty, Juno goddess of riches, and Pallas goddess of knowledge. The original equations are firmly ascribed to ancient authority, a claim with which the humanists could hardly quarrel. Then Habert goes on to state that these equations have their roots in real historical circumstances, in the hyperbolical praise lavished on certain women famed for beauty, worldly wealth and prudence respectively. The significances of the goddesses are thus explained and vindicated by assumptions derived from traditional euhemeristic rationalisations of pagan mythology. Allegorical similitudes give place to historical processes. In the case of Venus the historical explanation is complicated by some speculation on social psychology. For the original human Venus was not only beautiful but unchaste. Nevertheless, so captivated were her admirers and so cowed by her power and reputation that they praised her, literally, to the skies and drew a beautiful veil over her impurities. Only the most perceptive of the ancients saw the corruption beneath and revealed the truth in fables. So the moral ambivalence of Venus also has a rational explanation in history. But further than this Habert does not venture. None of the attributes of Venus appear; indeed she has no physical presence in the poem. Habert turns to a catalogue of the idolatrous errors of the pagans, which are totally alien to Christian truth and cannot be in any sense accommodated into a Christian context. Venus survives as an aberration in Christian society, as the sin of lechery, 'femme lascive'. This is Habert's only gesture towards allegorical interpretation, and the links he makes between lechery and the Venus of fable are tenuous. The language of pagan fiction and Christian truth sit uneasily together. There are no similitudes to bond them, and even the meanings which the ancients themselves accredited to fable lose significance for the Christian reader. All the wisdom of the pagans

> N'estoit sinon que doctrine apparente
> En jugement, et de raison parente.
> Non pas raison selon Christ temperée,
> Mais selon loix humaines moderée. (p. 51)

Also in 1545 Habert published another set of variations on the Judgement of Paris theme, consisting of three separate poems, *La Nouvelle Pallas*, *La Nouvelle Juno*, and *La Nouvelle Venus*. The Juno poem makes reference to the recent birth of the first son of the Dauphin Henry (the future Henry II) and his wife, Catherine de Medici; the *Nouvelle Pallas* is accompanied by poems about this birth; and the *Nouvelle Venus* appears to be slightly earlier, as it alludes to Catherine's pregnancy and unborn child. This enables us to date the poems to the end of 1543 and the early part of 1544, and indeed Habert tells us that they were presented to Henry and Catherine in a manuscript version and were considerably revised and augmented before appearing in print in 1545.[5] Here we have another transposition of the fable, or rather of the goddesses of the fable, for the narrative has now disappeared altogether. We are left with Pallas, Juno and Venus, but not the Pallas, Juno and Venus imagined by the poets of antiquity:

> Les anciens jadis sages tenus
> Une Deesse ont dit estre Vénus:
> Naïve et belle, et en biens fortunée,
> Mais d'amour folle, et trop desordonnée:
> Et que son filz Cupido triomphant
> Combien qu'il fust nud, aveugle et enfant,
> Brusloit d'amour les femmes et les hommes.
> Mais en ce temps veritable où nous sommes,
> Nous n'adjoustons à ce langage affable
> Aucune foy, ains le tenons pour fable,
> Laissons donc là Venus et sa sequelle,
> Car quant à moy je suis Venus nouvelle,
> Chaste et pudique, ou de grace y ha tant,
> Que mon amy en est rendu content.
> (*Nouvelle Venus*, p. 8)

Fable is replaced by 'truth', and the truth which Habert has his reformed goddesses express is the definition of true love in the case of Venus, and true religion in the case of Pallas and Juno.

Despite the implicit allusion to the Judgement of Paris made by the grouping of the poems under the names of the three goddesses, the model for Habert's new Venus belongs to another tradition altogether. She is sister to the celestial Venus much celebrated by Italian neo-Platonic thinkers, who by dividing the goddess of love into a celestial and a terrestrial manifestation were able to separate the beauty and love which for them opened the gates of heaven from the eroticism which Christianity assured them led to hell. This Venus is a philosophical allegory created to express an idea, and she is much more amenable to Habert's present purpose than the ambivalent figure of the fable. We have already seen his need to call in the assistance of the clearly defined abstraction, Lubricité, in order to fit the enigmatic Venus of myth securely into a moral context. His 'nouvelle Venus' is identified on three separate occasions with the celestial Venus of Plato:

> Mais en cela Platon soit mon autheur,
> De deux Venus contraires inventeur:
> L'une impudique, où tout crime est compris,
> L'autre pudique, et de trop plus grand preis:
> L'une d'amours fabuleuse Deesse,
> L'autre d'amour veritable maistresse.

> (*Nouvelle Venus*, p. 6)

She is a very unsophisticated, rather domesticated version of the Platonic allegory. The distinction she is brought in to make is a simple, straightforward moral distinction, without any of the metaphysical speculations of the Italian philosophers. She denounces promiscuous 'fol amour', which leads to jealousy and strife and which is associated with the Venus of fable and with the poetic fiction of ancient literature (Paris, Adonis, Narcissus, Dido, and Ovid's *Ars Amatoria*). Instead she extols the peace which follows perfect mutual fidelity, and finds her illustrations in the Bible, in the union of Adam and Eve before the Fall, and in the story of Pierre de Provence and Maguelonne, which belongs to modern literature and to Marot in particular.[6] Habert's subject in this poem, the definition of true love and perfect marriage, associates it very closely with the preoccupations of much contemporary literature, with the poems of the *Querelle des Amyes*, with the stories and discussions Marguerite de Navarre was writing for her *Heptaméron*, even, very remotely, with Scève's *Délie*. To move in that direction Habert has had to renew his image of Venus, substituting the Platonic dichotomy which is quite alien to the Ovidian narrative tradition, and almost severing her connection with fable altogether. On the one hand, this illustrates once again how intractable a vehicle for concepts mythological narrative had become for writers in the 1540s. On the other hand,

Habert is demonstrating that a good deal of freedom was now available to the writer in the way he developed the implications of the figures of mythology. He allows the influence of Venus to generate a great variety of themes and ideas, and he does this by a process of loose association and by the compositional device of making intermittent allusions to the original Venus in order to change the direction of his argument. By introducing one or other of her attributes he can expatiate on the erroneous view it represents and then digress into another long amplification where the goddess herself is lost from sight. This is not interpretation in the strict sense. Habert depends only very slightly on similitudes for the initial stages of a rhetorical development, introduces them only to refute them, and moves very quickly into a much more discursive mode, where he can deal not in the ambiguities of metaphor, but in straightforward propositions and arguments. We have altogether lost the controls exerted by the fixed interpretative schema of the *Bible des poetes* and by the contexts provided by Lemaire's cross-references. What we find in Habert is more in the manner of Erasmus's long digressions on the sentences he quotes in his *Adages* and the rhetoric of amplification which he taught in *De Copia*. This is also the manner which Erasmus used to comment on literary texts and to explore how they could be applied to the contemporary moral and social scene without making anachronistic equations between things ancient and modern.[7]

The directions in which Habert allowed Pallas and Juno to take him are perhaps more interesting to us than the marriage of true minds, but would deflect us even further from mythological narrative. His Pallas proclaims true knowledge, to be learnt only from the Gospel, and his Juno turns away from worldly wealth to lay up her treasure in Heaven. Both these poems refer in unequivocal terms to the religious conflicts of the day. They make a clear commitment to the translation of the Bible into French and to other tenets associated with the non-schismatic party advocating reform within the established Church. Professing full adherence to the Catholic creed,

> Car je veux croire et aymer sans feintise
> Tout ce que croit la catholique Eglise,
>
> (*Nouvelle Pallas*, p. 21)

Habert is no less direct in his attack on 'sophistes' and 'hypocrites' who keep the Word of God from the people, and he places his hope for peace within the French Church on the leadership of 'grands seigneurs de hault credit', and on a true Biblical understanding of the controversial issue of faith and works. In 1545, at precisely the moment when attitudes in the religious conflict were beginning to polarise, when the Sorbonne was organising its most authoritative attack on suspect books in response to the influx of French works from Geneva,[8] Habert published this very clear statement of the position of the centre party and placed it under the direct protection of the Dauphin Henry and Catherine de Medici. His poems, and the fact that they were reprinted in the next three years, are evidence for the early history of an articulate centre party, which was to re-emerge onto the political scene, again under the protection of Catherine de Medici, at the time of the Colloque de Poissy and Catherine's attempts at compromise in the early years of the Wars of Religion.

What is of more interest to our present investigation is the extremely wide range of themes which can be gathered under the mythological net. Of course, it can be done only by making the connections so loose that they hardly hold at all. Narrative disappears, so does physical description of the goddesses, so do the tropes that once linked description to concept. What remain are precisely the features which Habert stressed most in his telling of the Judgement of Paris: the rhetorical speeches and the structure. These poems are pure monologue, a concatenation of unambiguous statements and rhetorical arguments and exhortations, designed to persuade the reader to an intellectual point of view on clearly defined moral and religious issues. As far as structure is concerned, Habert seems to retain his interest in the tripartite design for which the traditional Judgement of Paris had given him the model, although the purpose of this composition is now quite different. The speeches of his new goddesses echo each other rather than present three divergent styles of life as the old ones did. But whereas in the earlier poem they were connected by the narrative of the choice offered to Paris, now when we look for the point where they converge we find it not in any fable, but in political choices to be made by the royal couple Henry and Catherine. The new Pallas speaks in Henry's ear, and Catherine is actually identified with the modern Juno and the modern Venus, with their repudiation of the old mythology, its style and vision, and with their very explicit statements on matters of current debate.

The *Nouvelle Pallas*, *Nouvelle Juno*, and *Nouvelle Venus* are Habert's most innovative elaboration of mythological material. They represent the limit of his copious variations on the theme of the three goddesses and mark the end of his obsession with the fable and its applications. Habert's vision is not poetic, as Lemaire and Boccaccio understood poetry in its purest sense (as trope and allegorical fiction). Nor does Habert's mode of exposition really make for new discoveries about the significances latent in the fable itself. He tends to replace rather than reread his mythological figures. They are not explored as concepts, but used as generators of rhetorical developments which lead the reader's attention outwards and away from the fable towards extraneous matters. The reader is also led safely away from the sensual and aesthetic seductions which Venus had held out to Lemaire. In these poems, Habert, like many another writer at this period engaging with the moral and aesthetic issues raised by mythological poetry, but denied the help of the traditional guides to reading it, allays his anxieties by in effect refusing to fable any kind of truth status and replacing it with Christian doctrine, neo-Platonic purity, and the language of the Bible.

Nevertheless, Habert's interest in mythological poetry continued and was about to take a significant new turn. He addressed himself to the *Metamorphoses* itself, forsaking his attempts to rationalise and transcribe fable in favour of exact translation, a form of writing mythological poetry in which, inevitably, the purely literal sense is authoritative and precludes elaboration. In the later 1540s Habert embarked on the task of completing Marot's verse translation, of which only two books had appeared. Habert published six books of his continuation in 1549 and the complete work in 1557.[9] This is the first literal translation into French of the whole *Metamorphoses* to appear in print. For the first time all Ovid's fables are told in Ovid's own manner. Habert's younger contemporaries, the poets of the Pléiade, may not have needed or appreciated his rather cumbersome efforts, but they certainly believed in the recovery and transposition into French of Ovid's authentic style. The Judgement of Paris, along with other accretions from the moralised Ovids, seems destined for oblivion.

TRANSITION: LECTION AND ELECTION

Despite the very significant differences between the Judgements of Lemaire and Habert, in one crucial respect our response to both variations of the fable is similar: in both cases reading is closely associated with choosing. Of course the very matter of the fable accentuates the notion of choice and predisposes the reader towards a response which falls in with the pattern of the Judgement story, based as it is on the presentation and selection of options. But Lemaire and Habert do reflect the models of writing prevalent at their separate moments in the sixteenth century. Therefore, the fact that both are drawn to the fable of the three goddesses as the form best for exploring the possibilities of mythological poetry suggests that in this field at least there is common ground between them, and that both instinctively connect reading with choosing, 'lire' with its close cognate 'élire'. The prologues to both works envisage a reader who will ratify the sense he uncovers in the narrative by making a specific moral choice:

> Brave je dis non point tant seulement
> De grande noblesse, ains d'ung vray jugement . . .
> Qui jour en jour accroist et continue
> D'aymer Pallas.   (Habert's *Jugement*, fol. 3v°)

The moment of choice, however, is not delayed to the end of the fable. Both authors stimulate in the reader a constant state of awareness that the process by which he elicits meaning from the text is simultaneously a process of selection.

In Lemaire the strategy of choice is based on a clear spatial structure and directed by language codes which initiate us into a hierarchy of levels of sense. Fully intelligent reading involves a series of guided choices by which we learn to discriminate between these senses and consequently between what they signify. A little later, and with a similar stress on progress between spatial locations, Lemaire was to explore even more fully the connections between reading

71

language codes and making moral choices in the contrasts he draws between his Temple of Venus and Temple of Minerva in the *Concorde des deux langages*. In Lemaire we have a very sophisticated elaboration in mythological terms of the complex tradition of medieval exegesis, which grew out of methods applied primarily to Scripture and kept as its paradigm the distinction which Christianity made between the spiritual and the physical, to the detriment of the latter. Its premises for interpretation derive ultimately from the application to difficult texts of St Paul's imperative to choose between the letter which kills and the spirit which gives life.[1]

Habert's Judgement is not so clearly defined in spatial terms, but its structure is still rigidly tripartite. And if the process of choice is no longer mediated through the language of tropes, the reader's response to the suasive rhetoric of Habert's goddesses is still essentially an act of choosing. The chief difference between Lemaire and Habert is that Lemaire's reader co-operates, as it were, in the discovery of meaning, picking up clues and applying directives which the author has implanted within the text. In Habert, however, we are faced with enigmas which are only resolved with certainty by interventions from outside the language 'selon le naturel . . . sans allegories' in which the mythological narrative is now confined, that is to say by the advent of allegorical personifications or the total refabrication of the goddesses. It is not difficult to find parallels for this feature of Habert's writing in the works of his contemporaries, especially those who share his evangelical leanings. When they apply the model of reading as choice, lection as election, to the contemporary debate on free will, they show rather less confidence than Lemaire and the orthodox of his generation in our capacity to read signs and choose aright unaided. In Rabelais's *Tiers Livre* of 1546, in which the reading of signs and the making of choices is the very nub of the work, Panurge's rhetoric might beguile us into opting for his nonsensical but speciously attractive universe of debts and debtors, were it not for Pantagruel's decisive intervention with words taken from the entirely different language code of St Paul's epistles.[2] The threefold subject matter of Marguerite de Navarre in her *Prisons* is exactly the same as that of our Judgements: the lives of love, of worldly power and of wisdom, which are the prisons of the poem's title. But the prisoner in each of these captivities would never read his situation aright were it not for illumination which comes to him from outside the walls which inhibit his understanding, from the rays of divine grace.

Nevertheless, despite their differences, our response to the mythological fictions of Lemaire and Habert, as to a great part of the literature of the first half of the sixteenth century, is predicated in terms of choice. Even Marot's epistles, half-serious, half-parody, make some form of choice the only possible reply to their special pleading. In the second half of the century poets will promote a rather different kind of reading, which will involve making connections rather than making choices, and they will review pagan fable from an altered perspective. There is, however, a very interesting book produced in France in the 1540s which, besides returning us to Venus, may provide us with a junction to what otherwise tends to look like a fairly abrupt change in the direction of writing around 1550. The *Songe de Poliphile* (Paris: L. Cyaneus for J. Kerver, 1546) is a translation of the Italian *Hypnerotomachia* of Francesco Colonna, originally printed by Aldus in 1499, although Colonna had completed the work in 1467. This is not, then, a new book, but it is typical of the reception of Italian literary fashions in France that there is often quite a gap between the publication of a particular work in Italy and the moment when it seems of special relevance to French readers. This is certainly true of editions of commentaries on classical texts. In the case of the *Hypnerotomachia* the moment is signalled by Jean Martin's translation, which in fact follows hard on the heels of a second Italian edition, and by the superb new engravings which were made to illustrate it. Once more, as in the case of the *Metamorphoses* time and again, a translation of an older work seems to bring contemporary literary developments into sharp focus.

The narrator of the *Songe de Poliphile* is led through an extremely complicated series of choices, conceived spatially as a journey and a succession of meticulously delineated places: architectural structures, temples, fountains, gardens, and so on. In the earlier stages of his journey his guides are allegorical personages, Logistique (Intellect), Thelemie (Will), the Five Senses, and a host of others. The significances of the places to which they lead him are transmitted in the most arcane of language codes, in 'difficult' tongues, Latin, Greek, Hebrew and Arabic, in emblems and hieroglyphs and in mythological tableaux. Despite its more stridently humanist pretensions and its antique dress, this still seems the universe of tropes and choices which for Lemaire constituted poetic discourse. But in fact Poliphile and his reader are progressing in the reverse direction to the journey Lemaire takes in the *Concorde des deux langages* from the aesthetic world of sense visited in the Temple of Venus to the intellectual truths which endure for ever in the Temple of Pallas. Poliphile is brought to a triple gate where he is presented, in terms of

5   The Three Gates: Colonna, *Hypnerotomachie, ou discours du songe de Poliphile*, Paris, 1546, fol. 46v°

allegorical abstractions, with a choice between the three lives which our goddesses of the Judgements were made to signify, between Gloria Mundi, Gloria Dei and Mater Amoris (Plate 5). Like Paris, he chooses the gate of love, but this time the reader's critical faculties are not alerted to dispute his choice. It is true that Logistique abandons him with dire forebodings, but we have no cause to regret her once Poliphile is met on the other side of the gate by a nymph 'avec un visage riant, et de si bonne grace, que Venus ne se monstra onques si belle au beau bergier Paris, quand il luy adjugea la pomme d'or'. This nymph is none other than his beloved Polia, the object of his quest, but Poliphile only half recognises her because of her dress, which for him obscures her identity, but which to the reader of Apuleius distantly recalls the Venus of his Judgement mime. Before they can truly know each other and the unalloyed delights of Venus herself, Poliphile and his nymph must pass through a long series of initiations, ever progressing by means of reading hidden senses from symbol to symbol towards the ultimate disclosure and fruition of bliss. It is not possible here to describe all the complexities of their tortuous path, but as the narrative proceeds the signs through which revelations are made are subtly changed so that personified concepts are largely displaced by pictures of mythological deities and fables. Certainly, the search which began with choices involving the interpretation of allegorical figures is consummated in the modes of narration, description and mythological fiction. The journey leads to a Temple of Venus and thence to the garden Isle of Cythera, where, at the climax of the quest, the naked Venus herself is unveiled in her fountain. The iconography of this figure is strongly reminiscent of the tradition exemplified by the *Bible des poetes*. But this Venus belongs to a totally different sensibility, resplendent now in the nudity which the *Bible des poetes* glossed over, from which Lemaire chose to turn his eyes and which Habert chose not to contemplate at all. She is the quintessence of sensual beauty, entirely divested of allegorical significances and undistorted by tropical disfigurations, a golden vision in which the aesthetic and the erotic are joyously conjoined and in which Poliphile finds his true felicity:

La deesse Venus estoit jusques au dessus des hanches en l'eau de la fontaine, tant claire et si subtile que toute la forme de son corps se pouvoit discerner selon la perfection du naturel, qui est contre l'effect de toutes autres eaues, lesquelles representent au double toutes choses plongées en leur humeur, les rendant plus grosses, courbes, difformes, contrefaictes, ou diminuées de leur entier. Davantage ceste eau rendoit une petite escume au long des rives, sentant ainsi que le Musc fondu avec l'Ambre, ou à peu pres. Là estoit assiz ce corps celeste, resplendissant comme un Escarboncle exposé aux raiz du Soleil. Ses cheveux estincelloient comme petiz filetz d'or, et estoient entortillez à l'entour de son front, puis pendans dessus ses espaules, où ilz faisoient un gracieux reply, et de la descendoient jusques à l'eau, sur laquelle ilz nageoient tout à l'entour de la deesse, qui avoit en sa teste un chapeau de fleurettes, meslées de pierres precieuses, les yeux amoureux et ryans, les joues vermeilles, la bouche petite et delicate, le col droict, rond, et uny, la poictrine relevée et polye comme Albastre, les mammelles rondes avec grand espace entre deux. Aux oreilles luy pendoient deux grosses perles orientales, plus belles et plus riches que ne furent jamais celles de la Royne Cleopatra. A telle beaulté je ne sauroye trouver que comparer entre les humains, car de si noble vision ne peuvent jouir sinon les dieux glorieux et celestes.[3]

Poliphile's passage from moral choice to aesthetic delight involves a shift from predominantly interpretative to predominantly descriptive modes of language, with a concomitant change in the function of figures of speech. Colonna's vision of Venus anticipates that of the Pléiade poets, and to a certain extent his language prefigures theirs. But it needed a more far-reaching reassessment of ways to read mythological fiction for Poliphile's special dream-world to become a commonplace literary experience. The most pertinent evidence for such a reassessment is to be found, as always in our period, in commentaries and adaptations of basic classical texts.

5

A PREPARATION FOR READING

Habert was not the only poet of the time to conceive the project of completing Marot's translation of the *Metamorphoses*. A contemporary in Lyons, Barthélemy Aneau, had already begun to tackle it independently, when Habert's publication of six books of his version in 1549 and news that he was progressing well with the remainder made it obvious that there was no point in Aneau continuing. Nevertheless, he published the only part he had managed to complete, the third book, along with a corrected version of Marot's translation of Books I and II in 1556.[1] The most active part of Aneau's career spans almost exactly the same years as François Habert's, 1540 to 1560. It was during that period that Aneau was Principal of the Collège de la Trinité at Lyons, the most important educational establishment in the city. Although he was something of a versifier, Aneau is best known as the probable author of the *Quintil Horatian*, in which he took issue on a number of points, major and minor, with Du Bellay's manifesto for the new poetry of the Pléiade, *La Deffence et Illustration de la langue francoyse* of 1549. In Aneau we are encountering a teacher and literary critic, rather than a practising poet, and, as a critic, he elaborates his ideas in essays and annotations, not in imaginative re-creations of his material. But he is a critic very much alive to the revolution in aesthetic standards and verbal expression in the vernacular which his young contemporaries had been promoting with such vigour in the seven years before he published his translation. In his introduction, Aneau includes Du Bellay among the 'bons poëtes du present' (fol. b 5 + 2) – perhaps a gesture of reconciliation with the new style? In any event, there is a shrewd and fertile mind at work in the long essay at the beginning of his *Metamorphoses*, and in it we can see reflected the major shifts in critical perspective which underlay the new directions given to writing by the poets of the 1550s and which their poetry in turn reinforced and stabilised for a time.

Aneau's introduction is called a 'preparation de voie à la lecture, et

77

intelligence de la Metamorphose d'Ovide, et de tous Poëtes fabuleux'. The very title of his essay stresses reading, and that is where Aneau begins. The sort of mental activity involved in reading had, of course, been implied in everything our previous commentators had said about interpreting Ovid's fables. Nevertheless, Aneau is the first to talk with such careful precision in terms of reading a text, rather than, as was especially true of the *Bible des poetes*, in language which could belong both to the process of reading and to the process of decoding a visual puzzle. In Aneau's analysis, reading involves the will and the intelligence. These two being faculties of the soul, they partake of the infinite, non-corporeal nature of the soul from which they derive, and, like the soul, they cannot be content with the mere literal sense of words or with the material, temporal, and insignificant world designated by words used and understood only in that sense:

Laquelle ame estant infinie en ces deux puissances et actes, ne se contente de la simple et nue declaration des choses: mais oultre ce a voulu y cercher aultre sens plus secret, et attaindre à plus hault entendre. (fol. a 4v°)

So the act of reading, by the very nature of the faculties engaged in it, is a searching out of meanings felt to be in some sense hidden in the text. The author may have deliberately written non-literal meanings into his text and used language to signal their presence to a reader already attuned to a certain kind of code. Or, if the reader can detect no such signals in the text, then it is part of the very process he is engaged in to read them into it, 'ou bien, si tel [aultre sens] n'y sembloit estre, le y a voulu adapter'. In either case, reading is active discovery, initiation, and re-creation, and the reader brings to his text unlimited potential for multiplying meanings, bounded only by the number of possibilities held within the text. Now, according to Aneau, it is of the very nature of poetry, as distinct from other forms of discourse, that it is able to carry the greatest number of simultaneous meanings and so satisfy most fully the reader's human search for plenitude and significance. On the one hand, true poets are divinely inspired, 'esmeuz, et haultement raviz par un vehement esp'rit divin, appellé des Grecz Enthousiasme' (fol. a 4v°), and have been privileged to see beyond the world of the senses to the eternal laws and patterns which constitute 'universal truth'. Nowhere is this more evident than in the poets' use of mythology, for it was under the guise of mythological fable, 'fiction miraculeuse, et non vraysemblable narration de fables elegantes, et joyeuses', that the earliest poets deliberately concealed their insights into the primordial order and harmony of things:

Ainsi donc les bons, et anciens Poëtes qui estoient estimez divins, et Prophetes ont couvert les nobles ars, la Philosophie et la Theologie antique . . . soubz mythologies. (fol. a 4 + 1v°)

On the other hand, these insights are mediated by the style of writing peculiar to poetry, by the harmony of its rhythms and, most especially, by its use of figurative langage. It is a

style plus hault monté que la pedestre, et simple prose des Philosophes, en parolle nombreuse de beaux vers mesurez, en forme de parler riche, et aornée de toutes figures, et couleurs. Soubz telle fabuleuse escorce couvrant verité et sapience. (fols. a 4 + 1v°–a 4 + 2)

So for Aneau the difficult and deeply rewarding enterprise of reading poetry involves paying most particular attention to the signals embedded in the language of mythology and in the language of tropes. There lie the clues to the polysemous meaning for which the soul searches:

D'ond aussi le literateur ne trouve plus grande difficulté, et ne se arrogue plus grande, ne plus propre gloire qu'en l'enarration des Poëtes, comme de ceulx qui ont tout comprins en leurs escriptz soubz plaisante feinctise.

(fol. a 4 + 2)

To read 'à la lettre' is to read 'froidement'; to read fables in their fullness of sense is to be

embeu d'esprit semblable à celluy des Poëtes c'est à savoir noble, bon, libre, et approchant, aumoins tendant au Divin. (fol. b 4)

Aneau's analysis of reading poetry (and, by implication, what he expects of modern writing) has evolved from some sort of amalgam of the traditions we have looked at previously. There is a strong neo-Platonic component, particularly in his passages about the God-given inspiration of the earliest poets and how they masked their profound intuitions in mythological fables. This was an important theme in the poetry of the early 1550s and one Ronsard had found particularly fertile for developing his ideas on the status of poetry and poets.[2] Aneau inclines to the view held by most neo-Platonic theorists that to interpret myths is not to play with mere similitudes, but to uncover substantial truths hidden by the author in his text. However, when he comes to describe and categorise the kind of meanings we should expect to find in mythological poetry, it is not towards the outer reaches of neo-Platonic speculation that Aneau leads us, but some way back to the paths of the four senses applied by the *Bible des poetes*. Aneau reduces these four senses to three, by rigorously excluding spiritual interpretation, or as he calls it:

tropologies anagogicques, [les fables] appliquant et tirant à gueulle torse au sens mystic des sainctes lettres, Car cela est mesler le Ciel avec la terre: et les choses sacrées avec les prophanes. (fol. c 5)

Aneau applies to his reading the historical standards of humanist scholars, and will not allow anachronistic equations between the truths available to pagan visionaries and the revealed truth reserved for Christians. He concedes to Ovid and mythological poets in general only those elements of the Christian religion which are attainable by natural reason. The theology of the ancients, he says, is 'la naturelle cognoissance de Dieu par ses effectz'. He precludes from it those truths which belong to faith:

Toute la Poësie ancienne autre chose n'est que la Philosophie, et faulse Theologie payanne qui a son respect seullement à Nature, pour n'avoir cogneu Dieu autrement que par ses effectz, ce que est la Nature des choses. (fol. b 4)

So far the bias of Aneau's interpretation is radically different from that of the *Bible des poetes*. We are made to feel a sense of total separation between Christian knowledge and language on the one hand and classical pagan poetry on the other. Habert, in his own way, had made just such a discrimination, tentatively with the allegorical abstractions introduced into his Judgement of Paris poem, clearly in the pronouncements of his three new goddesses. We shall have to see later how relevant this separation is to the world evoked by the mythological poems of the Pléiade, how far theirs is a self-contained fictional world created out of a literary heritage, an aesthetic vision coexisting with but independent of its authors' Christian belief. Aneau himself is clear that the fables cannot be made to correlate with the language of Christian doctrine, but he is equally clear that these fictions are true in some senses, and not purely self-referring. It is when he turns to the true senses he is prepared to allow to mythological poetry that we find ourselves on more familiar ground.

Toute fable Poëtique se doibt, et peut r'apporter par allegorie, ou à la Philosophie Naturelle donnant enseignement, et doctrine, ou à la Philosophie Moralle ayant commandement, et conseil, ou à l'histoire baillant memoire et exemple: et quelquefois à deux, et quelquefois à toutes trois. (fol. a 4+2v°)

He goes on to give examples of allegorical interpretation, physical, moral and historical, in substance very close to the tradition of the *Bible des poetes*, except that his physical allegorisations, for example

Jupiter as the world soul and principle of generation, have an imaginative splendour and elevation about them which makes one think of Ronsard's *Hymnes*. The old directives, temporarily in abeyance in the *Grand Olympe*, are reasserted and the mind's infinite capacity for finding significances is set on an already well-charted course.

Aneau's map for exploring mythological texts involves reference to other guides as well as to the key familiar to us from the *Bible des poetes*. Like Lemaire, he derives his interpretations from a range of accredited authorities. The other texts Aneau brings into play represent a culture with a large Greek component unknown to Lemaire: Hesiod, Theocritus, Callimachus, and Lycophron among others, and their interpreters. But Aneau does have authorities in common with Lemaire: Fulgentius, Albericus,[3] and Boccaccio. In addition, and perhaps more realistically, Aneau refers us to modern compilers, to the commentaries of J. Willichius on Virgil (1539 and 1547), to Xystus Betuleius in his commentary on Cicero's *De Natura Deorum* (Basel, 1550) to Giraldi's *De deis gentium* (Basel, 1548), and, with particular enthusiasm, to the *Miscellanea* of Jean Brodeau de Tours (1555). These more contemporary works of reference are primarily concerned with facts and historical evidence, and they are often highly critical of the texts they annotate. Historical inquiry is developing its own standards of rigour, and its own reading methods, despite Aneau's assumption that it is still one of the modes of allegorical interpretation. We are entering the great age of Renaissance mythography, when comprehensive encyclopaedias based on critical principles begin to replace original works of fiction like the *Metamorphoses* as repositories of knowledge.[4]

Although Aneau is careful to ground the equations and analogies made in his interpretations on 'auctoritez receues et approuvées de toute ancienneté', as humanists like Rabelais had insisted, he is very different from Lemaire (and Rabelais) in the way he uses them and expects his reader to use them:

Et soient advertiz les lecteurs que de toutes les Mythologies je n'en allegue pas un auteur, pource que le destroict de marge où elles sont apposées ne le peut comprendre et aussi que pour eviter ostentation de grande lecture, je les laisse à recognoistre à ceux qui les ont leuz, et à recercher à ceux qui ne les ont veuz: me contentant avoir en ceste preface baillé indice quelz ilz sont, ou où on les doibt cercher, et peut trouver.   (fol. c 5+1–c 5+1v°)

The fruits of Aneau's research are not presented in the form of direct quotations and there are no cross-references. The reader is expected to bring to the text in hand an assimilated culture which will alert him to signals, echoes and reminiscences embedded in the language he is reading. Aneau is referring at this point to his own annotations in the margin of his translation, but we shall find the same principle at work when we come to look at original re-creations of mythological narrative by contemporary poets. Verbal allusion becomes the most important key to understanding. The range of allusion is controlled to some extent by the boundaries of the literary culture common to poet and reader, and by the fact that, broadly speaking, writers do continue to think in terms of the models of interpretation bequeathed to them by the traditional 'senses'. But there remains an area in the reader's response where he is a free agent answerable only to his private encounter between his personal bank of associations and the work in front of him. Aneau's essay suggests a mode of reading which is not as carefully subjected to external controls as that promoted by the *Bible des poetes* or even Lemaire, but which is more disciplined an exercise than the (rather daunting) licence to interpret and amplify at will which seemed allowed, at least in theory, by the *Grand Olympe*.

Aneau recommends the same sort of controlled initiative when he talks about the actual process of reading senses into mythological fiction. He allows some scope for original interpretations, provided they deal in analogies which are judged to be rational and in accord with nature. His stress on 'jugement', 'sens naturel' and 'raison' (fol. c 5v°) disallows mere ingenuity and subscribes to the sort of criteria defined as 'inductions de nature' on which Rabelais insists in Chapter IX of *Gargantua*. As an example of interpretations discredited by these criteria, Aneau points to alchemical readings of the *Metamorphoses* (fol. c 5–c 5v°). Although he does not specify, he may be alluding to an alchemical version which we know to have been written in the 1540s, and of which only seventeenth-century manuscripts survive.[5] It is worth noting that this extravagant interpretation was contrived, and apparently gained some currency, at the very period when editions and translations of the *Metamorphoses* generally appeared as plain texts whose exegesis was left to the reader's discretion. On the other hand, Aneau also argues forcibly against the detailed, systematic, point-by-point equations which we found in the *Bible des poetes*. The art of reading does not consist for Aneau in a mechanical retroactive translation of all the information in a text into a particular code of interpretation. It is a more subtle operation altogether:

Tousjours ne fault exactement chercher es fable Poëtiques raison, suycte et Lyaison convenante et consequente en une chescune menue partie d'icelles

82

mais sufict aucunement avoir trouvé, et monstré ce que en somme les Poëtes ont voulu en toute la fable signifier . . . Ainsi es mythologicques expositions des fables, ne fault trop scrupuleusement cercher les Allegories menues par celles, qui par aventure ne conviendroient aucunement à la principalle allegorie de toute la fable laquelle sans plus de scruple doibt suffire.[6]

(fol. c 5v°–c 5+1)

This analysis of reading sees it as a continuous sequence of contacts and adjustments with a passage of writing. Significance emerges, or is created, in the actual process of reading and rereading, and it is coextensive with the whole text. Aneau rejects not only the too-simplified model of the *Bible des poetes*, but also the brutally reductive attitude of some humanists who seemed to want to compress and contract mythological fables into brief moral *exempla* and discard narrative as inessential.

In some ways we have moved back to a tropical understanding of mythological narrative, reading it not only literally, but as a 'fabuleuse escorce couvrant verité et sapience', and transposing the meaning of words from one sense to another. The anxieties and hesitations which writers of the previous decade or so seemed to harbour about this kind of transference and the similitudes on which it depends have somehow been dispelled. This is primarily because the meanings are derived from the text itself in what is felt to be an authentic manner, rather than imposed upon it. But it is also because the education of Aneau's young contemporaries had made them totally familiar and at home with many forms of tropical expression. In describing poetic language, Aneau refers not only to the philosophy and ancient theology hidden beneath its 'fabuleuse escorce', but also to its 'style plus hault monté . . . en forme de parler riche, et aornée de toutes figures, et couleurs'. These are the figures of ancient rhetoric, figures of speech and figures of thought or tropes, and among the latter are metaphor, metonymy, synecdoche, hyperbole, allegory, all figures which involve a transference of meaning, that is, as Erasmus put it, when 'a word is transferred away from its real and proper signification to one which lies outside its proper sphere' (*De Copia*, p. 333). The generation of the Pléiade had been introduced to these in the context of ancient literature, and taught to identify them, define them, and imitate them in the forms described by ancient and modern writers on rhetoric, with illustrations from Latin poetry.

We must keep our eyes open to observe every figure of speech that they [the great authors] use, store it in our memory once observed, imitate it once remembered, and by constant employment develop an expertise by which we may call upon it instantly.   (Erasmus, *De Copia*, p. 303)

With increasing frequency, and clearly responding to a growing demand, Latin editions after 1550 point out tropical expressions in their texts for students to collect, learn and copy. Numerous compilers published manuals of definitions and examples drawn from ancient sources and from the thorough investigation of Latin usage undertaken by philologists in the fifteenth and early sixteenth centuries. In France, the rather complicated treatises on figures-of-speech by Despauterius and Pontanus, published in the 1520s, had been replaced by the clear and popular expositions of Mosellanus, Susenbrotus, and then Talaeus (Omer Talon), whose *Rhetorica* was put into French by Antoine Fouquelin in 1555. In a closely related field, the *Specimen Epithetorum* of Ravisius Textor, first published in 1518, continued to be printed at frequent intervals throughout the century, both in expanded versions and in handy epitome.[7] It provided lists of appropriate Latin adjectives for every conceivable noun, taken from ancient and neo-Latin authors, and very often metaphorical in their meaning, 'epithet's decorative effect being greatest', as Quintilian had said, 'when it is metaphorical'. The vernacular theorists, significantly in the light of the comparative absence of metaphor in French poetry of the 1530s and 1540s, to which we have already alluded, were much slower to make figures of thought a major factor in their analysis of poetry. Neither Fabri (1520) nor Sebillet (1548) has much to say on tropes. But with the advent of the Pléiade poets in 1549, the situation changes dramatically. Du Bellay, Ronsard, Peletier du Mans, all define poetic language largely in terms of:

methaphores, alegories, comparaisons, similitudes, energies, et tant d'autres figures et ornemens, sans lesquelz tout oraison et poëme sont nudz, manques et debiles.[8]

The understanding of tropes which writers in the 1550s derived from their classical and humanist authorities is very different from the medieval concept of their function, which lay behind allegorical interpretation and was aimed at the systematic substitution of one set of significances for another. The humanists regarded tropes primarily as an adjunct to style, a means of varying expression and giving it 'richness . . . embellishment, dignity, clarity, sublimity, charm' (Erasmus, *De Copia*, p. 335). Metaphor and allegory, or 'extended metaphor', as the humanists defined it, were now seen as constituent elements of the text, not external mechanisms for interpretation, or, as the earlier humanists claimed, misinterpretation. Tropes as found in classical literature may indeed carry a transference of sense at the conceptual level, but they also operate as modes of variation at the purely literal level and make analogies between material things. Their function is not primarily explanatory, but descriptive and ornamental, always bearing in mind that ornament in Renaissance poetry does not mean mere superfluous decoration, but a careful direction of the reader's attention to contexts and associations from which the overall significance of the poem is derived. This is metaphorical expression as a poet like Ovid understood it and as a translator like Aneau tried faithfully to reproduce it. Interestingly, Aneau reserves his severest criticism of Marot's style as a translator for precisely those points where Marot's French is inadequate to re-create the more complex figures of rhetoric typical of poetic language in Latin:

Car à la verité comme ce bon Poëte François feu Clement Marot de sa propre et naturelle invention, vene, et elocution Françoise escrivoit tresheureusement, et tresfacilement: Ainsi autant en estrange translation, de langue à luy non assez entendue traduisoit il durement, et mesme les Poëtes Latins qui sont assez scabreux artificielz, et figurez de schemes qui a pene se peuvent rendre en François.   (fol. c 4vᵒ–c 5)

And it is precisely here that Du Bellay claims that translation fails and imitation must begin:

Je ne croyray jamais qu'on puisse bien apprendre tout cela [i.e. style, and tropes in particular] des traducteurs, pour ce qu'il est impossible de le rendre avecques la mesme grace dont l'autheur en a usé.

(Du Bellay, *Deffence*, p. 87)

The recovery through close analysis and imitation of the way tropes were used in ancient poetry seems to have overcome humanist uncertainties about this mode of writing, and in the vernacular the plain, discursive and prosaic style of an Habert pales before the sheer linguistic vitality and imaginative brilliance of a poetry based on metaphor.

All Aneau's comments on reading, significances, and tropes presuppose one thing, and that is the presence of the original text. He does not start from brief summaries of fables as Bersuire had done, or from paraphrases as in the case of the *Bible des poetes* and the *Grand Olympe*. His references to his French predecessors are very dismissive:

Les François l'ont voulu avoir en leur langue vulgaire premierement mise en prose par un Quidam: puis defigurée en un livre intitulé le grand Olympe, par. [   ]   (fol. b 5 + 1)

Aneau, like Marot and Habert in his complete version, works with the fables as Ovid wrote them, and he is scrupulously concerned with the accuracy of his translation. The meaning of the tales is conveyed by the language Ovid uses, and this makes synopses and paraphrases totally inadequate. The narrative itself signifies, or, rather, generates significance in the mind of the reader supplying context and association. This guarantees a certain autonomy to the text and gives to its literal sense an importance which the traditional interpretative schema of the *Bible des poetes* had denied it. It is not now replaced by new substitute texts appropriate to each of the senses, but remains as the primary element from which meaning is re-created at each rereading.

The privileged position of the literal sense is reinforced by the illustrations with which Aneau's book is liberally provided. Most of them had first appeared in Guillaume Rouillé's 1550 edition of Marot's translation of the first two books of the *Metamorphoses*, again a literal translation. They are very elegant, finely detailed engravings of episodes described in the fables, and very accurate in their representation of the text. In his introduction Aneau explains their purpose: to give a clear and easily grasped visual résumé of the narrative, and to bring out its aesthetic qualities.

Pour embellir et enrichir l'œuvre est apposée à chescune histoire ou fable l'image figurée d'icelle tant pour plus grande evidence, et plaisir à l'œil: que pour plus facile intelligence et recreation à l'esperit.   (fol. c 5 + 1v°)

The 'plaisir à l'œil' is the pleasure of beauty. If for Aneau reading activates the infinite longings of the soul in its search for significance, it is also an aesthetic experience, and this experience he seems to locate in the beauty of material forms mediated through their mimetic representation in art. The nature of this response to the aesthetic qualities of the literal sense of Ovid's fables is clearly another factor to be taken into account when we come to look at how Aneau's contemporaries reworked them. The many illustrated editions of Ovid in the latter half of the sixteenth century, both Latin and French, provide plenty of evidence about the value attached to pictorial images of the *Metamorphoses*.[9] Advances in the engraving techniques to which we owe these exquisite miniature works of art obviously quickened a sense of delight in the beguiling kaleidoscope of scenes and figures which Ovid's stories set before the reader's eyes before ever he starts to make an intellectual response to them. But this fascination with the mimetic aspect of Ovid's poetry cannot be understood simply in terms of improvements in printing. Janot's 1539 edition of the *Grand Olympe* had contained some pretty woodcuts but few of them actually illustrated the text. There are very complex relationships of cause and effect in the links to be traced between book illustrations and the aesthetic value now ascribed to the literal sense of mythological poetry. Certainly the illustrations fixated the literal sense, making it instantly accessible at a single glance and lifting it clear of the verbal ambiguities in which it may be embedded in its linguistic expression in the text; and they located it, often in an elaborate picture-frame border, in the category of pictorial art.

The illustrated Ovids printed in the latter half of the sixteenth century are not only very many, but very varied in the kind of associations they make between mimetic representation, the verbal text, and the text's significances. The most famous Ovid picture-book is the *Metamorphose figuree* of 1557 (the year after Aneau's translation and the same year as Habert's). In this case non-literal significances are rarely brought into play, and the text itself almost evaporates altogether. There are pictures on every page, accompanied by short, literal summaries of each story in rather doggerel verse, which itself is based on an Italian intermediary, Gabrielo Simeoni (Plate 6).[10] On the other hand engravings are not always tied to the literal sense of the fables they illustrate. Aneau himself had already used some of the engravings to be found in his translation in a completely different way in his *Picta Poesis* and *Imagination poétique* of 1552. This is virtually an emblem-book, published in a Latin and a French version, of which about a quarter of the pictures are in fact engravings for the first three books of the *Metamorphoses*, due to appear in their proper context and with another text by Aneau four years later. Aneau appends to the pictures explanatory verses which sometimes relate to the fable illustrated, but as often as not bypass the fable and interpret the emblem-picture as if it had no connection at all with Ovid's text. These little poems, in contrast with those of the *Metamorphose figuree*, are all about significances, and although they are put in the up-to-date and critically respectable guise of an emblem-book, they in fact resort to the arbitrary equations typical of the *Bible des poetes*, and make the same sort of anachronistic translations into a modern context. Aneau's poem on the Pan and Syrinx picture (*Imagination poétique*, p. 27) concocts a story to fit the illustration and then translates it by means of exactly the same sort of similitudes as one finds in the *Bible des poetes*: the satyr (not identified with Pan) is a youth 'suyvant l'Amour, vertus à dos laisant'; his seven pipes are the seven liberal arts; the hollow reed, bending in the wind, is a prostitute (Plate 7).

Aneau's *Imagination poétique* is a good example of the tenacious survival of the medieval manner of systematic allegorical interpret-

Salmacis & Hermaphrodit.

Salmacis voit le bel adolescent
En sa fonteine : & de lui amoureuse
Tresardemment, lors prend le fruit recent:
Mais qu'auient-il? chose tresmeruueilleuse,
Que lon peut dire estrangement honteuse:
Des deus n'est qu'un personnage, qu'on dit
Masle & femelle, en couple unique hideuse:
Et autrement, c'est un Hermaphrodit.

6   Salmacis and Hermaphroditus: *La Metamorphose d'Ovide figuree*, Lyons, 1557,
sig. d 4

CONVERSION DES AMOVRS A L'ESTVDE DES LETTRES.

VN SATYR ieune, & paillard, pourſuyuoit
La belle Nymphe ou s'amour mis auoit.
Elle fuyoit: & luy la pourſuyuant
Sans viſer ou: le tourra ſi auant
Pour cheuaucher en lieu mol ſans houſeaux:
Qu'en vn mareſc entra plein de roſeaux.
Et la ayant mainte larme eſpandue
Et maint ſouſpir pour la Nymphe perdue,
Là ſouſpirant pour ſa tresbien aimée,
Qu'il penſoit eſtre au mareſc abyſmée,
Il s'apperceut que des cannes yſſoit
Par ſes ſouſpirs, vn ſon qui gemiſſoit
Treſdoucement. Parquoy au treſord lieu
Et à l'amour il diſt vn grand Adieu.
Ie dy l'amour de la Nymphe paluſtre,
Que deſchaſſa autre amour plus illuſtre
De Muſicalle harmonie inuentée.

ation, despite the criticisms of the humanists; the *Metamorphose figuree* is an extreme example of the reductive effect of total concentration on the literal sense. The editions of Ovid, and illustrated editions in particular, show how wide a variety of ways of reading mythological narrative was available in the 1550s: literal, 'selon le naturel du livre', or in brief, prosaic summaries; as a visual picture, or as a set of general intellectual truths in coded form; as moral *exemplum*, or as emblem; as material for allegorical interpretation by similitudes, or as a repertory of literary reminiscences and associations. When, as at this period, under the direction and example of the Pléiade, writing is envisaged primarily in terms of the art of imitating and transposing literary models, reading in all its varying modes becomes more than ever a crucial formative influence on composition.

6

JEAN-ANTOINE DE BAÏF

Imitation

In turning to the work of Jean-Antoine de Baïf (1532–89) for our first examples of how the poets of the Pléiade handled mythological narrative, we move almost imperceptibly from translation, as envisaged by Aneau, to literary imitation. In his narrative poems Baïf fulfils almost exactly the rôle of the diligent and meticulous imitator of Latin literature to whom Du Bellay looked in his *Deffence* for that much-desired transformation of French poetry into 'une forme de poësie beaucoup plus exquise, la quele il faudroit cercher en ces vieux Grecz et Latins' (*Deffence*, p. 189).[1] As the concept of literary imitation developed in the poetry produced by the Pléiade, it divided, very broadly speaking, into two types, both of which were derived from the practice of humanist schools and the methods of composition taught there. The poet may start from a theme, a subject, a scheme for a poem, and look for ways of developing it in a diversity of authors. Behind this notion of composite imitation, or *contaminatio*, lies the commonplace book, both the abundance of material it could supply and the sort of reading and writing habits it inculcated in students used to collecting together extrapolated passages from different authors on common literary themes. This method of imitation engages the reader with a complexity of styles and literary allusions on which the writer has himself to impose some sort of order, or at least direction. Into this mode of imitation Ronsard injects the vigorous energy with which he seizes on ideas and images from different sources and fuses them together to explode into new life.

However, at the beginning of the Pléiade's enterprise, in the *Deffence*, Du Bellay seems to look more frequently to the other type of imitation to increase the range of expression of the French language. This required the writer to take a single author as his model and recreate the style of that one author systematically and exclusively in an extended passage or a total poem, se proposant, chacun selon son naturel et l'argument qu'il vouloit elire, le meilleur aucteur, dont ilz observoient diligemment toutes les plus rares et exquises vertuz. (*Deffence*, p. 99)

In this case we start from the text to be transposed, and the skills required are the essentially linguistic skills, experience and judgement of the translator (and this despite Du Bellay's attempts to distinguish here between translation and imitation). It is indeed language which primarily concerns Du Bellay in the *Deffence et Illustration de la langue francoyse*, and his recommendations are most often couched in formal rhetorical terms, in stipulations about language and forms of expression. This is precisely the area in which Baïf is working in most of his narrative poems, using his sophisticated knowledge of both Latin and French to create in the vernacular a scrupulously exact reproduction of the linguistic register, the tone, the figurative expressions, and the rhythmical periods of a particular Latin poem. It seems a fairly circumscribed aim, even a humdrum one perhaps compared with the quest for large significances and theological allegories of all sorts. We are back with the 'naturel du livre', although Du Bellay and Baïf would have refused to recognise the *Metamorphoses* of Ovid in the loose paraphrase of the literal sense offered in that name by the *Grand Olympe*. For them a book's nature is its language and its style. Nevertheless, style is vision. These apparently simple stylistic exercises are an important part of the revolution brought about by the 'ancienne renouvelée' poetry of the Pléiade, a revolution not only in poetic language, but in ideas and attitudes to life.

Poems and patterns

Baïf's mythological narratives include imitations of various Greek, Latin and Italian poets, but his predilection seems to be for Ovid. His versions of fables from the *Metamorphoses* are to be found in nine books of *Poèmes* published as part of his *Euvres en rime* in 1573 (Paris: L. Breyer).[2] They are as follows:

(1) *Le Laurier* (Book I, pp. 43–55) which tells how Apollo pursued in chase the unwilling nymph, Daphne, and how, in answer to her prayer, she was changed into a laurel tree to keep her virginity for ever (*Metamorphoses*, I, 474–567);

(2) *Le Meurier, ou la Fable de Pyrame et Thisbe* (Book IV, pp. 165–82) that unhappy pair, already the subject of a poem by Habert, who were forbidden by their parents to associate, but found a secret way of speaking to each other through a chink in the wall between their

92

adjoining houses; by this means they were able to agree to meet, but at the place of assignation Thisbe, arriving first, was surprised by a lion and ran away; Pyramus killed himself because he thought that she was dead, leaving Thisbe to take her life in her turn with his sword (*Metamorphoses*, IV, 55–166);

(3) *Salmaci* (Book IV, pp. 190–5), whom we met in the *Bible des poetes*, the nymph who embraced the reluctant Hermaphroditus in the pool which bears her name and was physically united to him for ever as a single hermaphrodite (*Metamorphoses*, IV, 285–388);

(4) *L'Amour de Medee* (Book VI, pp. 298–304), largely a description of how Medea struggled with her new-born passionate love for Jason (*Metamorphoses*, VII, 9–99);

(5) *Atalante* (Book VI, pp. 310–16), the tale of how Atalanta promised herself in marriage to whoever should beat her in a running race, of how Hippomenes won by diverting her attention with the golden apples from the garden of Venus which he rolled along the ground at her side, and of how they profaned a temple sacred to Cybele by making love there and were transformed into the lions which draw her chariot (*Metamorphoses*, X, 560–704);

(6) *Amour de Vertun et Pomone* (Book VIII, pp. 387–91), which relates how Pomona, a nymph of gardens and orchards, was wooed by Vertumnus, who could change himself to many shapes, but who finally won her when he reverted to his own (*Metamorphoses*, XIV, 622–94, 765–71).

The first two of these poems belong to the early 1550s; the rest are of uncertain date.[3]

So closely does Baïf imitate Ovid that before we look at any of his poems in detail we must examine their status as literature: imitation, or translation? Of the poems we have listed, four (*Salmaci*, *Medee*, *Atalante*, and *Vertun et Pomone*) render Ovid almost word for word. The remaining two (*Le Laurier* and *Le Meurier*) supplement translation with amplification at particular points. However, apart from *L'Amour de Medee*, none of these are said to be translations; they are presented as original poems. To the modern critical sense this may seem like deliberate deception and worse, particularly if we have in mind Du Bellay's scathing condemnation of translation, especially of poets, which he calls:

chose laborieuse et peu profitable, j'ose dire encor' inutile, voyre pernicieuse à l'accroissement de [notre] langue.   (*Deffence*, p. 97)

However, it would be naïve of us to suppose that Baïf ever assumed that he could mislead the well-informed reader for whom the poets of the Pléiade consciously wrote. Baïf presents his 'translations' as poems because he wants them to be read as poems, not translations. It is a signal to the reader to make the sort of initial response appropriate to a poem, not a translation. For example, the sign 'translation', particularly of a Latin work as easily available as the *Metamorphoses* was in the Renaissance, would perhaps direct the reader solely to make comparisons between the Latin and French texts, and judge Baïf's poem as a rendering. But if we approach his texts as poems, reading becomes a different process. Among other things, the reader will apply himself to detecting significant relationships between elements in each individual poem, and, if he is aware of a set of poems such as these narratives constitute, he may look for configurations which link the poems within the set. These links would certainly be Baïf's creation, not Ovid's, even if the ingredients from which such patterns were made were taken from Ovid. Making this precise selection of passages and isolating them from the continuous narrative of the *Metamorphoses*, Baïf has transformed these poems into quite different modes of literature, stimulating a reading attentive to similarities and contrasts unlikely to be detected in their original context.

Baïf marks the difference by giving his narratives a particular genre name: *poème*. He himself has little to say on genre definition of this kind. But Ronsard, rather later, in a poem published posthumously in 1587, was to make pertinent distinctions between *poésie*, by which he meant an epic sequence of incidents (his definition applies perfectly to the *Metamorphoses*) and *poèmes*, based on a single fable from mythology:

> D'Homere l'Iliade et sa soeur l'Odyssée
> Est une Poësie en sujets ramassée
> Diverse d'arguments: le Cyclope eborgné,
> D'Achille le boucler, Circe au chef bien peigné,
> Prothée, Calypson par Mercure advertie,
> Est un petit Poëme osté de sa partie
> Et de son corps entier.   (XVIII, p. 284)[4]

Ronsard defines the two genres in a series of tropes, comparing the multiplying of themes and fables in *poésie* to a field of many flowers:

> Poésie est un pré de diverse apparence,
> Orgueilleux de ses biens, et riche de ses fleurs,
> Diapré, peinturé de cent mille couleurs,
> Qui fournist de bouquets les amantes Pucelles,
> Et de vivres les camps des Abeilles nouvelles.   (p. 283)

The *poème*, in contrast, has a single subject, and may be represented figuratively as a single flower or a particular species of tree:

> Poëme est une fleur, ou comme en des Forés
> Un seul Chesne, un seul Orme, un Sapin, un Cyprés.   (p. 283)

But Ronsard's extended metaphor embraces more than the contrast between single and plural objects. The flowers of *poésie* grow wild. They are nature's bounty, albeit carefully arranged for the artistic effect implied by 'diapré'. The *poème* however is described solely in terms of artifice, craft and cultivation. As a tree it is diligently worked by the carpenter and transformed into agents of civilisation, the plough and the ship:

> Qu'un nerveux Charpentier tourne en courbes charrues,
> Ou en carreaux voutez des navires ventrues,
> Pour aller voir apres de Thetis les dangers,
> Et les bords enrichis des biens des estrangers. (p. 284)

Later, Ronsard compares the single mythological narrative extracted from an epic and imitated in French with an offshoot of a laurel tree, which a gardener transplants with careful art so that its beauty may be seen to better advantage on its own. Ronsard's similes imply that the *poème* fulfils certain literary functions. Like a ship, it brings home riches from foreign lands; and like a cultivated laurel tree, it gives sensuous and aesthetic pleasure to the gardener:

> elle croist et s'augmente,
> Puis de fueilles ombreuse, et vive de verdeur,
> Parfume le jardin et l'air de son odeur.
> Le Jardinier joyeux se plaist en son ouvrage. (p. 284)

The ramifications of Ronsard's metaphor establish certain conditions for the *poème*: it is a form in which art is more evident and more to be sought than natural inspiration; it is a vehicle to domesticate and display riches imported or transplanted (or imitated) from other cultures; and it is essentially a source of aesthetic pleasure, but for the cultivated connoisseur perhaps, rather than for the children of nature who roam the flowery meads of *poésie*.

Baïf is essentially a poet of formal gardens, defining his *Euvres en rime* in the preface as 'un jardinet planté diversement'. He begins his Ovidian poems with short dedications to friends and patrons, and in three cases these lines refer to the succeeding poems in metaphorical language remarkably similar to Ronsard's. Two of Baïf's *poèmes* are in fact trees, *Le Laurier* and *Le Meurier*. The laurel attracts associations from its symbolic rôle as protector of poets, but Baïf attaches them to a single, carefully planted garden tree,

> Ce Laurier que de sa dextre,
> Fizes, le vertueux maistre
> De ce jardin, a planté
> Pres ce pourmenoir, pour estre
> Rampar encontre l'esté. (pp. 43–4)

In *Le Meurier* and *Salmaci* poems are called flowers and the poet appears again as a cultivator of gardens. And although there are no flowers at the beginning of *Atalante* and *Vertun et Pomone*, the garden image is maintained in the poems, in the golden apples culled from the garden of Venus for Hippomenes, and, in its most fully elaborated form, in the fruitful orchard which is the setting for Pomona,

> Qui à dresser jardins sa pareille n'avoit,
> Et planter les vergiers par sus toutes sçavoit
> Dont elle tient son nom.   (pp. 387–8)

As in Ronsard's *Au Lecteur*, the key metaphor for the mythological *poème* is the cultivated garden. Its value is primarily aesthetic (nothing is said about 'meanings') and its beauty is the product of art.

Another term which Baïf uses to define his *poèmes* is the gift. The poems are given to friends and patrons, to honour them (*Le Laurier*) as a deposit towards the full sum of the gift which is the patron's due (*Le Meurier*), as a repayment for kindness (*Salmaci*), as a pleasurable distraction from business (*Atalante*), as an artistically fashioned present (*Vertun et Pomone*).[5] It is a quite different model from that of Lemaire and Habert. The paradigm for Baïf's narratives is not moral choice. They are part of the discourse of civilised society, and the model is an economic one, an equal exchange of services and goods, whose chief function is to promote harmony and give pleasure. Baïf is careful in these poems not to use mythology as systematic metaphor, but all the concepts he evokes when talking about his narratives can be subsumed in the Latin word 'gratia' and in its personified form, the three Graces of mythology. Their dance unites the idea of gifts and gratitude, of concord and aesthetic delight. Moreover, the Graces are companions of two deities, of Apollo, god of poetry, and of Venus, goddess of beauty and of sexual love. Baïf's poems are gifts from both these worlds.

It is possible to link Baïf's narratives thematically as well as by genre, although we can only speculate about the circumstances of their composition. The collected edition of 1573 does not arrange poems in chronological order. Guy Demerson in his edition of the first book of the *Poèmes* has suggested that all the books are grouped by themes: investigation of nature, poetry, life in the city, social diversions, and so on, and he finds in the tales of metamorphosis what he calls a 'pensée secrète' uniting all nine books.[6] In the case of poems which reproduce whole narratives from Ovid (as distinct from incidental allusions to the *Metamorphoses*) one principle of organisation does seem to emerge, and that is that the fables appear in the same order as they occur in the *Metamorphoses*, starting with Daphne from Book I and ending with Vertumnus and Pomona from Book XIV. Does this indicate a sense of progressive development through the fables? Certainly one is tempted to see a pattern in the stories Baïf has chosen to relate. We move from the sterile flight of the ever-virgin Daphne and the frustrated sublimations of Apollo, through successively more successful, if threatened, attempts at sexual union (Pyramus and Thisbe, Salmacis, Atalanta), to the happy, fruitful marriage of Vertumnus and Pomona at the end. Between the five narrative poems (excluding the maverick Medea) it is possible to detect all sorts of thematic relationships. There are two poems of pursuit, with two races, one of which the lover loses and one of which he wins (Daphne and Atalanta); lions appear twice, to frighten the unhappy Thisbe and as the ultimate transformation of Atalanta and Hippomenes, whose uncontrolled sexual passion, though consummated in marriage, eventually identifies them with the violent beast which had stalked Pyramus and Thisbe and precipitated their innocent deaths; two deviant nymphs refuse to serve Diana, goddess of chastity, to whom Daphne had consecrated herself, but whereas Salmacis dallies in idle ease before she entwines herself round Hermaphroditus in her emasculating embrace, Pomona, industriously cultivating her garden, comes gladly to see that the natural interdependence of elm and encircling vine is an image of fertile marriage. Once alerted, the reader senses that the possibilities for arranging and rearranging patterns of similarities and contrasts are inexhaustible. If we replaced the Ovidian poems in their proper context in Baïf's *Poèmes*, or looked at them in juxtaposition with his narrative poems from other sources, we should doubtless pick up all sorts of additional parallels.

But what exactly are we doing? We are recording echoes of the literal sense from poem to poem and, as it were, plotting them to create an intelligible whole, but we are not at any point provided with equations or similitudes with which to relate the fictional world of the poems to the 'true' world of religion, the natural order, the moral law, the facts of history. Nor are we offered cross-references to other texts as a key to defining the meaning of any one individual poem. As we explore the patterns made by the relationships between the poems we become aware of a network of images and ideas (mostly clustering round sexual union and marriage), but we do not feel, I think, that this network of connections leads us to a clear-cut and definitive interpretation of any particular fable. The mode of reading which Baïf seems to invite does not impel us to translate his text retroactively into different codes of meaning. He does not alert us, like Lemaire, to significant differences in language modes. Still less does he imply that the reader exercises a choice between them. What Baïf does activate in the reader is an awareness of patterns and harmonies. In other words, reading such texts has become an essentially aesthetic, less a moral, enterprise. Moreover, the most fertile ground for such patterns lies with precisely those elements in mythological poetry which earlier translators and commentators had valued least: with the detail of the narrative exposition in the original text, and with its rhetorical figures. This shift to an aesthetic base for reading is most obvious in relatively simple narratives like those of Baïf. And, as they are clearly exercises in reproducing a Latin model, they demonstrate how directly it is derived from the imitation of ancient writing.

Reflections in the pool of Salmacis

Baïf's poem *Salmaci* (pp. 190–5) recounts the fable of Hermaphroditus to which we have already referred when describing the *Bible des poetes*. There the story was told in a very plain style, reduced to action and dialogue, but converted by the interpretations added at the end into allegories of the Incarnation of Christ, of the womb, and of the temptations of female allurements. The *Grand Olympe* had reproduced this paraphrase, divested of its interpretations, and this version would certainly have been current in the third quarter of the sixteenth century, although, perhaps significantly, the years between 1554 and 1570 are a gap in the history of the frequent publications of the *Grand Olympe*. Nor had allegorical interpretation been forgotten with the last printing of the *Bible des poetes* in 1531. Aneau's emblem-books of 1552 have two engravings connected with the myth.[7] In one a bisexual, bicephalous Hermaphroditus appears as 'l'Image d'un convenable, et bienfaict Mariage' at the centre of a complicated arrangement of symbolic figures, all illustrating the idea of perfect marriage and explained in the text (Plate 8). Hermaphroditus here is the allegorical representation of an idea, equated with the Platonic androgyne, and totally abstracted from Ovid's fable. The fable does appear in a more recognisable form in an engraving obviously derived from Ovid's text, which shows Hermaphroditus and Salmacis embracing in a fountain (Plate 9). The text for this emblem describes the emasculating properties of the pool and equates it with the female sexual organ. Both Aneau's emblems translate the story in the same manner if not the same sense as the *Bible des poetes*. They work with a

FIGVRE DE MARIAGE.

L'HERMAPHRODIT est icy en pincture
A double face, & à double Nature.
Lvne de Masle, & l'autre de Femelle,
En vn seul corps, ou l'vn l'autre se mesle.
Puys deux baisers sont baillez, & renduz
Par les deux chefz l'vn vers l'autre estenduz.

    QVI sont plaisirs d'Amour perpetuel
De l'vn vers l'autre, en effect mutuel.
D'vn des costez, est des sages quelqu'vn:
Qui dict, q̃ L'HOMME, ET FEMME NE SONT QV'VN.
Daultre costé est vn Satyr hydeux
Qui dict, q̃ QVAND SE BATTENT, ILZ SONT DEVX.

---

8 *Figure de mariage*: Aneau, *Imagination poétique*, Lyons, 1552, p. 19

FONTAINE DE SALMACIS, PAIL-
LARDISE EFFEMINANTE.

Av lieu profond d'vne combe encombreuſe,
Eſt vne foſſe obſcure,& tenebreuſe.
Et au mylieu vne fontaine eſtrange:
Mais l'imonneuſe,& de bourbeuſe fange
Son eau troublée.En laquelle fontaine
Quiconque vient,pour ſa chaleur ſoubdaine
Y refroidir: & qui à corps ſuant
Se vient baigner en ce mareſc puant:
Celle fontaine à Nature tant malle:
Que quiconque eſt là entré homme maſle:
Effeminé en ſort,& demy homme,
De doubteux ſexe, Androgyne on le nomme.
    Ceste Fontaine ont les Poëtes ſincte
De Salmacis,Nymphe laſciue,& cointe.
Ou fut faict Homme & Femme Hermaphrodit.
Tant ſa Nature,& chaleur refroidit.

---

summary version of the narrative, and use similitudes to draw the reader outside the text to make a total conversion of its literal code into other combinations of meaning, part physical and part moral. The interpretative mode of reading was certainly being perpetuated in the 1550s, and the sense it attached to fables would have been reinforced by humanist reference works on mythology. Giraldi, for example, whom Aneau recommends in his 1556 translation of Ovid, associates the fountain of Salmacis with 'vitium impudicitiae'.[8] Returning to Baïf, however, we find that he scrupulously refuses to make such substitutions of meaning, and avoids the use of language which operated them. His language is modelled exclusively on Ovid's and this means that the way figurative expressions are made to function by Baïf creates very different effects from the complete translations of sense produced when similitudes are applied as agents of conversion.

Only in the first four lines of his *Salmaci* does Baïf stand aside from the text of Ovid's *Metamorphoses*, and that is to define his poem and its status. Presenting his work as an act of gratitude to his friend or patron, Mandat, he calls it a gift and, metaphorically, a flower:

> Mandat, il ne faut pas que de ta courtoisie
> J'aye cueilly du fruit, sans de ma poësie
> Te donner quelque fleur, par qui soit confessé
> Que tu m'as le premier en plaisir davancé.   (pp. 190–1)

The syntax, the word-order, and the rhymes of the first two-and-a-half lines all associate 'poësie' and 'courtoisie', poetry and the refinement of civilised social relationships. In the fourth line their common factor is revealed: 'plaisir'. Baïf's *Salmaci*, defined in terms of a gift and a sophisticated form of pleasure, is thus linked to Baïf's other Ovidian poems, whose opening lines all use similar language. The beginning of *Salmaci* also initiates the reader straight away into Baïf's use of tropical language. The poem is a metaphorical flower, and this identification of poem and flower is the product, as it were, of the fairly complicated logical equations made in the first two-and-a-half lines, whose careful symmetry is underlined by the parallel arrangements of words within the half-line phrases: 'courtoisie' and 'fruit' are a pair, mirrored in 'poësie'/'fleur'. So our first context for metaphor is a logically coherent pattern, in which reading is primarily the clarification of relationships. The conceptual meaning of the association poem/flower is only implicitly conveyed by this context, by implication from the parallel pair 'courtoisie'/'fruit'. Nor are we ever given a precise statement of what we are to understand by the equation poem/flower. The metaphor is open-ended and accumulates meaning according to the number of associations we make during the process of reading. We could recognise, for example, its long pedigree in classical literature, back to Seneca and beyond, and with it, Baïf's claims for his poetry as part of that heritage; we could associate it with the rôle of flowers in the narrative of *Salmaci* itself (p. 192); we could remember the way Ronsard and others defined the *poème* as a cultivated garden flower transplanted from the wilder, natural terrain of *poésie*; we could note that this close association of flower and fruit comes as a prelude to the middle one of Baïf's five Ovidian narratives, in which the imagery of flower and fruit is dominant and reflects a progression within the five poems from the unfruitful leaves of Daphne's virginity, through the ambiguous union of Hermaphroditus and Salmacis, to the stable, fruitful marriage of Vertumnus and Pomona. All these associations, and others, make our understanding of the metaphor more complex and more meaning-full. Our reading is still motivated by the impulse Aneau had recognised, the impulse to thrust beyond the 'simple et nue declaration des choses' in order to 'cercher aultre sens plus secret'. But in Baïf's poems (as in the poems they imitate) this sense of layers of significance is not the product of precise translation of metaphor into concept, as had been the case with poetry rooted in the tradition of allegorical interpretation. Here, one of the primary functions of metaphor is to generate patterns, and it is in discovering relationships and patterns that we feel the sense of exhilaration and aesthetic excitement peculiar to meaningful reading. Moreover, the patterns we discover (or create) are, in poems like Baïf's mythological narratives, exclusively literary. They are created from within the text, or from within a familiar literary tradition by means of textual allusions. The mode of allegorical interpretation, on the other hand, requires that tropes should make relationships between the fiction (the text) and the true nature of things. It is instructive to compare Baïf's metaphorical definition of his poem *Salmaci* with Lemaire's prologue to the *Illustrations*. All the way through Lemaire suggests that reading his fiction is essentially a process of relating it correctly to the truth, to the facts of history, to a proper sense of moral choice, to the concepts represented by the goddesses, and so on. He ends by applying the garden metaphor to his work, but with the clearest indication of exactly what sense we are to give each of its terms:

Parquoy tous nobles coeurs qui voudront cueillir fruit ou flouriture, cestadire, doctrine ou passetemps dedens ce jardin, remply et illustré de singularitez [a reference to the title of the work], seront bien si humains, qu'ilz en rendront graces à la tresnoble fleur, pour laquelle il est ainsi cultivé [i.e. Marguerite, to whom the work is dedicated]. (p. 8)

The 'nobles et clers entendemens' who can appreciate the flowers and fruits of Lemaire's garden are those for whom tropes and mythological narratives are equations for conceptual truth, and who read aright because they choose aright from among the senses they recognise. Baïf's play of relationships uncovers other delights.

Chief among these is visual pleasure. As we have seen in connection with Aneau, Baïf is composing his mythological narratives at a time when Ovid's tales were more closely associated with the visual arts than ever before and when some illustrated books had almost completely reduced them to pictures. This was a major trend of the 1550s, with publications like the *Metamorphose figuree*, and it was at this period that Pontus de Tyard gave instructions in the following terms for a picture of the Salmacis fable designed for the château at Anet:

Faudroit que dedans un fleuve, sur le bord duquel seroient les vestemens de Hermaphrodite, une Nymphe nue tint ledit Hermaphrodite embrassé, et Hermaphrodite essayant de luy eschaper et de se deffaire d'elle: leurs deux corps seroient (comme un commencement de transformation) desja joints ensemble, comme s'ils n'estoient qu'un, combien que la teste, les bras, et les jambes fussent encores separez. Venus et Mercure se verroient en quelque image par l'air, qui, comme parlans ensemble, regarderoient ceste Metamorphose.[9]

The Pléiade poets are preoccupied with the power of words to create powerful visual images and with the relationship between language and painting. This is doubtless a large part of the attraction which the literal sense of Ovid's narrative held for an imitator like Baïf. In stark contrast with the *Grand Olympe* he re-creates every visual aspect of Ovid's scene. He follows Ovid almost word for word in his brief description of the young Hermaphroditus, but where there are discrepancies it is because Baïf tends to substitute seeing for knowing. Ovid says of Hermaphroditus's face that his mother and father could be recognised in it ('cognosci possent'); in Baïf it becomes a picture:

> dans sa face le trait
> De la mere et du pere estoyent en un portrait. (p. 191)

Similarly 'studio minuente laborem' becomes more specifically an enthusiasm for seeing:

> Le desir et plaisir qui de voir luy venoit
> Amoindrissant tousjours le travail qu'il prenoit.[10] (p. 191)

The association of sight with pleasure and desire is already more explicit in Baïf's poem than in Ovid, and it will become a dominant theme later in the narrative. In the *Grand Olympe*, on the other hand, all references to sight are converted to knowledge, 'enquerir' and 'scavoir', and we pass immediately from the physical characteristics of Hermaphroditus to his moral qualities, 'moult estoit simple et peu malicieux'. Baïf's description of the fountain to which Hermaphroditus comes in the course of his travels reproduces his source exactly, including the negative formulation which both evokes vegetation with precisely visualised epithets, and denies it:

> Là ny le jonc pointu, ny la canne estulee,
> Ny le gresle roseau de l'onde reculee
> N'entoure le bassin. (p. 191)

This form of amplification by negatives is contrary to normal usage and its strangeness draws attention to the special feature of language which distinguishes its mimetic powers from those of the visual arts. Language can say not only what is, but also what is not. This paradox, impossible in painting, is repeated in the initial description of Salmacis, who is presented almost entirely in terms of what she is not:

> Une Nymphe s'y tient: mais qui le tems ne passe
> Ny à tirer de l'arc, ny à suivre la chasse,
> Ny à courre à l'envy. Seule Naiade elle est,
> Qui de Diane viste en la court ne se plaist.
> On dit que bien souvent ses sœurs l'ont avertie:
> Salmaci, pren le dard, pren la trousse garnie,
> Pren l'arc dedans le poing: le loisir que tu as
> Employ'-le de la chasse aux honnestes ébats:
> Mais étant, Salmaci, de tes sœurs avertie,
> Tu n'as pris ny le dard ny la trousse garnie,
> Ny l'arc dedans le poing, ny ton loisir tu n'as
> Employé de la chasse aux honnestes ébats. (p. 191)

There is an implied contrast here between two different styles of life, that of Salmacis and that of the more orthodox nymphs. In the description of the pool Baïf seems to miss Ovid's barren sedge (the 'steriles ulvae' of line 299), which establishes a link in the pattern of positives and negatives between, on the one hand, the vegetation which is not here and the lives of the nymphs dedicated to barren virginity, which Salmacis does not follow, and, on the other hand, the evergreen turf which does edge the pool and Salmacis's devotion to her own sexuality. Instead, Baïf hints at a moral antithesis between the leisure of Salmacis and the 'honnestes ébats' of Diana's nymphs.

What he does follow with meticulous care is the patterning of Ovid's schemes, the formal division of his three negative sentences into three separate visual entities, the precise repetition of words and their disposition within the line. The investigation of language's negative potential is balanced by a demonstration of its power to impose formal control and pattern. This may be just an exercise in stylistic imitation, but from such exercises will grow the most beautiful and disturbing visions of Renaissance literature:

> Vous n'estes pas en drap d'or habillée
> Ny les joyaux de l'Inde despouillée,
> Riches d'email et d'ouvrages, ne font
> Luire un beau jour autour de vostre front:
> Et vostre main, sans artifice belle,
> N'a rien sinon sa blancheur naturelle . . .
>
> (Ronsard, *Elegie*, XIV, p. 152)

As the poem moves towards the meeting of Salmacis and Hermaphroditus, the association of beauty with the sense of sight becomes more prominent. It is made in terms of the narrative exposition, in the self-reflection of Salmacis in the pool and at the moment she catches sight of Hermaphroditus:

> Mais tantost dans son eau son beau cors elle baigne,
> Tost d'un buys dentelé sa chevelure peigne:
> Par fois en se mirant au transparant sourjon,
> S'y conseille que c'est qui luy sied bien ou non . . .
> Elle le voit venir: et le voyant sur l'heure
> Desire d'en jouïr: mais quelque tems demeure
> (Bien que bouillant d'amour) à ses cheveux tresser,
> Agencer sa vesture, et sa face dresser,
> Tant qu'elle merita vraiment de sembler belle.   (pp. 191–2)

Baïf stresses the immediate conjunction of sight, physical beauty and sexual desire, already present in Ovid's 'visumque optavit habere', but somewhat obtrusive in the disconcerting phrase 'bouillant d'amour', which is peculiar to Baïf. The phrase disconcerts because of its watery connotations, and because Salmacis, in the familiar classical tradition transmitted in the humanist commentaries and discreetly suggested by both Ovid and Baïf, is to be in part identified by the reader with the fountain that bears her name. 'Bouillant d'amour' could then imply that love heats the temperature of the pool to boiling-point, and if we read it in this way it becomes our first example of a conceited metaphor. There is no model for it in the passage Baïf is imitating, although, like all conceits, it derives from a careful study of how metaphor is made to work in classical poetry, transferring words from their proper meanings to other, but related meanings. Conceits are a product of an exaggerated fascination with such relationships, and they often amplify conventionally accepted associations of meaning (here, love/heat = metaphorical boiling) by adding further connotations to the basic metaphor, which relate it back in a surprising but logical manner to the physical elements already denoted by the text (here, heat/water = physical boiling or bubbling, as in a bubbling spring). It is a mode which requires sharp wits and sharp sight on the part of the reader, but it does not point him outside the text. It is an example both of the essential literariness of Renaissance writing (Baïf plays with the possibilities for metaphor of this partial identification of nymph and pool, he does not use it to rationalise the fable) and of its tendency to stress the physical constituents of tropes, and more especially the visual.

In placing this stress on the visual, Baïf sometimes alters and sometimes amplifies his model. The grass and leaves on which his Salmacis lies are assertively 'drue' and 'épesse'; Ovid's are enervatingly soft, 'mollibus . . . mollibus'. Baïf's feeling for the picturesque tends to obliterate Ovid's appeal to other senses which in fact are more intimately involved in the fable (Ovid's Salmacis will soften the young man's hardness at the climax to the story, 'mollitaque in illis [undis] membra', but Baïf confuses the point by twice describing Hermaphroditus's body as 'douillet'). Nevertheless, Ovid's language is also highly visual, and especially in his similes. After Salmacis has propositioned Hermaphroditus, he blushes; a specific colour is mentioned three times in the text, and each time as a variant of the word 'rubor'. Baïf both imitates and amplifies, using seven different shades of colour and adding more detail to each of the comparisons:

> une honte naïve
> Les jouës du garçon peignit de couleur vive,
> Qui les ruses d'Amour encor ne comprenoit:
> Toutefois le rougir ne luy mesavenoit.
> Une telle couleur sur les pommes éclatte,
> Qu'à demy le Soleil a teint en écarlatte:
> Tel est l'ivoire peint de sanguin vermillon:
> Telle est la Lune aussi, quand le haut carillon
> Du resonant érein n'a puissante efficace
> Pour rendre clair-bruny l'argenté de sa face,
> Lors que les charmes forts de sa trouble paleur
> Ont taché la clarté de vermeille couleur. (p. 192)

Tropes, and perhaps similes in particular, not only challenge the reader's wit in making relationships but represent the physical world with a sensuous immediacy typical of painting and surpassing it in language's ability to reproduce the variety of nature in little compass. Here we are near the source of countless numbers of Renaissance poems which anatomise a woman's beauty in terms of a variety of seemingly unconnected natural phenomena described in vivid detail. It is a triumph of the material world and of the literal sense and of mimetic art, although here, as is often the case with poetry in this manner, the centrifugal tendencies of such an accumulation of similes are carefully controlled. Baïf puts a limiting frame, as it were, round his sequence of images by bringing us back at the end, with words like 'trouble', 'taché', to the initial generator of the figure, 'honte'. He does not systematically relate his tropes to specific moral categories, but he does use the idea of modest shame to make his similes cohere at the conceptual as well as the sensuous level, and this had not been the case in Ovid, where the repetition of variants of 'rubor' had alone performed this function. Nevertheless, there could not be a more markedly different sense of language from that of the *Grand Olympe* where the whole passage is reduced to:

Hermaphroditus ne sonna oncques mot, comme celluy qui moult estoit honteux et qui oncques n'avoit senti que c'estoit d'amours et par vergongne rougit. (ı, fol. 61vº)

Beauty emerges from figures of rhetoric into the action of the narrative as Hermaphroditus divests himself of his clothes to enter the pool to bathe. Salmacis is all eyes, and Baïf stresses the sexual indiscretion of her stare by adding three positive words of sight to Ovid's lines, which have only one:

> et derriere
> Des arbrisseaux branchus s'embuchant se plia
> Sur un genoil en terre, et l'enfant épia.
> Tandis, comme celuy qui ne se donne garde
> Pour le happer d'aguet qu'on le guette et regarde,
> En enfant qui n'a soin, le voicy le voila . . . (p. 193)

Seeing becomes voyeurism; the relationship between human beauty and its beholder becomes linked, however delicately, with ideas of rape, albeit without the slightest hint of the moralising inferences which for Lemaire were inescapable. All this is implicit in the narrative of the fable, but Baïf's small amplification brings it nearer the surface, and familiarity with imitations of this kind helped to make it part of the normal language of love poetry. At this point also, strong involuntary emotion resulting in physical change is again expressed in terms of simile. The language of the poem becomes altogether more tropical as we near the conclusion and the change of

107

nature effected by sexual union. The mirror image, already present in Salmacis's self-reflection earlier, reappears as reflected sunlight:

> Lors Salmaci s'éperd et brusle de desir
> De celle beauté nuë, esperant la saisir:
> Ses yeux estincelloyent comme un miroir éclaire,
> Qui du Soleil serein reçoit la flamme claire;   (p. 193)

and as refraction, when the youth's white limbs shine through water as through glass:

> Luy de ses creuses mains bat ses flancs et ses hanches,
> S'élançant dans l'étang: là où ses cuisses blanches
> Et ses bras sous l'eau claire à secousses jettoit,
> N'étant non plus caché, que si quelcun mettoit
> Des images d'ivoire ou des lis sous un verre,
> Qui net et transparant sans les cacher les serre.   (p. 193)

Again, it is our sense of sight which is most immediately involved in responding to these similes, followed by the mind's capacity to relate, as our memory moves back and forward through the text, collecting images of water as it reflects and refracts, recalling two previous references to the ivory of Hermaphroditus's body, and Salmacis's fondness for gathering flowers. Again it is the literal sense and the material world which provide the patterns, suggesting also, but never stating, a possible transference of sense which would identify Salmacis with her pool, reflecting sunlight and enclasping all that enters it. The tropical language of the text permits such interpretations, but our reading does not depend upon them. The figure of thought involved would be *allegoria*, defined by humanist rhetoricians according to classical usage as 'continuous metaphor', but allegory here is added delight not explanation, an option not a necessary choice. As it happens, Baïf's French fails to render the metaphor which most conspicuously affirms the identification of nymph and water. Ovid's Salmacis, after leaping into her pool, is poured round Hermaphroditus, 'circumfunditur'. Baïf makes the sexuality of her embrace more explicit, but loses the ambiguity contained in Ovid's metaphor:

> Bon gré maugré le tient: et quelque resistance
> Qu'il face, luy ravit plus d'un baiser d'avance:
> Met les mains dessous luy: de ses tetins étreint
> Son estomac douillet qu'ardante elle contreint:
> Et tantost d'une part, puis de l'autre s'attache
> Alentour de l'enfant.   (pp. 193–4)

Nevertheless, the water image remains very much part of the poetic vocabulary of Renaissance poetry, modulated from metaphor to metamorphosis by Ronsard:

> Que ne puis-je muer ma resamblance humaine
> En la forme de l'eau qui cette barque emmeine!
> J'irois en murmurant sous le fond du vaisseau,
> J'irois tout alentour, et mon amoureuse eau
> Bais'roit ore sa main, ore sa bouche franche . . .
>
> (*Le Voiage de Tours*, x, pp. 224–5)

The accelerated accumulation of tropes towards the end of the narrative is most marked in the coupling of Salmacis and Hermaphroditus, ambiguously described both as union and as struggle:

> car elle le retient
> Empetré, comme on voit un serpent que soustient
> En l'air l'oiseau royal, et qu'amont il emporte:
> Il luy ceint des replis de sa queuë retorte,
> Jambes, aisles et col: ou comme court lacé
> Le lierre importun sur le chesne embrassé:
> Ou comme les pescheurs souvent prennent le poupe
> Dans le fond de la mer, qui veincueur enveloupe
> Son ennemy surpris jettant de toutes pars
> Les liens étreignans de ses fouets espars.   (p. 194)

In Baïf's words the similes are presented more explicitly as visual comparisons, 'comme on voit', but, as in Ovid, the common factor which links them is the upward reach of the eagle and the trees ('longos truncos' in Ovid), which the logic of the comparison associates with the male, and the downward pull of entwining serpent, ivy, and suffocating polyp. Baïf reproduces the detail and also the shape of Ovid's sequence of similes, which begin in attempted ascent through the air and end, as the narrative does, in the hidden underwater recesses of the pool. What Baïf omits perhaps is the full phallic implication of the 'spatiantes alas' of Ovid's eagle and of his long trees, and there is a loss in concentration when Baïf introduces his obtrusive fishermen, who are not in Ovid's text.[11] Nevertheless, we have here a series of pictorial images of sexual union from which the reader, by careful attention to the elements which unite them to each other and to the narrative in which they are embedded, can derive an intelligible view of the sexual relationship of man and woman. Here the predatory female threatens the male with castration, and his fears seem justified by the conclusion of the narrative. Their physical union is complete, but their individualities are destroyed:

> Ainsi les membres pris d'une étroitte meslee,
> Ils ne furent plus deux: leur forme fut doublee,
> Si qu'on ne pouvoit dire ou fils ou fille il est:
> Car où l'un seul n'est pas, l'un et l'autre apparoist.   (p. 194)

Moreover, it is the male who suffers the most obvious physical change, and the generalisation of his experience which Hermaphroditus makes in his prayer at the end allows us (but does not impel us) to read it as a metaphor for the sexual act:

> Quiconques abordant dans cette source forte
> Homme entier entrera, que demy-homme en sorte,
> Et depuis qu'il sera teint de cette liqueur,
> Sente amollir soudain sa premiere vigueur.   (pp. 194–5)

The *Grand Olympe*, by labouring the reciprocity of the sex change, entirely loses this possibility:

Octroyez moy tel don pour la demonstrance que'en ceste eaue ay perdu la moytié de ma nature masculine, que tous hommes qui ceste eaue attoucheront, puissent devenir demy femme et les femmes qui s'i laveront deviennent demy hommes.   (I, fol. 62v°)

Aneau in his *Picta Poesis*, makes the same basic equation which we would need to make if we read the fable as to some extent a metaphor for sexual congress: 'At revera hic fons nihil est aliud nisi cunnus.' Baïf is not being particularly daring or perceptive here. But in following Ovid, he is writing an altogether different poem from a text that would result from an amplification of Aneau's emblem verses. Aneau describes his fountain as a dark, muddy, turbulent, marshy bog (!) and the intelligible moral sense to be read into the fable is an unequivocal condemnation of lust. Baïf's vision is totally dissimilar. His is an aesthetic, virtually amoral world where the full sensuous response to human beauty merges closely into erotic fascination, that very world which Lemaire had seen in Venus and rejected. Physical beauty is here a sensual delight and a property of observable particulars. For Baïf, the function of poetic language is to denote such particulars and to suggest patterns of relationship between them. The reader is invited to explore these patterns, but the text retains its autonomy and the reader his freedom to create relationships within it. It is not a code that can be totally translated or reread in another sense, and Baïf suggests no overall interpretation of the poem which can make sense of it in moral terms. The patterns formed by vocabulary, rhetorical schemes, and tropes give the poem form, but basically its model is that of narrative, of evolving experience which realigns the relationships perceived and rearranges the patterns continuously as we read. We respond to a tension between this shifting fluidity of Baïf's matter and the linguistic control which attempts to give it form. And this tension is mirrored in the sexual ambiguities at the heart of this poem, where victory is defeat and union destroys. The earlier interpretative modes of reading mythological narrative may have offered a choice of senses, but they were not normally ambiguous; their formula for each rereading was Aneau's 'nihil est aliud nisi'. But close imitation of classical narrative and rhetorical styles revealed to the Pléiade a vision of art and life where beauty and sexuality, Venus herself, beguile by their very ambiguities:

> Quel plaisir est ce, ainçoys quelle merveille
> Quand ses cheveux troussez dessus l'oreille
> D'une Venus imitent la façon?
> Quand d'un bonnet sa teste elle Adonise
> Et qu'on ne sçait s'elle est fille ou garçon
> Tant en ces deux sa beauté se desguise.
>
> (Ronsard, IV, pp. 77–8, 1578 variant)

Pyramus and Thisbe: amplification to excess

Baïf's *Salmaci* is a very close imitation of Ovid, diverging so slightly that in some cases where he shifts the perspective it is impossible to tell whether we are looking at deliberate changes, awkward translation, or unconscious inaccuracies. His poem about Pyramus and Thisbe, *Le Meurier*, takes us a stage further in the development of the sort of writing which may evolve from imitating the style of a single author. The writer still adheres closely to his model, but adds variations of his own. Like the practice of imitation itself, such elaboration is very much the product of humanist rhetorical teaching. The *De Copia* of Erasmus is wholly devoted to varying means of expression in order to achieve an abundant style, 'copia'. Among the exercises Erasmus recommends are both imitation and emulation of classical authors:

It will also be very helpful to emulate a passage from some author where the spring of eloquence seems to bubble up particularly richly, and endeavour in our own strength to equal or even surpass it.   (*De Copia*, p. 303)

Baïf's additions are stylistic exercises of this kind, amplifying his text in what he judges to be the manner of his author, outdoing him as it were. What and how he chooses to elaborate can tell us more about his attitude to mythological narrative, and a brief glance at his *Meurier* will perhaps show the direction in which this kind of imitation could move.

The first deviation alters the reader's approach to the fable quite significantly. Baïf begins his narrative with 'Chante Deesse', a normal formula for epic rather than for a sentimental love-tale. It is certainly very different from the opening context of Ovid's story, which is one of several told by women spinning together. Baïf reinforces the serious note struck by his invocation when he summarises what is to follow as

> l'amour mutuelle
> De deux amans, et la fin trop cruelle
> Pour telle amour: qui teignit de leur sang
> Le fruit d'un arbre à l'heure encore blanc.   (p. 166)

Ovid mentions the change in the tree but gives no hint of its sad cause. What Baïf introduces here is dramatic irony. The reader is in a privileged position, knowing the end to which the protagonists are destined and of which they are pathetically unaware. Habert had already conditioned the reader's response in a similar way in his version of the tale, albeit using completely different means, when he had fabricated jealous and powerful rivals for Pyramus in the persons of Cupid and Mars. Baïf makes no such accretions to the plot. But he does repeatedly, and much more frequently than Habert, remind the reader of the 'piteux issue', the 'triste nuit', the 'mort douloureuse' which await his lovers. Moreover, Baïf makes much of the rhetorical figure *aversio*; Ovid certainly uses it once in this fable (IV, lines 68–9), but Baïf employs it on several occasions, turning from the narrative third person to apostrophise his characters thus:

> O vostre amour saintement fortunee,
> Si de ce trein vous l'eussiez demenee!
> Heureux vraiment on vous pourroit vanter,
> Si le devis vous eust peu contenter.
> Mais, hé! vouloir tousjours plus entreprendre
> Avec malheur vous fit ainsi méprendre.   (p. 168)

The aim doubtless is dramatic vividness, but combined with the superior knowledge accredited to the author and the reader, the effect is rather patronising. Certainly the *aversio* device tends, I think, to distance the reader from the action described in the text by making him a knowledgeable third party, or audience, in the dialogue suggested between the author and his characters. Relatively disengaged from the progress of the narrative itself, the reader's attention is all the more wholly focused on the manner in which it is told.

The pace of Baïf's tale is very much more leisurely than Ovid's and the reader is continually diverted from the narrative to Baïf's amplifications. These include long protestations of love, which Baïf puts into the mouths of Pyramus and Thisbe, as Habert and the *Grand Olympe* had done before him. But unlike them, Baïf is just as much concerned with amplifying the intervening narrative passages, which means that direct speech does not become the predominant feature of the story, as it had been for his predecessors. Even within speeches Baïf reserves his most complicated variations for what clearly interests him most: rhetorical figures. A few examples will have to suffice, for the poem is long and Baïf seizes on every possible occasion for a scheme or trope. Ovid describes the growing and forbidden love of the young couple with a metaphor (love as fire) and a proverb (hidden fires burn fiercest) (IV, lines 61–4). In his amplification of this passage (eighteen lines to Ovid's four) Baïf begins with an additional metaphor, the flower of youth:

> Lors que déja leur âge fait plus meur
> Epanissoit de jeunesse la fleur. (p. 166)

Then, with a repetition of the initial conjunction, he continues with a mythical allegory of love under the figures of Venus and Cupid:

> Lors que Venus, de rire coutumiere,
> Aux jeunes cœurs fait sentir sa lumiere,
> Les allumant du petillon brandon
> Que porte au poing le raillard Cupidon. (p. 167)

This is clearly a trope. Baïf is not tempted, as Habert was, to take the idea literally and add it to his plot. Baïf is more interested in the potential of the rhetorical figure, and turns it into a double metaphor (*metalepsis* or *transumptio*), making Cupid's torch lead into the next metaphor, love/fire, which Baïf expands from Ovid's single verb 'ardebant' as follows:

> De Thisbe alors la mere trop soigneuse
> Fit reserrer sa fille vergongneuse:
> Cuidant ainsi de ce feu l'empescher,
> Mais elle fit la belle trebucher
> En plus grand feu. (p. 167)

The next phrase makes an epigrammatic generalisation about things forbidden, which would have been familiar from any commonplace book and which is properly a *sententia*, indicated by quotation marks, as such figures often were:

> "La chose deffendue
> "Plus âprement est tousjours pretendue. (p. 167)[12]

Then Baïf proceeds to amplify the fire metaphor, stressing the reciprocal effect of love by a reversal of word order (*reversio*):

> Ce qui n'estoit qu'amitié simplement
> Se fait Amour, qui brusle egallement,
> Deux cœurs d'un feu, qui Thisbe de Pyrame,
> Pyram de Thisbe ard d'une egalle flamme.   (p. 167)

The paragraph concludes with a second *sententia* based on the proverb in Ovid's text:

> "Et ces feux sont, entre eux n'estant ouverts,
> "D'autant plus chauds qu'ils sont moins découverts.   (p. 167)

The original shape of Ovid's four lines (narrative, then metaphor, narrative, then proverb) is retained, but in an amplified and more complex form (narrative, then metaphor, then *sententia*, narrative, then metaphor again, then a second *sententia*).

  Le Meurier is much more diffuse and centrifugal in its structure than *Salmaci*. As in the example just quoted, the reader is continually diverted into the detail of the complicated patterns of rhetorical figures whereby Baïf varies each separate element of his model text. Far from promoting a coherent reading of his poem, Baïf's pursuit of abundance or *copia* not only distracts our eyes with vivid visual detail, literal and metaphorical, and inveigles our wits into over-elaborated schemes and tropes. The tendency to diversify also affects the tone of the poem, as Baïf mixes styles proper to different genres. As we have seen, his exordium belongs to epic, as do some of his similes in their length and subject matter, for example the tempest of Thisbe's thoughts (p. 171), of which there is no sign in Ovid. Other similes and metaphors are more appropriate to the world of sentimental romance and aim at pathos, not tragic grandeur; to this belong also the patterns of antithetical words in which Bäif schematises the strange, paradoxical fate of the lovers:

> Et Pyrame sur l'heure
> Apres l'ennuy d'une lente demeure
> Vient arriver, pensant le malheureux
> Cueillir le fruit du desir amoureux:
> Mais se hastant à la joye amoureuse
> Il se hastoit à sa mort douloureuse,
> Pour faire, mort, son amante mourir.   (p. 175)

At the end of the poem, as dawn breaks, we even have a short pastoral interlude with happy shepherds (p. 181). This mixture of language codes appropriate to different genres is not part of the overall meaning of the mythological narrative, as we found it to be in

Lemaire. There is no clear conceptual scheme to give an intelligible sense to Baïf's excursions into different styles. On the other hand, he does very carefully establish for the reader a consistent point of view throughout the narrative by his dramatic irony and by his frequent apostrophes to the lovers, in which they are always addressed as objects of our sympathy and pity. This juxtaposition of stylistic virtuosity with a rather simplified and unified emotional response foreshadows the manner of later humanist poet–playwrights like Garnier. Moreover, the delight in experiment, in pushing rhetorical ideas as far as they will go, has a definite mannerist air about it. And, like later mannerist poets, Baïf can produce some incongruous effects. There is an awkward moment when Baïf amplifies his description of Thisbe's distress with a simile:

> Comme en Hyrcargne une lyonne esmeuë,
> Quand, cependant qu'en queste elle se ruë,
> Le caut pasteur ses petis a tirez
> De leurs taniers, les trouvant adirez,
> Single en courroux ses flans, son dos, sa teste
> De sa grand'queuë: et rugist et tempeste . . .   (p. 178)

Hircanian tigers have a good pedigree and are much associated with the cruelties of love in classical literature; but to identify Thisbe with a lion, though not without a certain neat symmetry, seems in the circumstances like ridiculous excess. Here, and elsewhere, Baïf does seem to be sacrificing the whole to the part, decorum to versatility, and the interrelated structure of the total poem to the elaboration of single ornaments. On other occasions the temptation of metaphor can produce effects not only incongruous, but grotesque, another aspect of style which later sixteenth-century poets were to pursue in tropes arresting as they were strange. Pyramus has a pretty wit if not a very nice imagination:

> Mais vous Lyons, qui l'avez devoree,
> Lyons oyez cette voix esploree,
> Puis que je n'ay ce seul piteux confort
> Que de la voir toute morte à ma mort:
> Faittes de moy, faittes vostre pasture,
> Vos gorges soyent au moins la sepulture
> De deux amans, et vos ventres comblez
> Soyent le cercueil de nos cors assemblez.   (p. 176)

What engages the reader here is certainly not verisimilitude, either in a literal sense or in any other. It is gratuitous wit, rhetoric reflecting on itself and exploring its own potential. Art's mimetic function is all but obscured by a display of virtuosity, but the machinery on which the performance depends is the rhetoric of classical poetry and Baïf's thorough understanding of Latin. The root of this particular flower of rhetoric is the Latin word 'bustum' and its two meanings: a tomb and the maw of an animal. Ovid has provided the idea of union in death (lines 156–7) and the wish to be eaten (lines 112–14), and in another part of the *Metamorphoses* (VI, line 665) he has provided the seed for Baïf's trope.[13]

Neither metaphor nor level of style gives coherence to Baïf's *Meurier*. In Lemaire they were clues to meaning, codes through which the reader related fiction-writing to truth. In Baïf they generate an infinite variety of ways of expressing the literal sense of mythological narrative, but they remain reflections of the literal sense. Nor do the schemes and tropes of *Le Meurier* discover unifying patterns, as was the case in *Salmaci*. The reader is continually led into intricate figures, and it would be possible in theory to establish correspondences between them. But there are far too many and the reader's memory is too soon baffled for this quest to be an aesthetic and intellectual pleasure in this instance. Abundance turns to excess, entropy leads to collapse, and the poem tends to disintegrate into its separate rhetorical particles. Similarly, although our emotional involvement with Pyramus and Thisbe is solicited so stridently by the author, it is in fact dissipated by his calls on our wit and rhetorical *savoir-lire*.

Le Meurier exemplifies one extreme form of developments implicit in the humanist practice of imitation. It also exemplifies its inherent literariness (and here we touch on a point which will need much more elaboration when we come to Ronsard). In this sort of poetry the primary function of tropes is not, as in Lemaire, to relate the text to universal concepts and truths of quite another order than literary creation. Baïf takes his tropes, both their form and their content, from literary tradition and uses them to graft his text securely back into that same tradition. This is true of all his similes and metaphors. Pyramus persuades Thisbe to meet him by arguing from the ways of nature, but it appears that nature can only be persuasive about general truths if she speaks the language of literary *topoi*:

> Quoy? ne vois-tu que le brassu lierre
> De longs fueillars son chesne aimé reserre,
> Et que la vigne en ses pampreux rameaux
> A tout souhait enlasse ses ormeaux? (p. 169)

The image is used because it is a familiar commonplace, not because it is pertinent to the language of this poem. The same image inserted into Baïf's *Vertun et Pomone* (p. 389) or Ronsard's *Voiage de Tours*

116

(x, p. 224) has quite a different effect because it also belongs to a network of nature-references within these poems. In *Le Meurier*, where it has no such context, its main function is to recall a literary tradition. Similarly, Baïf's *sententiae* or moral generalisations are all tags from Latin authors. However, his mode is not really allusive, for he does not stir memories of specific texts or bring in resonances from other poems to amplify his sense in subtle and particular ways. He relates it to anonymous commonplaces of no special character, to the clichés of the literary language of ancient Rome at its most trite and most proverbial, rather than to the insights of any of her writers. Nor does the commonplace-book origin of his similes and *sententiae* have a cohesive effect on his material. On the contrary, each incident or idea is related to a separate moral category of commonplace expressions, so his generalisations are only provisional, and their tendency is to fragment the text into unconnected truisms.[14] Baïf buries Pyramus and Thisbe beneath a baroque superstructure of ornaments and literary *topoi*, with a virtuosity which smacks more of rhetorical game-playing than of a serious investigation of poetic language. Poor Pyramus and Thisbe! Renaissance poets were more cruel to them than the lion! At least Baïf shrouds them decoratively before their ultimate metamorphosis into a literary joke at the hands of Shakespeare's rude mechanicals and on the point of Théophile's blushing dagger.

7

PIERRE DE RONSARD

Commonplaces and the effects of poetry

The poems by Baïf which concerned us in the last chapter were the product of an extended and very close imitation of particular Latin models. Their style and their vision grew out of a fastidious, sometimes virtuoso manipulation of words, which Baïf learnt in transposing texts from one language to another. Ronsard too acquired his linguistic skills from the same exercises and could imitate, when he chose to, in the same way. But for Ronsard such imitation was subordinate to the whole scope of his enterprise. He employed it selectively and adroitly to create specific effects in the wider vision projected by his expansive imagination and essentially syncretic mentality, which combined all sorts of insights and intellectual positions derived from his extensive reading.[1]

Syncretism is as much a hallmark of Renaissance humanism, of the Florentine neo-Platonists, of Erasmus, and of Montaigne, as is the careful, programmatic reconstruction of an ancient style. Indeed, the way Renaissance humanism assimilated classical culture nourished the encyclopaedic ideal and gave it a theoretical base. To start with, the texts which our writers studied in their formative years were not only accompanied by minute linguistic and rhetorical analyses, whether orally in the teacher's comments or in the margins of annotated editions.[2] They were also linked into the whole corpus of classical writing by constant cross-references to other authors who had treated the same topic, used the same words, or explained a particular phrase. So no single passage was read as an isolated unit, but all had latent affiliations with the immensely varied intellectual universe that was Greek and Roman literature. This sense of an integrated but multi-molecular whole found formal expression in the commonplace book, the humanists' main pedagogic aid, whose influence we were beginning to discern on Habert (see p. 63). The commonplace books are collections of texts without commentary selected from different authors, but nearly always from poets, and grouped according to the headings and subheadings chosen by the editor. These headings, mostly concepts and abstract ideas, represent an attempt to systematise all knowledge and give it expression. For the humanists who promoted the commonplace book with such fervour did not see themselves as making inconsequential and arbitrary arrangements when they put their material into categories, any more than they were willing to play merely verbal games with similitudes. These categories were, as Melanchthon put it, 'the forms and rules of things', that is to say, they represented and defined knowable reality, and they made it intelligible by arranging it in systematic divisions which really inhered in nature and which took the form of infinitely proliferating classes and sub-classes.[3] Moreover, nature, thus ordered, could be translated immediately into language, the privileged language of Greek and Latin poetry, in the extrapolated passages which filled the pages beneath the subheadings. The grouping of these passages emphasised the connections, the 'common ground' between them. So the corpus of classical poetry became not only a Book of Nature, but also a book which in itself contained an infinity of significant relationships to be discovered and explored.

This is the cognitive model which lies behind the practice of imitation by *contaminatio*, which Ronsard nearly always favours. Collecting textual allusions from diverse sources, then juxtaposing them and amalgamating them in a single poem, Ronsard imitates both the ordered synthesis of nature and her infinitely variable multiplicity:

> Mon Passerat, je resemble à l'Abeille
> Qui va cueillant tantost la fleur vermeille,
> Tantost la jaune: errant de pré en pré
> Volle en la part qui plus luy vient à gré,
> Contre l'Hyver amassant force vivres:
> Ainsy courant et fueilletant mes livres,
> J'amasse, trie et choisis le plus beau,
> Qu'en cent couleurs je peints en un tableau,
> Tantost en l'autre: et maistre en ma peinture,
> Sans me forcer j'imite la Nature.   (*Hylas*, xv, p. 252)

He also imitates the editor of a commonplace book, translating nature into a composite language of literary references. The commonplace book fostered certain ideas about literature and literary imitation which are implicit in much of the work of Ronsard's contemporaries, but which find their most sophisticated expression in the work of Ronsard himself. Among such ideas is the theoretical conviction that literary writing is not wholly self-referring, but does reflect a real world of created things and true concepts. However, nature has already been given form and significant expression, in classical literature. It is there, in the stylised representations of ancient art, that we can see, much more clearly than in the transient objects of our own private and partial experience, the universal truths of nature which transcend particular instances and endure beyond the personal moment. The contents of the books from which Ronsard selects in the lines quoted above are bright flowers already picked from nature's flux, 'absentes de tous bouquets', an elixir immune to time and winter's death. Ronsard's reference to flowers is not merely a pretty image or an erudite flourish, but almost technical, for the language of flowers was the common metaphorical language for talking theoretically about poetry. The same flowers were cultivated in Baïf's poem-gardens, and the most popular commonplace book of all was entitled *Illustrium poetarum flores*. In a brief introduction the humanist scholar Beroaldus refers to the quotations collected there as everlasting flowers culled from a lovely meadow:

veluti ex pulcherrimo prato flosculos hosce odoratissimos, qui spirant suaveolentiam iucundissimam, qui tanquam amaranthi, minime marescunt.[4]

Collectively the poets of antiquity provided Renaissance writers with a dictionary of privileged and interrelated themes, images and expressions. And just as the proliferation of examples in the commonplace book was deemed to prove the universal validity of the concepts they illustrated, so the modern poet represented nature most exactly and most persuasively by drawing on a multiplicity of literary associations with a common theme. But this is the very area where the writer, 'maistre en sa peinture' and no longer bound to a particular text as in the type of imitation restricted to a single model, could assert his own creative instinct and speak with his own voice. For *contaminatio* involves the writer in choice, arrangement, and making connections. Moreover, it is precisely at this point, when he identifies the poet's activity with making relationships between his flowers (or his texts), that Ronsard introduces the language of aesthetics:

> . . . J'amasse, trie et choisis le plus beau,
> Qu'en cent couleurs je peints en un tableau,
> Tantost en l'autre: et maistre en ma peinture,
> Sans me forcer j'imite la Nature.

'Le plus beau', 'tableau', 'peinture' – this is the language of painting, which, as we have already seen, the Pléiade poets associate closely with the depiction of physical beauty. The beauty of nature, 'belle . . . inconstante et variable en ses perfections', is rendered most tellingly by the assembly which poet and painter make of her diversities, mediated through the copious forms of expression with which classical writing had already matched them.

The commonplace book model can tell us something about *contaminatio* imitation, something about Ronsard's method of composition, and also something about his understanding of poetic language and the reasons why his own is so richly intertextual. It shows where to look for beauty, but it does not fully explain the aesthetic excitement of reading Ronsard's best poems, an excitement he himself knew from reading certain passages of classical poetry:

Relisant telles belles conceptions, tu n'auras cheveu en teste qui ne se dresse d'admiration. (XVI, p. 332)

Among such passages to which he refers in the *Preface sur la Franciade* (XVI, pp. 332–3) are the very same 'vers de Virgile' which Montaigne made central to his essay on sexuality and aesthetics whence our present investigation has derived. Cassandre's poet understood perfectly well the exquisite ambivalencies of this close association between aesthetic and sensual excitement, but as only one factor in the exegesis of 'telles ecstatiques descriptions'. The notion of the hair-raising effect of reading poetry belongs more properly to another context of ideas: the 'horror' of the sacred place where the poet (or reader) is initiated into a mystery, an intuition of truth which eludes the grasp of normal rational discourse.[5]

> Car la gentille Euterpe ayant ma dextre prise,
> Pour m'oster le mortel par neuf fois me lava,
> De l'eau d'une fontaine où peu de monde va,
> Me charma par neuf fois, puis d'une bouche enflée
> (Ayant de sur mon chef son haleine soufflée)
> Me herissa le poil de crainte et de fureur.
> (*Hymne de l'Autonne*, XII, pp. 48–9)

The system of ideas which made best sense of this for Ronsard and his contemporaries was neo-Platonism, and when Ronsard theorises about the feeling of excitement and fear conjoined which reading poetry can give, it is most often to neo-Platonic language and theories of divine frenzy that he has recourse.[6] But other characteristic features of Ronsard's writing are also relevant.

On the one hand, it is important, I think, to note that his attempts to define the effects of poetry on the reader usually occur in the context of narrative (our verse quotations so far have been from two such, from *Hylas* and the story of Autonne, and practically all his examples in the *Preface sur la Franciade* are from the *Aeneid*). Fable itself, 'car la fable et fiction est le subject des bons poëtes' (xiv, p. 16), and the temporal nature of narrative seem important factors in communicating a sense of unfolding discovery and initiation into truth. The neo-Platonists themselves, particularly the Italians, often employed mythological fables to communicate ideas, but by means of conceptual equations which petrify the narrative element. As we shall see shortly, Ronsard's narratives lead the reader on more complex and open-ended trails of discovery than the relatively simple, retroactive interpretations required in neo-Platonic allegorising.

There is another context to Ronsard's analysis of reading poetry, besides narrative. His reference to lines from Virgil in the *Franciade* preface come in between attempts to define poetic language in terms of rhetorical figures:

Figures, Schemes, Tropes, Metaphores, Phrases et periphrases eslongnees presque du tout, ou pour le moins separees, de la prose triviale et vulgaire (car le style prosaïque est ennemy capital de l'eloquence poëtique).

(xvi, p. 332)

The hair-raising effect of poetry is very closely allied to a tropical use of language which re-presents things by suggesting new relationships between particulars and between words and concepts, and enriches the poem's range of associations. What Ronsard is referring to here is clearly metaphorical expression, as understood in ancient rhetoric and as he encountered it in his reading of ancient texts such as the ones he cites in his *Preface*. He had already made a similar connection between an ecstatic response to poetry and the rich complexities of its language in a *Chant pastoral* of 1559. Two shepherd–poets, Bellot and Perot (Du Bellay and Ronsard), approach a grotto dedicated to the Muses (the Château de Meudon). Entry into the grotto involves sacred, threefold rites and an invocation of the nymphs and other deities of the place. Ronsard's language identifies it with all his other descriptions of the 'horror' of the poetic experience:

> Ilz se lavent trois fois de l'eau de la fontaine,
> Se serrent par trois fois de trois plis de vervene,
> Trois fois entournent l'Antre, et d'une basse voix
> Appellent de Meudon les Nymphes par trois fois,
> Les Faunes, les Sylvains, et tous les Dieux sauvages
> Des prochaines forests, des mons, et des bocages.   (ix, p. 77)

Crossing its threshold thrills the poets with a holy awe and initiates them into divine mysteries:

> ilz entrerent dedans
> Le sainct horreur de l'Antre, et comme tous ardans
> De trop de Deité, sentirent leur pensée
> De nouvelle fureur saintement insensée.   (IX, pp. 77–8)

But immediately afterwards this state of ecstasy is replaced by a critical analysis of the edifice more typical of the connoisseur, with lists of architectural terms:

> Ilz furent esbahis de voir le partiment,
> En un lieu si desert, d'un si beau bastiment:
> Le plan, le frontispice, et les pilliers rustiques,
> Qui effacent l'honneur des colonnes antiques,
> De voir que la nature avoit portrait les murs
> De crotesque si belle en des rochers si durs,
> De voir les cabinets, les chambres, et les salles,
> Les terrasses, festons, gillochis et ovales . . .   (IX, p. 78)

We are aware from the beginning that our shepherds are figures from an *allegoria* in the humanist sense of the term, an extended metaphor which demands precise elucidation carefully controlled by the text. The sacred grotto is a beautiful palace of art, a technically sophisticated edifice, to be understood in the sense of the metaphor for style which Ronsard applies to poetry later in the *Preface sur la Franciade*:

> Les Poëtes . . . d'une petite cassine font un magnifique Palais, qu'ils enrichissent, dorent et embellissent par le dehors de marbre, Jaspe et Porphire, de guillochis, ovalles, frontispices et piedsdestals, frises et chapiteaux.   (XVI, p. 340)

In the *Chant pastoral* the enumeration of architectural features introduces ideas of structure, variety, and decoration. Then, modulating by means of a simile (another rhetorical figure), Ronsard turns his palace into a flowery field:

> Les terrasses, festons, gillochis et ovales,
> Et l'esmail bigarré, qui resemble aux couleurs
> Des préz, quand la saison les diapre de fleurs.   (IX, p. 78)

By this image of flowers and the connotations which the words 'couleurs' and 'diapre' have with painting and with rhetoric (to 'diversifie with sundrie figures' is Cotgrave's rendering of 'diaprer'), the reader is returned once again to the commonplace metaphorical language which Ronsard and the poets of his time use to express poetry's transformation of nature into art. A vital agent of this transformation is rhetorical ornament. Ronsard asserts its totally indispensable rôle in the structure of poetic discourse by the tautologous nature of the language in which he writes about figures, itself densely figurative.

In the *Chant pastoral* various constants in Ronsard's concept of how poetry works its effects are brought together: the ecstatic intuition of higher truth, which seems possible only in a special poetic world of gods and nymphs, that is to say, the figures of mythological narrative; complex patterns and transferences of sense created by rhetorical figures; and literary allusiveness, presupposing a culture shared by writer and reader, of which the most typical and influential manifestation was the commonplace book. We have met these ideas together before. They are in substance the same as Aneau's in his *Preparation de voie à la lecture et intelligence des Poetes fabuleux*, with which he introduced his translation of the *Metamorphoses*.

Nevertheless, granted there are clear affinities between the mythological poems of Ronsard and of his friends and the analyses which contemporary critics were making of their models in classical literature, one question of major importance is still outstanding. Ronsard, in particular, and to some extent all the poets of the Pléiade use mythological narratives as metaphors for exploring the character of poetic discourse and the nature of poetic activity. In prologues and epilogues Ronsard time and again presents his narratives as examples to illustrate propositions about writing poetry. Time and again, as we shall see, the language in which he relates his fables recalls the metaphorical language in which he is accustomed to talk about the effects of poetry and the experience of being engaged in writing it. Already Lemaire had embedded an evaluation of different types of discourse in his telling of fables. But it is not until the Pléiade that mythological narrative is used to articulate that intense preoccupation with poetry and the poet which is the hallmark of so much Pléiade writing and which, for Ronsard at least, is a personal obsession. The practice of closely imitating other authors doubtless fostered this self-consciousness in so far as poets were trained with particular rigour to read a text simultaneously as an instrument transmitting meaning and as an essay in the art of verbal expression. They were taught to be sensitive to idiosyncrasies of style, and to project themselves into the mentalities of different, individual writers. The free-ranging metaphorical associations of humanist rhetoric also opened up the potential of mythological narrative for use as a symbolic language referring to areas well outside the categories of the old allegorical schemes. At the same time the stress placed on rhetorical figures by contemporary commentaries on classical texts encouraged authors to identify poetic energy with figurative writing, and hence to elaborate mythological fiction into patterns of metaphor. Conditions were favourable for Ronsard to revitalise mythological narrative by appropriating it to express his preoccupation with the dilemmas, the ecstasies and the sacrifices involved in writing poetry. Moreover, the language of neo-Platonism was available to give his enterprise ideological weight. But the impetus which set French poetry on this new direction probably came from an aspect of the poetic schooling of Ronsard and some members of the Pléiade which distinguished them from their predecessors: that is, their initiation into Greek literature. The first object of Ronsard's enthusiasm, the first author from whom he took the sacred flame, was Pindar, and in Pindar's odes the craft and status of the poet are inextricably bound with his function as a teller of fables. And it is precisely in the context of odes imitated from Pindar that we have to look for Ronsard's earliest experiments in narrative form.

'Le Ravissement de Cephale'

Le Ravissement de Cephale (II, pp. 133–47) belongs to the fourth book of Odes, published in 1550. The influence of Pindar, which predominates in the early odes as a whole, is evident in this poem where Ronsard is beginning to explore at length the techniques and potential of mythological narrative as a self-sufficient entity, divorced from the contexts into which it was fitted in Pindar's celebrations of young heroes. The tripartite pattern of the Pindaric ode, based on the repetition of groups of three stanzas, is deliberately recalled in Ronsard's division of his poem into three *pauses*.[7] In the first, sea-nymphs embroider a cloak for Neptune to wear at the marriage of Peleus and Thetis, and Ronsard describes the picture they are working. In the middle and longest section, one of the nymphs sings the tale of Cephalus mourning for his dead wife and ravished by the goddess of the dawn. In the final *pause*, Themis, priestess at the marriage of Thetis, predicts the birth and prowess of her son, Achilles. Already it is apparent that the poem is a *contaminatio* of at least two fables, the marriage tale with which we are already familiar and for which the major classical model was Catullus LXIV (but Ovid also refers to the prophecy about Achilles in *Metamorphoses* XI, lines 217–28), and the fable of Cephalus, for which Ovid is the main source (but here again, Ronsard has two models to conflate, for Ovid tells the story twice, in *Metamorphoses* VII, lines 690–756, 796–862, and in *Ars Amatoria* III, lines 686–746). Laumonier in his notes to his edition also picks up other subsidiary verbal parallels, especially from Virgil, and the Peleus and Thetis fable is a favourite with Pindar. Ronsard is orchestrating quite a complex set of textual themes and already focusing our attention as much on the pattern he makes of them as on his skill in transposing the style of classical poetry. The reader is alerted with particular force to the originality of Ronsard's perspective on his material by the extraordinarily oblique angles from which he tells the tales. His later narratives will be much more straightforward, more confident perhaps, but here nothing is direct or simple. Most of the first section describes a storm at sea, not as from nature but as it were in a picture. The story of Cephalus and Aurora comes to us not from the author–narrator but from one of the Nereides, and in the telling, she changes Ovid's point of view altogether, making Aurora the central character in place of Cephalus (as in the *Metamorphoses*) or Procris (as in the *Ars Amatoria*). Finally, the prophecy in the last part of the poem is a very oblique approach to Achilles and the war of Troy. All these modes of indirect narrative are found in ancient literature, the first and third most notably in fact in Catullus's Peleus and Thetis poem, but not juxtaposed in such an obtrusive way. Ronsard makes them a crucial factor in our reading, the more so because he divides the three modes of narrative discourse into three separate divisions of text.

The first part of the poem is what is known technically as an *ecphrasis*, an animated description of a painting, or, as here, an embroidered picture. We encounter again the fascination of Pléiade poets with pictorial art, the terms of which they so often employ to define their own aesthetic of poetry. And this is largely what Ronsard is doing here. The subject of the picture is named immediately:

> Au vif traitte i fut la terre
> En boule arondie au tour,
> Avec la mer qui la serre
> De ses braz tout alentour. (II, p. 134)

It is to be the whole physical world of nature reproduced in the small compass of Neptune's cloak. On the one hand, Ronsard suggests a definition of the artist's ambition, to imitate all nature, and on the other, he grasps what is wildly paradoxical in this enterprise. It is this bold sense of paradox which underlies the descriptions of the next five stanzas, hinting at the limitations of mimetic art and at the same time triumphantly compensating for them by the resources of language. The intricate and varied detail of the picture, impossible to crowd in or to discern on any real canvas, is possible to the poet, for language is free of the physical dimensions in which a painting is contained.

126

Language alone can match nature's infinite variety. Language alone can bring movement to the still surface of a picture, stir the wind, make lightning fall from the clouds, boil the sea, spread dark across the sky. Language alone can add sound to the dumb show:

> La mer pleine d'inconstance
> Bruit d'une bouillante eau . . .
> Les bords en vois effroiantes
> Crient, d'estre trop lavés
> Des tempestes aboiantes
> Autour de leurs piés cavés. (II, p. 135)

And language alone can free the painting from its eternal present, by introducing a narrative which moves in time, changes the scene and creates a future: Neptune in Ronsard's description of events rescues the sailors from the storm and calms the waves. The reader is dazzled by this virtuoso display of poetry's potential as mimetic art, but the facility with which the poet demonstrates the superiority of his medium over the painter's is not without disturbing omens. The challenge to contain the whole world in little room dissolves immediately into tempest. Are we meant to recall the commonplace image of the writer as navigator?

> Au meilieu d'elle un orage
> Mouvoit les flots d'ire pleins,
> Palles du futur naufrage
> Les mariniers estoient peins. (II, p. 134)

Only the intervention of gods and demigods restores order. Perhaps without some such divine epiphany, or without the potency of fiction, the same critical process which revealed the paradoxes of mimetic art in painting could be applied to language too. At any rate, as we already suggested when discussing Baïf's *Salmaci*, it is possible to detect that in their pursuit of the rhetorical virtue of *enargeia* or pictorial vividness,[8] writers were being made more aware of the fundamental nature of language and of its properties. This awareness was sharpened by a close imitation of classical models with their expertise in mimetic representation, but also, I would suggest, by the juxtaposition of pictures and text in contemporary editions of ancient poetry such as Ovid's *Metamorphoses* (and the spirit of emulation may owe something to the tendency of printers to promote the pictures at the expense of the text).

As the middle section of the poem develops, the reader begins to pick up signs of a complicated network of correspondences with the first part. Here too, bright promises are clouded, not least by the story

Ronsard chooses to insert at the centre of his poem. In the first *pause*, the initial ambition to capture the physical universe in art is associated with a metaphor of sexual embrace:

> Au vif traitte i fut la terre
> En boule arondie au tour,
> Avec la mer qui la serre
> De ses braz tout alentour. (II, p. 134)

Immediately before that, Ronsard has located his whole poem at the time of the preparation for the marriage of Thetis

> . . . où son mari l'appelle
> Aus dous presens de Venus. (II, p. 134)

The last part of the poem deals with their progeny. In the middle section, where the reader might logically expect the marriage ceremony, he is given the tale of Cephalus, occupying the same place in the whole poem as the storm does in the first section. The interrelationships which Ronsard establishes between his *pauses* are intricate and subtle, requiring the reader to be alert to the same sort of linguistic and metaphorical echoes as does Baïf, but in a poem which, compared with Baïf's, is labyrinthine in its complexity of themes and literary allusions. These relationships are effected by contrasts as well as similarities, and whereas the three sections of the poem are alike in their oblique approach to narrative and in the overall shape that narrative takes (progressing from insecurity to stability), their presentation of their material is significantly different. The first part is a framed picture, and examines art and language in terms of representational painting. The second part is a song, and in this section of the poem rhetorical figures, fairly discreetly used in the first part, play a much more salient rôle. Aurora herself, goddess of the dawn, slips in and out of her identity as amorous female and natural phenomenon, her rosy skin, her blushes, her fiery sky all functioning as metaphors for each other and combining in conceits:

> Elle qui a de coutume
> D'allumer le jour, voulant
> L'allumer, elle s'allume
> D'un brandon plus violant . . .
> En vain elle dissimule
> Ne sentir le mal qui croist,
> Car la flamme qui la brulle
> Claire au visage apparoist:
> Au pourpre que honte allume
> Par raions dedans son teint,

> On voit qu'outre sa coutume
> Son cueur est pris et ateint.   (II, pp. 138, 141)

The model for these conceits Ronsard found in Ovid, but their close juxtaposition here influences the way the reader reacts to the rest of this section, encouraging him to pick up latent hints of metaphor, even when Ronsard does not fully develop them. Aurora's emotional turmoil, for example, associates her and her story with the tempest of the first part:

> Ores pronte en ceci pance,
> Et ores pance en cela,
> Sa trop constante inconstance
> Ondoie deça et là.   (II, p. 142)

Nowhere does Ronsard's tropical language give a coherent interpretation of the sense of his narrative, but it does set up patterns of associations which hint at further associations to be discovered by the reader who, in Aneau's words 'ne se contente de la simple et nue declaration des choses: mais oultre ce a voulu y cercher aultre sens plus secret'.

In addition to persuading his reader to read metaphorically, Ronsard uses literary allusions to direct him to latent meanings. His poem is clearly modelled on Catullus, who also interpolates a fable (Theseus and Ariadne) in the middle of his account of the marriage of Peleus and Thetis. The knowledgeable reader will recognise at once that Ronsard has substituted the tale of Cephalus for the Ariadne story. He may also catch echoes of the parallel section of Catullus's poem, both in the symmetry between the two fables (a divorce between two earthly lovers followed by the intervention of a god who ravishes one of them up to heaven) and in the language Ronsard uses (Aurora's fluctuations reflect the marine images used by Catullus, for example his line 62: 'prospicit et magnis curarum fluctuat undis'). Moreover, Ronsard has deliberately altered Ovid's narrative in order to make the Aurora episode come after, not before, the death of Procris. He presumably means the reader to recall his models, and so to register the full extent of the contrast which his own substitution coupled with his reversal of the Cephalus and Aurora story presents. In Catullus, Ariadne's momentary unhappiness is turned into triumph in her joyful apotheosis under the influence of Bacchus. In contrast, the centre of Ronsard's poem is a scene of grief, the human Cephalus weeping over the dead body of his human wife, killed by his own error and the violence endemic in human love. Spying like the voyeur Salmacis on 'ce que voir ne devoit pas', Aurora is enflamed by a young man in a pool, but this time the sexual overtones are muted and the pool is a pool of his tears:

> Elle vit dans un bocage
> Cephale parmi les fleurs,
> Faire un large marescage
> De la pluie de ses pleurs. (II, p. 139)

It is Aurora who, again like Salmacis, propositions the young man, but the issues involved in his refusal are graver than any Baïf disclosed. It is immortality that Aurora offers to Cephalus, a union of his mortal state with gods and nymphs, and this entails his rejection of human love and of the world of mutability and death to which that love belongs:

> Elle à la mort fut sugette,
> Non pas moi le sang des Dieus,
> Non pas moi Nimphe qui jette
> Les premiers raions aus cieus:
> Reçoi moi donques, Cephale,
> Et ta basse qualité,
> D'un étroit lien égalle
> A mon immortalité. (II, p. 144)

Cephalus turns away from her, but she, again like Salmacis, ravishes him, not down into the pool, but up to heaven. The similarity between the actions of Aurora and Salmacis is emphasised by the simile Ronsard added in 1578:

> Puis comme un aigle qui serre
> Un liévre en ses pieds donté
> En luy faisant perdre terre
> Par force au ciel l'a monté. (II, p. 145)

The direction of the movement is different, but the eagle image is a common factor. Like Hermaphroditus, Cephalus is ravished against his will. His immortality is thrust upon him and he is taken reluctantly from the world of human love. Ronsard does not apply his textual parallels to interpret his fable, as Lemaire would have done. But the suggestive power of his allusions, precisely pointed as they are, opens his text to a proliferation of meanings controlled only by the reader's ability to make connections. The middle section of Ronsard's ode, which gives it its title, represents that amalgam of song, fabulous narrative, tropical language and literary allusiveness, which for Ronsard is the essence of poetry. Within this context, the reluctant ravishment of Cephalus is a curiously ambivalent comment on the divine fury which seizes on the inspired poet. Association with gods and nymphs seems to imply a loss or diminishment in human terms, a dubious compensation for human love, despite that love's fragility and pain.

In the third part of the ode the mode of discourse changes again, from poetic narrative to prophecy. According to the neo-Platonists, prophecy, along with mystical religious rites, love, and poetry, was a state of ecstatic intuition in which man could transcend his human limitations, and in Ronsard's circle, much influenced by Dorat's enthusiasm for it, prophecy was closely allied with poetry. Ronsard often speaks as both prophet and poet, overtly as in *Le Chat* (xv, pp. 39–47), more discreetly in the sonnets: 'Quand vous serez bien vieille'. In the *Ravissement de Cephale* Ronsard follows his model, Catullus, in ending his marriage of Peleus and Thetis with a prediction about Achilles, but in an abbreviated form which throws into relief certain themes which have pertinent links with the rest of his poem. Again, a mortal, Peleus, is elevated to the gods by union with a nymph. This time we are allowed to envisage a legitimate union of consent, albeit a rather joyless one. From it a child is to be born, a child immediately identified with the matter of epic poetry:

> tu dois enfanter
> Un qui donnera matiere
> Aus Poëtes de chanter. (II, p. 146)

The language of the last three stanzas of the ode invokes force and virility, victory and triumph. But the literary references embedded in it introduce a minor key: Telephus, over whom victory was mere illusion; the death of Memnon, Aurora's son; and the death of Achilles himself, which lurks beneath the apparently assertive and confident lines praising the epic hero to the skies:

> Le monde pour un tel homme
> N'est pas assés spatieus,
> Ses vertus reluiront comme
> Les étoiles par les cieus. (II, p. 146)

These lines are given their full dimension of meaning only by the addition of words unsaid, a subtext which the erudite reader, competent in the way Ronsard implicitly demands, will supply from his memory of Ovid or a commonplace book so as to complete the well-known antithesis on the measure of Achilles: while his fame fills the whole universe, his ashes scarcely fill a little urn (*Metamorphoses*, XII, 615–19).

Each of the three sections of Ronsard's poem has suggested a model for transposing nature into art: the physical world into painting, the world of emotions and ideas into mythological narrative and metaphor, the world of temporality into prophecy. In each, the triumphant assertion of poetic form is underwritten by a network of references to the official poetic language of classical literature. But all three hint at paradox, sacrifice, and ambivalence in the enterprise of writing poetry. The reader's response is syncretic, involving a delicate balancing of all the flashes of meaning struck from juxtapositions of figures and literary allusions. How different a response this is from that solicited by poets in the first half of the century may be summed up in the difference between the tripartite form of Ronsard's ode and the threefold divisions of our earlier Judgement poems. Ronsard's *pauses* postulate no moral choice. The subject now is poetic discourse itself, and its different but complementary forms. When Ronsard's shepherds hold a singing contest, their arbiter is asked to judge the aesthetics of their poetry, not the style of living it embodies.

Mythical transformations and the truth of things

At many levels Ronsard's poetry restates the sort of tensions between opposites which our analysis of *Le Ravissement de Cephale* has uncovered; but basic to them all is the tension between mutability and temporality on the one side, fixity and permanence on the other.[9] By art the poet strives paradoxically both to represent and to fixate the temporal flux, both to imitate nature in all its variableness and to make a graven image of enduring truth. His primary resource is language which itself is double, seeming temporal in its discursive, narrative, or descriptive rôle, where it unfolds sequentially, but universalising as it turns existential matter into names, patterns and concepts. Perhaps that is why Ronsard's tropes (figures of change) tend towards their extreme form, metamorphosis, where mutability expends itself in a total transfiguration into something rich and strange. The tension is most extreme in the Cassandre sonnets. There the excitement of the senses and the perturbation of the emotions in the experience of love can lead to an apparent dislocation of language, expressed in the ambiguous order/disorder of *vers rapportés*, a verbal figure which is both disjunctive and synthesising:

> Œil, main et crin, qui flammez et gennez,
> Et r'enlassez mon cuœur que vous tenez
> Au labyrint de vostre crespe voye. (IV, p. 21)

But the poet can do more than match emotional tangles in a scheme of words. Tropes can perform a miracle of change, transferring

temporal experience into the timeless dimension of the aesthetic. The
sonnet continues and ends:

> Hé que ne suis je Ovide bien disant!
> Œil tu seroys un bel Astre luisant,
> Main un beau lis, crin un beau ret de soye.   (IV, p. 21)

The miracle-worker is the poet Ovid, poet of metamorphosis and
master of rhetoric; the vehicle is metaphor. But more than that, the
metaphors Ronsard chooses are the consecrated metaphors of the
literary tradition: eyes as stars, skin as white as lilies, hair a silken net.
The conjunction of these images belongs to the Petrarchan heritage
rather than to Ovid, although the first two are also Ovidian. Ronsard
is not proposing to imitate Ovid. He is predicating a composite
language of literary commonplaces. The beauty into which plain
humanity is transformed is a product not only of tropes, but of
translation into a privileged poetic language; and the affinity of this
beauty with poetic ecstasy is impressed on the reader by the almost
ritual, threefold application of the epithet 'beau' to the transcending
metamorphoses. Yet the tension between life and art remains. The
aesthetic epiphany at the end of the poem is hedged about by the
tentative, uncertain mood of the verbs, interrogative and conditional,
with negative overtones. This is so often the case in the Cassandre
poems. The aesthetic metamorphosis is a dream, a picture framed off
from life, a fiction.

Ronsard's exploration of poetic language in the Cassandre
sequence is inextricably enmeshed with the experience of sexuality
which the sonnets probe. In the poet's vision, Cassandre is an avatar
of Venus. The timeless quintessence of her physical beauty is
captured when she is related back to the goddess, not by a vague and
casual reference, but by very precise allusions to Venus painted in a
particular picture, the Venus *anadyomene* of Apelles. Moreover, this
lost painting of antiquity is preserved only in verbal descriptions of it.
It is art alone, and, supreme among types of artistic expression, it is
literature that allows us to enter a world of timeless universals.

> Quand au matin ma Deesse s'abille
> D'un riche or crespe ombrageant ses talons,
> Et que les retz de ses beaulx cheveux blondz
> En cent façons ennonde et entortille:
> Je l'accompare à l'escumiere fille,
> Qui or peignant les siens jaunement longz,
> Or les ridant en mille crespillons
> Nageoyt abord dedans une coquille.   (IV, p. 42)

However, our response to Ronsard's Venus/Cassandre also recalls

Lemaire's naked goddess, object both of aesthetic wonder and of erotic desire. Ronsard's sonnet resolves into a catalogue of her physical attributes, infinitely more discreet, but the product of the same sort of fascinated gaze with which Paris lingered on Venus:

> De femme humaine encore ne sont pas
> Son ris, son front, ses gestes, ny ses pas,
> Ny de ses yeulx l'une et l'autre chandelle:
> Rocz, eaux, ny boys, ne celent point en eulx
> Nymphe, qui ait si follastres cheveux,
> Ny l'œil si beau, ny la bouche si belle.   (IV, p. 42)

Aesthetic ecstasy is compounded with erotic delight. Ronsard's vocabulary for sexual union, like Baïf's description of the embrace of Hermaphroditus and Salmacis, is a nexus of tropes, but transfigured into metamorphoses, and thus into the very language he uses for the creative act of poetry, when eyes, hands and hair are turned to stars, lilies and nets of gold:

> Quand en songeant ma follastre j'acolle,
> Laissant mes flancz sus les siens s'allonger,
> Et que d'un bransle habillement leger,
> En sa moytié ma moytié je recolle: . . .
> Mon dieu, quel heur, et quel contentement,
> M'a fait sentir ce faux recollement,
> Changeant ma vie en cent metamorphoses.   (IV, p. 100)

But the recalled embrace is 'faux' in this poem, an erotic dream, a fiction, as the metamorphoses of art are fiction. Similarly, Ronsard embodies his sexual desire in images of metamorphosis from the literary tradition: the bull, the swan, the shower of gold, which seem images of plenty and of beauty:

> Je vouldroy bien richement jaunissant
> En pluye d'or goute à goute descendre
> Dans le beau sein de ma belle Cassandre . . .   (IV, p. 23)

But these fabulous things are also empty fiction, as unreal as the imagined embrace, and furthermore, beneath these beautiful forms we can read disturbing allusions to tales of cruelty and rape. The tercets close this sonnet on a watery image from the same mythological and symbolic world as the pool of Salmacis, an ambiguous death-in-love, but death all the same:

> Je vouldroy bien afin d'aiser ma peine
> Estre un Narcisse, et elle une fontaine
> Pour m'y plonger une nuict à sejour:
> Et vouldroy bien que ceste nuict encore

Durast tousjours sans que jamais l'Aurore
D'un front nouveau nous r'allumast le jour.

These ambiguities haunt Ronsard's verse. The paradise of Helen's kiss in the *Chanson* (XVII, p. 235) is a garden of art and an illusion, and the immortal, poetic figures of love which inhabit it (Procris among them) are consecrated symbols of violence, pain and death.

So Ronsard's Venus not only offers the delights of Lemaire's, but also her darker side of fragility and death. However, we read her differently. Lemaire provides his reader with a precise code with which to decipher his text and make a moral judgement on his Venus. Ronsard does not give us a key for interpretation, nor does he shift our response into the area of moral choice. There are no explanatory references or interpolations in these poems. Our reading is a process of constant adjustment to textual relationships, as it was for Baïf, although now these function across a much wider field, potentially the whole literary language. The sense we make of such relationships is not predetermined to fit separate and alternative categories of interpretation, historical, physical, moral and spiritual. This freedom of association liberates the writer (and reader) to explore areas difficult to accommodate in the old interpretative scheme. No moral sense, for example, diverts Ronsard from his evocation of sensual delight. At the same time the exclusively literary nature of the world within which the poets make these relationships turns them (and us) towards a narcissistic preoccupation with a self-referring poetic language and with the conditions of writing. This tendency marks the Cassandre poems from the start. In an introductory sonnet which gives a programme synopsis of the sequence to follow, Ronsard draws attention as much to himself as writer and to his mode of writing as to the matter of his verse:

> Il cognoistra que foible est la raison
>   Contre son trait quand sa douce poison
>   Corrompt le sang, tant le mal nous enchante:
> Et connoistra, que je suis trop heureux
>   D'estre en mourant nouveau Cygne amoureux
>   Qui son obseque à soy mesme se chante.
>
> (IV, p. 6, 1578 version)

The syntax of the poem impels the reader towards the culminating metaphor/metamorphosis whose multiple senses can only be discovered by understanding the literary language from which it derives. The swan is the bird of Venus, image of love and of rape (from the Leda fable); it is also the bird of Apollo, image of poetry as a mode of transfiguration and escape from temporality (see, for example, Horace, *Odes* II, xx), and at the same time of an art which prophesies the certainty of failure and death, its own and its creator's (the song of the dying swan is a commonplace in all reference works of the period).

The mythology Ronsard chooses for his narrative poems tends to reiterate the complex of themes already present in the Cassandre sonnets. The lovers of his tales, for example, contemplate the beloved both as an aesthetic object and as an object of sensual desire, sometimes also as a means of spiritual elevation, but they are impotent voyeurs, sexually flawed: Narcissus by his self-obsession, Atys by his self-castration, Cyclops by his monstrous ugliness, Hercules by his suppressed homosexuality, while Eurymedon, the hidden spectator of the *Baing de Callirée*, identifies himself with the sexless hermaphrodite, Caeneus.[10] Behind such images may lie the paradox of Ronsard's own life, poet of love and celibate cleric, which he hardly ever mentions directly except in the *Sonnets amoureux* dedicated to Sinope in 1559. These few sonnets are the furthest he goes towards autobiography in his love poetry, an experiment with 'realism' adumbrated in some ways in the less intense and less erotic Marie sonnets of 1555–6, and they are remarkable for their lack of mythological language. However, Ronsard's instinct that art in its proper imitation of nature transcends the world of accidental particulars reasserts itself in the mythology of the narrative poems. The paradox of Ronsard's hermaphrodite state becomes the essence of art's relationship with life. For the Renaissance artist beauty is a sensual delight charged with eroticism, yet his mistress eludes him as she is fixed within the picture-frame or subsumed into Venus. Art creates timeless icons; human love belongs to the world of flux and generation. Ronsard puts this commonplace through many textual variants: Aurora and Procris; the image of Narcissus in the pool and wasting Echo; Atys as ascetic and self-destroyer; Cyclops as poet of hyperbole and failed lover; Hylas lost to Hercules; Eurymedon and Caeneus, whom the metamorphoses of art and the promise of immortality compensate for their lack of manhood. Ronsard has struck the dilemma to which post-Renaissance poetry returns again and again, but whereas Yeats will opt for the 'changeless metal' of Byzantium and Valéry in *Cimetière marin* for the fluctuating ocean of life, Ronsard does not present the paradox as choice. He holds its terms in tension and equilibrium. The flowers of his poems are preserved for ever at the very moment of their evanescence, 'fueille à fueille décloses'. But the effect of such contradictions, deeply felt, is to

10 Nymph emasculating a drunken satyr: engraving after Primaticcio, *c.* 1544

alienate poets from the normal life of men and turn them into two-
natured monsters, hermaphrodites and satyrs:

> Ils ont les pieds à terre et l'esprit dans les Cieux,
> Le peuple les estime enragez, furieux,
> Ils errent par les bois, par les monts, par les prées,
> Et jouyssent tous seuls des Nymphes et des Fées.
>
> (*Elegie à J. Grevin*, XIV, p. 197)

The nymphs that haunt Ronsard's poems and lie just below the
surface of his natural world embody exactly his sense of how poetry
functions, disclosing an enduring permanent essence within a world
of growth and decay. They are beautiful, erotic and elusive. They
belong to the universe of classical poetic language and gather their
substance from it.[11] Yet they are also fabulous creatures, perhaps
figments of the imagination which pursues them, 'fantastique
d'esprit'. In the *Hymne de l'Autonne* it is nymphs who first awaken in
the pre-pubescent Ronsard an instinct to mark the rhythmic pattern
of their dance:

> Je n'avois pas quinze ans que les mons et les boys,
> Et les eaux me plaisoient plus que la court des Roys,
> Et les noires forests espesses de ramées
> Et du bec des oyseaux les roches entamées:
> Une valée, un antre en horreur obscurcy,

> Un desert effroiable, estoit tout mon soucy,
> A fin de voir au soir les Nymphes et les Fées
> Danser desoubs la Lune en cotte par les prées . . .
> J'allois apres la danse et craintif je pressois
> Mes pas dedans le trac des Nymphes, et pensois,
> Que pour mettre mon pied en leur trace poudreuse
> J'aurois incontinent l'ame plus genereuse.   (XII, pp. 47–8)

It is in the secret places of the nymphs that Ronsard experiences the true poetic effect of hair-raising 'horror', and it is there that his true subject and vocation are revealed to him – poetry itself and himself as writer:

> Tu vivras dans les boys pour la Muse et pour toy. (XII, p. 50)

By using the autobiographical mode, Ronsard persuades us of the authenticity of his initiation; by recalling the fictions of Hesiod, Lucretius, Horace, Seneca and others, which form the ancient commonplace of poetic inspiration, Ronsard identifies his own experience with theirs.[12] It is the traditional language of poetry which turns into fabulous shapes the poet's intuitions of 'forms of things unknown', and its commonplaces which give them a local habitation. The reader's only path into this sacred grove is by way of narrative, signposted by mythological and textual allusions. The poetic place he enters is an introverted world of literary significances created by a language of cross-references, where patterns of interrelationships grow and evolve as in a fictional universe.

However, the nymphs do not complete the education of the growing boy, and the narrative mode is abruptly halted, to be replaced by lessons and demonstrations.

> Ainsi disoit la Nymphe, et de là je vins estre
> Disciple de d'Aurat, qui long temps fut mon maistre,
> M'aprist la Poësie, et me montra comment
> On doit feindre et cacher les fables proprement,
> Et à bien deguiser la verité des choses
> D'un fabuleux manteau dont elles sont encloses. (XII, p. 50)

With this reference to Dorat, Ronsard confronts 'la verité des choses' and the responsibility of the writer to the external world. It should be recalled that the humanist compilers of commonplace books had themselves stressed that their quotations not only initiated students into their literary heritage, but taught them knowledge, giving them insights into the moral life and an understanding of nature. So Beroaldus promotes the useful and sanitary information purveyed by Mirandula's *Flores*:

Sunt haec ex sylva poetarum scitissime decerpta, quibus aut sententia moralis naturalisve, aut laus virtutis, aut censoria morum castigatio, aut praecepta saluberrima continentur. (fol. a + 1v°)

Dorat himself was much concerned with the application of mythology. In his teaching he inclined to a Christian neo-Platonic interpretation of ancient fable, especially of Homer, and his own poetry is mostly a commentary on contemporary political affairs.[13] For Ronsard the poet's engagement with the world of external reality was another facet of his imitation of nature and of his artist's calling to extrapolate from it permanent and persuasive truths. But he was fully conscious that poetry whose subject is the public, external world creates its effects in a different way from poetry which is primarily concerned with literature itself, a way as different as are the clear equivalences taught by Dorat from the suggestive play of associations in the grove of the nymphs. What he says about Dorat's lessons in fable-writing supposes a clear-cut distinction between mythological story on the one hand and the conceptual meaning to be attached to it or hidden in it on the other. It leads us back to a mode of reading which works retroactively on the text as a whole in order to translate the literal narrative into a coherent account of 'la verité des choses', to allegorical interpretation in effect. This involves a process of matching the text against a specific set of preconceptions, whereas the sorts of meanings we have been finding our way towards in the earlier part of this section were generated sequentially by the narrative itself, by the tropical expressions within the text, and by its literary analogues. There are, of course, areas of overlap, and poems where Ronsard demands of his reader a great deal of agility in adjusting now to one mode of reading, now the other, most notably perhaps in the Season hymns (where, perhaps significantly, the two modes are juxtaposed in the introduction to the *Hymne de l'Autonne*). Normally, however, Ronsard will signal a passage for allegorical interpretation, often by using explicit personifications (Ignorance, for example, in the early odes, the Seasons themselves in their hymns, Justice and other abstractions in the *Hymne de Justice*) or by an intervention directing the reader to a particular set of correspondences.

Very few of Ronsard's poems are rigorously controlled throughout by a systematic application of allegorical equivalents. Rather, his use of interpretation recalls Aneau's description of the mode in his *Preparation de voie à la lecture et intelligence des Poetes fabuleux*. There is the same flexibility of practice, and there is the same basic identification of the kinds of truth in the external world to which mythological narrative can properly be made to relate: historical, physical and moral.[14] Moreover, Aneau's exclusion of interpretations which bear on the spiritual life is reflected in the definition of the scope of allegorical interpretation with which Ronsard introduces his *Hymne de l'Hyver* (XII, pp. 70–2). Basically in agreement with the general drift of Aneau's analysis of interpretative reading, Ronsard says that the reader can detect substantial truths with confidence that they are intentionally present, coded in the text by the author and deliberately revealed by signals enticing the reader to draw certain parallels which rationalise the fable. But the context in which this interpretation is made to work, for both Aneau and Ronsard, is an essentially pagan one. The neo-Platonic type of allegory which Ronsard claims to insert into his poem is modelled on readings of Hesiod and Homer, and the truths about nature and man so revealed relate to cultural history, public and political morality, and natural science (p. 71). The highest to which such knowledge can aspire is to natural law as it is accessible to reason, and to an understanding of God which is, as Aneau had defined it, 'la naturelle cognoissance de Dieu par ses effectz'.

> Hardis furent les coeurs qui les premiers monterent
> Au ciel, et d'un grand soing les Astres affronterent:
> Là, sans avoir frayeur des cloistres enflamés
> Du monde, où tant de corps divers sont enfermés,
> Par leur vive vertu s'ouvrirent une entrée,
> Et virent dans le sein la Nature sacrée:
> Ils espierent Dieu, puis ils furent apres
> Si fiers que de conter aux hommes ses secrets.   (XII, pp. 70–1)

Ronsard stresses that this truth is not to be confused with the truth of revealed religion, by pointedly imitating a single author in these lines. They are a close paraphrase of Lucretius's eulogy of the arch-pagan Epicurus (*De rerum natura*, I, lines 60–73), instantly recognisable to the humanistically educated reader.

However, Ronsard is not content with Aneau's limitations. Throughout his career one finds traces of attempts to incorporate the truths taught by Christianity within his interpretative model.[15] Most of his contemporaries, Du Bellay, Jodelle and Belleau in particular, were intermittently concerned with the problem of mediating Christian truth through the classical rhetoric which had given them their poetic language. Ronsard, as always, was bolder. In his *Hercule chrestien* he even experimented with the medieval manner of spiritual equivalences, turning the story of Hercules into a series of anachron-

istic similitudes which reproduce exactly the reading methods of the
Bible des poetes:

> Premierement, qu'est-ce des trois nuittées
> Que Jupiter tint en une arrestées
> Quand il voulut son Alcmene embrasser,
> Qu'un nombre d'ans qui se devoient passer
> Ains que Jesus prist naissance de Mere,
> Tant il y eut dans le Ciel de mystere
> Avant que luy celast sa Deité
> Souz le manteau de nostre humanité?   (VIII, pp. 215–16)

But the experiment is not repeated. Ronsard's humanist critical sense
ultimately disallows such parallels. It also puts certain limits on his
application of neo-Platonic models for allegorising, for in practice it
inhibits him from arbitrarily imposing meanings by way of accidental
likenesses (the process by which the neo-Platonists, despite their
ambitious claims, arrived at a large part of the mystical senses they
attributed to mythology).[16] The solution which Du Bellay outlines in
the *Lyre Chrestienne* of 1552 was to prove more productive because it
starts from the classical language in which his contemporaries had
been taught to express themselves, not from the discredited medieval
models in which Christian poetry seemed atrophied. For Du Bellay
the key lies in style, not in conceptual equivalences. He proposes to
appropriate the figures of classical rhetoric to express Christian
themes, using, incidentally, exactly the same Augustinian commonplace about converting the gold of the Egyptians to the good of
true religion that Bersuire had cited in support of his allegorical
method. The approach taken by Du Bellay was to prove the way
through to the resurgence of Christian poetry in the later part of the
century, and, coupled with a revaluation of the language of the Bible
and the resources of allegory which exegesis still allowed to Scripture,
this was to produce Christian epics from the Protestants D'Aubigné
and Milton. Every page of *Les Tragiques* is a tissue of rhetorical
figures derived from classical usage and its apocalyptic vision of
history is profusely illustrated with examples from the classical past;
yet of the fictions of classical mythology there is scarcely a trace. But
this is not epic as Dorat envisaged it after the neo-Platonic example of
Landino's commentary on the *Aeneid*, a model which demands a
pagan scenario interpreted in a mystical sense closely analogous to
Christian language and concepts. Nor indeed does it correspond to
Counter-Reformation ideas for Christianising contemporary writing
and its pagan culture. The Counter-Reformation literary theorists of
the time, while promoting the language of the Bible and the Fathers,

seem also to look back to medieval methods of assimilating paganism in the hope of bringing them up to modern standards of literary elegance without discarding the basic premise that there were viable conceptual parallels between Christianity and mythology.[17] Perhaps we have here yet another reason why Ronsard failed to complete his epic, *La Franciade*, caught as he was in an impasse between the classical model to which Dorat's education, humanist and neo-Platonist, directed him and his critical standards of decorum which forbade him to infuse it with a spiritual sense. But without the dimension of man's spiritual nature, both his neo-Platonic background and perhaps his Christian belief told him that the project fell short of the encyclopaedic ideal of epic, the total poem. Nevertheless, in the less official, less inhibiting genres of narrative and discursive epistle he continued to exploit the potential of ancient myth with ever more versatility, bringing together in original and often disconcerting appositions his various approaches to fable and its capacity for meaning.

'Le Satyre'

The sixth and seventh books of Ronsard's *Poemes*, published in 1569, contain poems written during a prolonged period of retirement from his public life at court. He lived in relative isolation at his country priory at Saint-Cosme and at various times between 1567 and 1569 he was subject to recurrent attacks of illness. This we know from his writing of the time, for it is punctuated with references to himself, to his private musings and day-to-day activities. The relaxed tone of the 1569 collection is curiously different from the vibrant tensions of much of the earlier poetry, and so is the loose, centrifugal, rambling structure of the longer poems of this later period.

Le Satyre (xv, pp. 67–76) is presented as a simple imitation or transposition of Ovid's tale of Faunus and Iole (*Fasti*, ii, lines 303–58):

> Le doux Ovide a la fable autrefois
> Ditte en Romain: je la dis en François. (xv, p. 67)

The statement is baldly direct, deceptively simple as it turns out, for this is anything but a straightforward exercise in imitating a single model. The reader is immediately disarmed and promised an easy read, without either the taxing calls on his memory or the changes in narrative angle which kept him constantly on the alert in the *Ravissement de Cephale*. He is also promised mere entertainment:

> Amy Candé, pour bien te faire rire
> Je te feray le conte d'un Satyre,   (xv, p. 67)

lines which exactly reproduce Ovid's 'fabula plena ioci' (line 304).
But Ronsard takes a giddy leap away from Ovid in the next four lines:

> Ce n'est moins fait d'honorer son langage
> Qu'au Prince armé, qui de louange a soing,
> Borner veinqueur son Empire plus loing:
> Par ces deux poincts s'augmente la Patrie.   (xv, p. 67)

He gives his poem a heroic dimension and then retracts it just as
suddenly:

> Mais, mon Candé, il est temps que l'on rie.   (xv, p. 68)

The hint of irony in the rhyming of 'Patrie' and 'rie', even reminds
one of the mock-heroics of fables in the genre of Marot and La
Fontaine. The opening lines of Ronsard's poem set a style which is
disjunctive, discursive, juxtaposing contrasting registers of tone,
slightly bewildering perhaps to a reader used to a poetic language
which worked towards pattern and synthesis.

Hercules and Iole walk together through a natural landscape, 'Par
tertres, bois, par bocages ombreux'. It is a scene devoid of literary
denizens or associations, and the couple are described with an
attention to precise physical detail (similar in manner to Ovid's text,
but much elaborated) which creates no context of meaning other than
the severely literal. Even Hercules's club and lion-skin lose their
strangeness and their epic proportions by being put in apposition to
Iole's dress and ornaments and overshadowed by them:

> Luy, herissé desoubz la peau veluë
> Du grand Lion, empoingnoit sa massuë
> Ferme en ses doigtz, grosse de clouz d'airain.
> Elle portoit mille affiquets au sein,
> Ses mains estoient de bagues bien chargées,
> Son col estoit de perles arrangées
> Riche et gaillard: son chef estoit couvert
> D'un gay scoffion entrelassé de verd
> Sa robe estoit de pourpre Moeonine
> Perse en couleur, chancrée à la poitrine.   (xv, pp. 68–9)

An extended simile then makes another enormous jump, on this
occasion a jump in time:

> Ainsi qu'on voit au retour de beaux mois
> Se promener ou noz dames de Blois,
> Ou d'Orleans, ou de Tours, ou d'Amboise

143

> Dessus la greve où Loire se desgoise,
> A flot rompu. (xv, p. 69)

The original couple is multiplied in a geometric progression of Renaissance ladies walking 'deux à deux' and followed by their lovers. It is an ordinary scene, neither morally nor historically significant, nor does it present to the reader any moral or historical sense to be read back into the fable. The similitude suggests no conceptual parallel; it merely notes a proliferation in time of the original binary pattern. These people in their riverine procession exist in time's flux, and where Ronsard does bring them within the purview of literary commonplace, it is to mark their transience, like water and like grass and flowers:

> et joingnant la riviere,
> Joingnant l'esmail de l'herbe printanniere,
> Prennent le fraiz, fieres en leur beauté:
> En cependant leur jeune nouveauté
> Croist à l'envy des herbes qui fleuronnent. (xv, p. 69)

A further set of associations is brought discreetly into play by the metaphor which closes the digression from Ovid and brings us back to Hercules and Iole. In the modern scene, the sexes are divided and lovers do not walk with their ladies:

> Leurs amoureux en les suivant s'estonnent
> De leur beau port, (xv, p. 69)

They marvel at their beauty and at night they meditate alone on their icons:

> Ayant sans cesse au cœur le doux portrait
> Que trop d'amour en peinture leur colle:
> Ainsy qu'Hercule avoit au cœur Iole. (xv, p. 69)

Hercules's love of Iole is already identified with the transformation of physical beauty into art and a concomitant loss of virility. The contrast with the brute eroticism of Faunus is made immediately:

> Faune, qui est des femmes desireux
> Vit cette Dame, et en fut amoureux, (xv, p. 69)

and it is emphasised by the simile Ronsard adds to Ovid's 'vidit et incaluit', a rustic image of fitful warmth in winter, which places Faunus firmly outside Ronsard's metaphorical code for sophisticated and durable art:

> Son cœur ardoit de flames consomé
> Ainsy qu'un chaume en criquant alumé,
> Qu'un bergere enflamme d'aventure
> Au temps d'Hyver pour tromper la froidure. (xv, p. 70)

The next section of the narrative, describing preparations for supper and Hercules exchanging clothes with Iole, veers between the polarities of the poem, serious and humorous, ceremonial and domestic, epic and bucolic. Even its most stylised moment, the double periphrasis with which Ronsard amplifies Ovid's 'Hesperus et fusco roscidus ibat equo' (line 314), points in both directions, to images which in themselves echo the binary pattern of the whole poem: to a procession of personifications, Vesper drawing star-clad Night through the sky, and then to a domestic detail, as the ox drags homeward the plough. Ronsard amplifies Ovid's brief reference to the supper arrangements (line 317) and makes it a picture of domestic activity, but one which the *Preface sur la Franciade* will define as proper to the high seriousness of epic, 'car en telle peinture, ou plustost imitation de la nature consiste toute l'ame de la Poesie Heroïque' (xvi, p. 345).

All sorts of ambiguities are potentially in play as Hercules and Iole exchange clothes: the sexual ambiguities which the Renaissance delighted to discover in the erotic; the carnival humour of such a masquerade; the hermaphrodite theme which runs through so much of Ronsard's love poetry. But Ronsard keeps them in abeyance, occupying the reader's attention with a meticulously judged and amplified imitation of Ovid's literal denotation of the physical absurdities immediately visible to a spectator of the scene. Only at the close does Ronsard's vocabulary begin to create a context of meaning other than the literal, transferring the reader to a place with recognisable associations:

> Là tout joingnant estoit l'horreur d'un Antre
> Où le Soleil en nulle saison n'entre,
> Sinon l'Hiver que son rayon tout droit
> Passe dedans et amortist le froid
> Pour donner vie et force et accroissance
> Aux belles fleurs qui là prennent naissance.   (xv, p. 73)

Ovid's brief reference to the cave comes earlier in the tale, as a location for the meal (lines 315–16). Ronsard expands Ovid's two lines to twenty-four and moves them to a later point in the narrative so that it becomes a place reserved for Hercules and Iole alone, only after they have metamorphosed themselves and only after Hercules has discarded his masculine attire and the signs which identified him with heroes and giants. Our mode of reading also is transformed. Ronsard gathers into the cave a cluster of words which signal a particular set of associations: 'horreur' and its special connection

145

with the sacred tremor of aesthetic experience; the defeat of winter's cold; beautiful flowers which grow unnaturally. This is the figurative language in which Ronsard is accustomed to talk about poetry. The cave is a *locus amoenus*, a place of natural beauty mimetically reproduced in minute detail:

> De vif tufeau tout à l'entour estoient
> Des bancs sans art qui d'herbes se vestoient,
> Faisant d'euxmesme une pauzade aizée
> De poliot et de mousse frizée,
> Tendre, houpuë, et de trefles qui font
> Naistre en leur fueille un croissant sur le front.   (xv, p. 73)

It is also a *locus poeticus*, a hallowed place of secret and protected mysteries, where the nymphs may stay their flight and give their treasure up, and where wild nature awaits the poet who will translate it into the enduring world of literature:

> Aupres de l'huis, gardien de l'entrée,
> Sonne un ruisseau à la course sacrée,
> Où les Sylvains, où les Nymphes d'autour
> Se vont bagner et pratiquer l'amour
> Au chaud du jour, quand Diane, ennemye
> De leurs plaisirs, dort es bois endormie.
> Dessus la porte une lambrunche estoit,
> Qui de ses doigts rampante se portoit
> Sur un ormeau.   (xv, p. 73)

By the analogies of language the clover leaf discloses the crescent moon, and the wild vine clinging to the elm is subsumed, for the reader able to make such associations, into the cultured literary topos 'Plus estroit que la Vigne à l'Ormeau se marie . . .'.

At first sight there seems no source for such a development in the *Fasti*. Nevertheless, there are three lines which Ronsard omits to transpose (lines 328–30). If the reader chooses to look closely at Ovid's text, to which he was clearly directed at the beginning of Ronsard's narrative, he will find that Hercules and Iole were forbidden to make love that night because the next morning they were to celebrate a feast of Bacchus. Bacchus, a god of metamorphosis and ecstatic inspiration, whom Ronsard frequently associates with poetry, imposes a sexual taboo on our already hermaphrodite couple. The sacrifice of erotic potency to art is, as we have already seen, a recurrent preoccupation with Ronsard. To an imitator without this preoccupation, Ovid's parenthesis would hardly have delivered such a sense. Yet Ovid's three lines and the key word 'antra' seem to have motivated Ronsard's appropriation of the tale to his own obsession

146

11   Faunus, Hercules and Iole: engraving after Primaticcio

with the genesis of poetry and the conditions of writing. At the same time, only the reader with Ovid's text in mind can perhaps fully relate the ambivalent sexuality of Hercules to the poetic associations of the cave. It is not only through verbal reminiscences but also through a cross-fertilisation of texts that Ronsard generates meaning.

The same process, implying intertextual reading, comes into operation in a less complex way at the end of *Le Satyre*. After Hercules and Iole are asleep, Ronsard recounts the furtive intrusion of Faunus and his mistaken attempt to rape the disguised Hercules. For this he reverts, as in his description of the dressing-up, to a close imitation of Ovid's narrative, barely amplified with added visual detail and at times turning into simple translation. Faunus and his stealthy approach are, as in Ovid, objects of ridicule. But at the end of this episode the reader is once again taken abruptly away from the source-text. In Ovid both Hercules and Iole laugh good-humouredly at the satyr's discomfiture (lines 355–7). Ronsard's Hercules rises in fury at the desecration as, indeed, does Hercules in the painting of the scene which Ronsard doubtless knew at Fontainebleau (Plate 11):

> Le feu venu, Hercule se colere,
> S'enfle de fiel, vous l'eussiez ouÿ braire
> Parmy cet Antre, ainsy qu'un grand taureau:
> D'un coup de poing il cassa le museau
> Du Dieu paillard, et d'une main cruelle
> De poil à poil tout le menton lui pelle,

> Et tellement s'enaigrit de courroux
> Que l'estomac luy martela de coups.   (xv, p. 75)

Just as in his excursus into the cave, Ronsard alerts the reader to the extra-literal meaning he is about to add to the narrative by diverging from close imitation. Hercules's voluntary hermaphrodite state within the cave is not to be confused with weakness, nor does the poet whose subject is poetry itself lack a voice (and a harsh, plain-speaking voice) to castigate with vigour the vices of the present age:

> Que pleust à Dieu que tous les adulteres
> Fussent puniz de semblables salaires!
> Paillards, ribaulx, et ruphiens, qui font
> Porter aux Jans les cornes sur le front.   (xv, pp. 75–6)

The end of the poem reasserts the moral responsibility of the writer to 'la verité des choses'. Ronsard does not do this by way of a definitive and reductive interpretation of the fable, either by giving it a retroactive allegorical sense or by turning it into an *exemplum* of some moral truism. The application to the state of modern society comes in the form of a digression, leading us out of the narrative and into a judgement expressed privately to the friend whom Ronsard had addressed at the poem's start. The tone is in stark contrast with the humour promised at the beginning, and this picture of the realities of civil disorder is as far removed from the social ceremony by the banks of the Loire as is the satyr's rampant sexuality from the decorous world of Hercules and Iole.[18]

> On ne voit plus qu'un filz resemble au pere,
> Faute, Candé, qu'on ne punist la mere
> (Qui se debauche, et qui honnist sa foy)
> Par la rigueur d'une severe loy.   (xv, p. 76)

The rapid variations in tone of *Le Satyre* and the way the poem digresses from the base text and then returns to it, only to diverge onto another tangent: all these discontinuous and centrifugal tendencies are characteristic of Ronsard's later manner. So too is the apparent lack of cohesion between the contexts into which the fable is put at different moments in its telling. For by the very nature of their business the long poems of Ronsard's 1569 collection tend to strain against any attempt to make sense of them in terms of patterns. What Ronsard is doing now is taking the great constants of his poetic output and setting them against the vagaries of his private experience and the variables of the historical moment. The stable element in *Le Satyre* is the humanist practice of imitating classical writers, represented in the poem by passages where Ronsard carefully transposes

Ovid's text and imitates his style. Similarly, in other poems of this period of retreat and introspection, the major commonplaces of Ronsard's poetry reappear: neo-Platonic theories of ecstatic inspiration in *La Lyre* (*A Monsieur de Belot*), prophecy in *Le Chat*, Nature set against social ambition in *La Salade*, pictorial art (perhaps) in *L'Ombre du Cheval*, metamorphosis in the *Discours à maistre Juliain Chauveau*, Cassandre herself in *A Cassandre*. They lose nothing of their prestige or their power, but they are brought up against external reality in a more brutal and more perturbing way than ever Ronsard learnt from Dorat. For the reality which now preoccupies Ronsard is not primarily the reality of moral truisms or general laws of nature, but the reality of his own knowledge of himself and of the contingencies of contemporary history. The reader is persuaded into the intimacy of Ronsard's own private view of temporality, of intermittences and swings of mood in his personal responses, of public disorder and mutability in all things. It is a world where the language of poetic commonplaces alone is constant, but it coincides only fitfully with things as they are, and more often than not, especially in the *Sonnets pour Helene*, exists in ironic juxtaposition with the realities of experience. The form of Ronsard's longer poems in the late collections mirrors this attempt to catch 'la verité des choses' as Ronsard now perceives it. They are rambling, inconclusive, digressive. In the mythological poems he intervenes more and more frequently into his narratives in order to multiply the contexts in which his fictions may be read; and these interpolations are unsystematic, discursive, multifarious in their formulation, sometimes even tending to contradictions between narrative content and interpretation (as in *Le Pin*), and without any apparent unity of vision. The extreme example is the very late *Hynne de Mercure* (XVIII, pp. 265–74), fragmented into so many quicksilver pieces, as each short section of the poem takes a discrete view of the protean god of language and offers the reader a different mode of interpretation with which to make provisional links between the ambivalent figure created from literary references and the chaos of deceiving and contradictory appearances we call reality. These poem–essays, flowers of the 'longues nuicts d'Hyver' of illness and introspective solitude, bring Ronsard close to Montaigne. They both come to see reality in terms of the particularities of private experience, and the other mode of experience most important to them both is the experience of reading. Both look for insight to the juxtaposition of texts with texts, and of texts with their own perceptions. But whereas Montaigne sometimes allows his intelligence to play so critically on his interpolated texts that he comes close to destabilising them, Ronsard's faith in the immunity of the intertextual language of poetry remains intact. That language alone for him arrests the flux of time. Helen's beauty comes within the compass of Montaigne's 'branloire perenne', but still her name remains, 'de louange immortelle'. Through the language of commonplaces Ronsard's last poems compose one continuous text with his first. Cassandre's swan-poet endures; thirty-five years add but one more layer of literary allusion, one more variation on the commonplace, as with poignant irony Ronsard extends his frame of reference to include Ovid's fable of Cygnus and his metamorphosis from young man to old (*Metamorphoses,* II, lines 367–80: 'canae capillos dissimulant plumae'):

> Et deviendray un Cygne en lieu d'un Corbeau noir.

(XVIII, p. 221)

EPILOGUE: THE THREE
GODDESSES AGAIN

The change in poetic language which we have analysed in key texts
from sixteenth-century France points to a revolution in sensibility
and thought. Its repercussions permanently altered the relationship
between language and truth, which seemed to Lemaire so securely
established on a hierarchy of senses to which allegorical interpretation, supplemented by textual cross-references, gave the reader
access. The humanists' critique of the similitudes on which medieval
tropical language depended and their reintroduction of the figurative
modes of classical rhetoric had a profound effect on assumptions
made about literature's status as truth. It is in mythological poetry,
the most unequivocally fictional of all modes of writing, that this
change of status is most sharply perceived. Poetic discourse no longer
pointed the discriminating reader with any clarity or assurance to
moral and spiritual truths beyond the literal sense. It tended rather to
generate a universe of self-reflecting patterns and allusions, an almost
autonomous world of textual references and commonplaces, 'stile
apart, sens apart, œuvre apart'. This is the world of aesthetic
experience proper to literature, and the Renaissance poets explored
their new-found land with all the excitement of discovery. It was
fertile territory and from it was to spring the main tradition of
European poetry. Romanticism stimulated new growth, but if we
turn to the post-Romantics who were most preoccupied with the
larger questions of art's relationship to life, to writers like Keats,
Nerval, Baudelaire, Mallarmé, Valéry, Proust, Yeats, we find clear
traces of paths first taken by our humanist poets, and landscapes and
figures with which they taught us to be familiar. Their inheritors still
reap the fruitful ambiguities in the overlap of our responses to beauty
and the erotic; the poet still feels himself the hermaphrodite child of
the union of Venus and Mercury, sexuality and language; nymphs
beckon the adolescent Marcel to long-deferred discoveries in art and
love; the thrill of genesis still 'bids the hair stand up'; the everlasting
flowers of poetry find their true counterparts not in any Renaissance

garden, but in Mallarmé's Book; and mythological fable is still the epitome of fiction, unreal, but immune from time and death. 'Ces nymphes, je les veux perpétuer', claims Mallarmé's impotent faun, and Yeats affirms:

> And he that Attis' image hangs between
> That staring fury and the blind lush leaf
> May not know what he knows, but knows not grief.[1]

But there is a corollary to all this. With hindsight, we can see more clearly than the Renaissance poets themselves that the discovery of artistic autonomy was to produce a definitive rift in the always unstable alliance between the modes of language thought proper to literature and the language of knowledge and intellectual inquiry. Whereas Montaigne and Ronsard might still revel in the play of associations engendered by reading texts, Descartes was to dismiss literature, fable, rhetoric, even language itself as irrelevant and hostile to his pursuit of truth, clarity and moral self-assurance. For a long time the model code for most serious philosophical thinking was to be mathematics. Of course, there were other factors which determined the status and scope allowed to imaginative literature in the post-Renaissance period, religious, sociological, and technological not least. But on literature itself the influence of humanism was paramount, precisely because the focus of humanism was on language. That is why it makes sense to look for the causes of many developments in early modern culture to the minutiae of the humanists' reading of classical texts, to their promotion of literary imitation, and to the mentality of the commonplace book.

The poetry of the Pléiade has all the ebullience of discovery and experiment. We shall conclude this study by examining briefly how mythological poetry fared in the first decade of the seventeenth century, when the developments initiated by poets of the last half of the sixteenth century had been consolidated and we can see clearly some of the features which will remain constants of the established manner of the ensuing period. As far as non-narrative verse is concerned, the poetry of the early years of the seventeenth century fulfils exactly some of the predictions we were able to suggest when looking at how Baïf began to amplify his style of close imitation in *Le Meurier*. Metaphor is over-elaborated into conceit, producing the mannerism and, too often, the superficiality which Montaigne detected in the poetry of his time when he compared it with the language of his 'vers de Virgile':

J'ay desdain de ces menues pointes et allusions verballes qui nasquirent depuis. A ces bonnes gens [Virgil and Lucretius], il ne falloit pas d'aigue et subtile rencontre. (p. 976)

At the same time, the range of mythological allusion in short poems at this period is limited to a fairly restricted set of commonplace references, largely divorced from any textual context.[2] When we come to mythological narrative, we are in for more of a surprise.

In 1606, Nicolas Renouard published a prose version of the *Metamorphoses* 'avec XV discours contenans l'explication morale des fables', which was frequently reprinted over the next fifty years at least. By 1608, Renouard had responded to popular demand by producing *Le Jugement de Pâris et le ravissement d'Helene, avec ses amours*, which he appended to his *Metamorphoses* at the latest in 1612, because:

ceux qui n'ont pas leû les Vers Latins des Metamorphoses d'Ovide, où il n'y a rien du Jugement de Pâris, et l'ont veû inseré dans une ancienne Traduction, autrefois publiée sous le titre de Grand Olympe, ont jugé que la derniere Traduction des mesmes Metamorphoses, entierement conforme au Latin, estant defectueuse, n'y trouvant pas cette Piece; qui est une des plus agreables inventions que l'Antiquité nous ait laissée. Ce defaut presumé a fait naistre en plusieurs le desir de la voir, d'un style pareil à celuy des Metamorphoses.

(*Jugement*, p. [5])[3]

The Pléiade poets had shown no interest in the Judgement of Paris, apart from Baïf, who had rendered Lucian's dialogue with typical exactitude and with a typical predilection for an authentic classical version of the story (the one, moreover, furthest removed from the guise in which it was to be found in the first half of the sixteenth century).[4] Yet here we have an early seventeenth-century translator deliberately searching out 'ça et là ce qui en a esté escrit' to satisfy readers whose acquaintance with Ovid clearly goes no further than the *Grand Olympe*. Nor was Renouard mistaken about the current interest in the story, for there is at least one other notable version of the fable from the same period, the *Jugement de Paris* of Siméon de La Roque, published in his *Œuvres* of 1609.[5]

It is not only Renouard's Judgement of Paris that recalls the literature of the pre-Pléiade period. His fifteen discourses on the fables of the *Metamorphoses* seem at first sight to bring us back to a programme of rigorously applied retroactive interpretation, at least according to the categories recognised by Aneau:

Vous sçavez que ce n'est pas à l'escorce de l'invention fabuleuse, qu'il se faut arrester, et que si l'on penetre plus avant, on trouve le tronc de quelque estrange et veritable evenement, ou un effet de la Nature, ou quelque beau precepte moral, qui a servy de sujet à la feinte.   (*Discours*, p. 6)

For example, it is suggested that Mercury was said to have fathered Hermaphroditus because Mercury is a neuter planet and because rhetoric can both stimulate and mollify, whereas Salmacis is identified with the vices of sensual pleasure and idleness. There is no doubt that the instinct to go beyond the 'nue declaration des choses' is still activated in a particularly acute way by mythological narrative, and the old senses of allegorical interpretation still provide an intelligible and satisfying metalanguage for Ovid's book. Renouard is by no means an exception to his times. His discourses are largely derived from the *Fabularum Ovidii Interpretatio* of Georgius Sabinus, which was first published in 1555, and the traditional interpretations were kept very vigorously alive in the most important mythological dictionary of the second half of the sixteenth century, Conti's *Mythologia*. Indeed, the best-known French dictionary, the *Dictionarium historicum ac poeticum* of Charles Estienne, was vastly expanded in 1620 by the addition of moral interpretations from Conti. So the survival of the familiar schema of allegorical interpretation as modified by writers like Aneau must not be underestimated. But it is also important to look closely at exactly how the reader is invited to apply these interpretations. The text of Renouard's translation of the *Metamorphoses* is quite distinct from the discourses, which form a self-contained, separately paginated section of the book. Their use is entirely optional and not forced on us by inclusion in the text. Moreover, the justification given for them is that they constitute a reply to the moral disapproval of a critic for whom the *Metamorphoses* are nothing but an indecent display of lust and sexual perversion. This is the first time that we have heard allegorical interpretation linked so specifically with censure and presented not so much in terms of truth as in terms of a need to make literature morally and socially respectable. It is a subtle change, but it is a real one, and it is symptomatic of that revolution we have already noted. Literature's sphere of operation is recognised as autonomous and distinct from that of philosophical inquiry; but its practitioners need to maintain good diplomatic relations with the moral and social *bienséances* which condition the response of their readers. Typically, Renouard discounts attempts to find equivalences for Ovid's fables in the theories of the philosophers: 'ce seroit un travail à mon avis plus hautain et plus vain que profitable'; his emphasis is on their essential morality:

Je me promets de vous faire connoistre, que tant s'en faut qu'il y ait de scandaleux allechemens au vice; qu'au contraire, il ne s'y trouve rien en vain inventé, et que ce Livre est un patron, pour regler nostre vie et guider toutes nos actions à la vertu. (*Discours*, pp. 6–7)

There is another major difference between Renouard's discourses and interpretation as we have met it so far. He presents his material in the form of a leisurely discussion between two educated gentlemen who make polite suggestions about reading the *Metamorphoses* rather than dogmatic assertions. Their conversations are a sophisticated pastime characterised by elegance, refinement and tact, and they wear their learning lightly. We recognise the beginnings of a new style of discourse, deceptively facile and faintly ironic, modelled on polite social intercourse and as far removed from the scabrous complexities sought out by Lemaire as from the passionate personal involvement of Ronsard.

Renouard's *Jugement de Pâris*, not being part of his translation of the *Metamorphoses*, has no commentary, but a prefatory paragraph sets it firmly in the moral context with which we are familiar. The goddesses represent the three lives between which man has to choose: worldly ambition; the life of virtue and knowledge which leads to tranquillity and 'repos' (a more Stoic Pallas perhaps than we have met before); and the life of sensual pleasure, 'qui enchante nos sens, pour nous endormir parmy les delices' (*Jugement*, p. 7). The morality expressed by Renouard has a robust simplicity and self-confidence which must affect the reader's response to the tale. 'Volupté' is summarily and emphatically rejected in favour of 'Vertu'. Venus poses no real threat to rational man: 'elle ne remporte victoire, que les forces de la raison ne luy puissent oster' (*Jugement*, p. 7). Nor is our freedom of moral choice at any point in question:

Nous reconnoistrons en [ce] Tableau, que la liberté de nos actions n'est point forcée par les Puissances du Ciel, que du mal et du bien qui nous arrive, nous en sommes les ouvriers; et qu'il n'y a que nostre aveuglement qui attire sur nous les infortunes. (*Jugement*, p. 7)

So, the reader's choice is pre-empted, and unperturbed by any real sense of engagement in the moral issues raised by the story, but with a clear conscience on the score of its respectability, he can give himself to the delights of stylistic virtuosity offered by the fable, to the 'Poësie' which preoccupies Renouard in his narrative rather more than the 'Histoire' (*Jugement*, p. [5]).

The *Jugement* of La Roque has no moralising preamble and introduces straight away a rather different perspective on the subject.

The divinities assembled for his marriage scene are described in much more detail than Renouard's. It is unequivocally a feast of the senses, an earthly paradise for human eyes, in which the musical notes of Apollo, Pan and the Sirens echo from Lemaire, but are heard now only as a pleasant harmony, without the slightest hint of any distinction between them.[6] Lemaire's heaven of transcendental significances has become a pastoral idyll in which the goddesses play the rôle of shepherdesses:

> Sous l'ombre d'un grand chesne, où les fleurs bigarrees
> Donnoyent un plaisant lustre à leurs cottes dorees,
> Où seules à l'escart au point des grand's chaleurs
> Se faisoyent des bouquet de diverses couleurs. (p. 611)

There is no hint of allegory in La Roque's description of the goddesses. They are scarcely distinguished in substance from Paris, for if he recognises the divine in them, they too are ready to recognise godlike qualities in him, qualities which are identified specifically with grace and beauty:

> Et voyant sa beauté et sa Royale face,
> Sa façon, sa douceur toute pleine de grace,
> S'esbahirent par fois qu'un petit corps humain
> Eust les perfections dont il estoit si plain:
> Comme si par plaisir la sçavante nature
> L'eust d'un pinceau divin tiré sur leur peinture. (p. 619)

Nor are the divine and human separated by any outward signs in La Roque, for he omits altogether to describe the goddesses' attire. This is not so in Renouard's version, but his description of their clothes is radically different from any we have met before. His goddesses all wear dresses which put them firmly in an exclusively literary context, embroidered as they are with pictorial representations of the mythological narratives in which the goddesses play a major part. On the gown of Venus we read examples of the effects of love, presented as a list of twenty-three fables. This is neither the vernacular of the material world of sense, nor an encoded language of tropical signifiers. It is the language of fiction, a language which works through allusion to a familiar literary corpus, and out of which the Pléiade poets had created their autonomous universe of art and poetic discourse. All that remains to Renouard's Venus of the elaborate apparel of her previous avatars is her girdle, now totally unloosed from any moral constraint and revealing its hidden sense in words which compound sexual delight and the pleasures of fiction:

fatale ceinture, qui pleine d'un secret bon-heur, recelle dans ses replis les delicatesses, les mignardises, les agreables feintes, et les douces tromperies qui forcent à aimer.   (*Jugement*, p. 13)

The one passage which unites La Roque and Renouard in their telling of the tale is the moment when all nature holds its breath at the beauty of the naked goddesses. Habert and the *Grand Olympe* had declined to reproduce Lemaire at this point. But it is precisely here that La Roque and Renouard adhere most closely to Lemaire's exposition of the scene and indeed to his very words. Perhaps it is here that they feel most akin to Lemaire, recognising as their own the aesthetic vision which he had rejected a hundred years before. Moreover, the style of this vision has by now merged with the other vocabularies of physical beauty current in the Renaissance, notably with the Petrarchan, to form a standard composite poetic language, as in La Roque's description of Venus herself, where the commonplaces and conceits peculiar to Petrarchism are woven in and out of Lemaire's own words:

> Alors ce beau berger à loisir contempla
> Ceste divinité qui son feu redoubla,
> Son marcher, sa façon à nulle autre seconde,
> Et les flocons divers de sa perruque blonde
> Sans nul ordre espandus, dont les ondes encor
> Sembloyent non des cheveux mais un long fleuve d'or:
> Ses bruns sourcis voutez, ses arcs inevitables,
> Et de ses deux beaux yeux les soleils admirables,
> L'espace de son front esgal en sa rondeur,
> Où l'Amour establit son siege et sa grandeur,
> Et ce gracieux teint de beaux lis et de roses
> Qu'on voit au doux printemps nouvellement escloses:
> Ceste bouche riante et ce rang blanchissant
> Qui va de son thresor l'Indie enrichissant,
> Ses levres de corail, qui font naistre l'envie
> Et l'ardeur qui souvent à baiser nous convie.[7]   (p. 632)

To this, Juno and Pallas have, literally, no reply and no defence. La Roque's own judgement of Paris is unequivocally clear:

> Lequel sans aveugler sa raison naturelle,
> Ne fit aucun erreur la jugeant la plus belle.   (p. 634)

For La Roque, the moral consequence of the vision of Venus as goddess of physical beauty is pure hedonism.[8]

The early seventeenth-century Judgements point in two directions: to the moralising mythological fables so elegantly retold by Puget de

La Serre in the 1620s, and beyond them to the evolution of prose fiction as a genre inseparable from a serious moral context; but also to the world of exquisite pleasures and delicious ironies which is La Fontaine's *Amours de Psyché*. In both Venus is gradually retired from the stage, to be replaced by human figures projected with ever-increasing confidence within a purely human frame of reference. But the potential of Venus and her fable is far from exhausted. Her revenge lies with Racine.

NOTES

Introduction

1. It is perhaps invidious to single out a particular study from among several which have projected contemporary critical insights onto Renaissance literature, but for sixteenth-century France, especially for Rabelais, Ronsard and Montaigne, the most stimulating book is probably T. Cave, *The Cornucopian Text: Problems of Writing in the French Renaissance* (Oxford, 1979). A curious and fascinating example of the affinity between modern theories of writing and humanist commentaries on literary texts is to be found in the novel by R. Pinget, *L'Apocryphe* (Paris, 1980). The interesting and relevant book by T. M. Greene, *The Light in Troy: Imitation and Discovery in Renaissance Poetry* (New Haven, 1982), was unfortunately published too late for me to take account of it here.

2. See J. Seznec, *La Survivance des dieux antiques*, Studies of the Warburg Institute, 11 (London, 1940; 2nd edn, Paris, 1981), trans. B. F. Sessions (New York, 1961); R. R. Bolgar, *The Classical Heritage and its Beneficiaries: from the Carolingian Age to the End of the Renaissance* (Cambridge, 1954; reprinted New York, 1964); E. L. Eisenstein, *The Printing Press as an Agent of Change: Communications and Cultural Transformations in Early Modern Europe*, 2 vols. (Cambridge, 1979); E. R. Curtius, *European Literature and the Latin Middle Ages*, trans. W. R. Trask (London, 1953). Subsequent footnotes will direct the reader to supporting literature of more recent date. The history of specific mythological themes and figures, which is clearly germane to the subject matter of the present work, has become a favoured topic of late, and a useful critical survey of relevant studies, together with constructive suggestions for a methodology, will be found in R. Trousson, *Thèmes et mythes: Questions de méthode* (Brussels, 1981).

3. As far as Latin editions are concerned, this survey of the history of the *Metamorphoses* in the sixteenth century may be supplemented by the much greater detail given in A. Moss, *Ovid in Renaissance France: A Survey of the Latin Editions of Ovid and Commentaries printed in France before 1600* (London, 1982).

4. References are to Montaigne, *Essais*, ed. A. Thibaudet (Paris, 1950). For a fuller exploration of Montaigne's own treatment of some of the themes

broached in this Introduction, see R.D. Cottrell, *Sexuality/Textuality: A Study of the Fabric of Montaigne's 'Essais'* (Columbus, 1981), and M. B. McKinley, *Words in a Corner: Studies in Montaigne's Latin Quotations* (Lexington, 1981).

1. The Allegorical Tradition

1. The basic, and still the most exciting, history of allegorical interpretation is Seznec, *La Survivance des dieux antiques*; a great deal of fascinating detail is added to the story by D. C. Allen, *Mysteriously Meant: The Rediscovery of Pagan Symbolism and Allegorical Interpretation in the Renaissance* (Baltimore and London, 1970). For an analysis of allegorical interpretation in its medieval context, see J. B. Allen, *The Friar as Critic: Literary Attitudes in the Later Middle Ages* (Nashville, 1971).

2. *Ovide moralisé: poème du commencement du quatorzième siècle, publié d'après tous les manuscrits connus*, ed. C. de Boer and J. T. M. van't Sant, 5 vols. (Amsterdam, 1915–38)

3. The precise sources of Mansion's compilation have proved rather intractable to scholars. The most succinct account of their conclusions to date is to be found in E. Panofsky, *Renaissance and Renascences in Western Art*, 2nd edn (Stockholm, 1965), p. 78. A detailed analysis of one particular passage has proved very illuminating about the relationship between the *Bible des poetes* and manuscripts still extant: see W. G. van Emden, 'L'Histoire de *Pyrame et Thisbé* dans la mise en prose de l'*Ovide moralisé*: Texte du manuscrit Paris, B.N., f.fr. 137, avec variantes et commentaires', *Romania*, 94 (1973), pp. 29–56. Unfortunately the Pyramus tale does not include some of the problems presented by other passages in the *Bible des poetes*, which do not derive directly either from the prose version of the *Ovide moralisé* as we have it, or from the *Ovidius moralizatus* of Bersuire in the form in which it was printed in 1509 (although it was from a manuscript belonging to the same tradition as that used for the 1509 printing that Mansion took Bersuire's description of pagan divinities at the beginning of his book). It would appear that as well as the prose version, Mansion may have had to hand a copy of the verse *Ovide moralisé*, for, curiously, he retains several lines of this in his Orpheus story. He almost certainly also used a manuscript containing elements of a later augmented version which Bersuire had made of his work on Ovid, and for which he had borrowed interpretations from the French *Ovide moralisé* (this longer version was never printed). Interpretations translated from the augmented Latin text of Bersuire, which are distinguished from passages derived from the *Ovide moralisé* itself by Bersuire's habit of making analogous quotations from the Bible, are to be found, for example, in Mansion's allegorisation of the fables of Phrixus and Helle and of Hero and Leander. This still leaves moralisations which differ from both Bersuire and the *Ovide moralisé* and which may be Mansion's own invention, for example the moralisation of Actaeon.

4. The relationship between the four senses of allegorical interpretation and similar categories in medieval Biblical exegesis has been analysed by H. de Lubac, *Exégèse médiévale: les quatre sens de l'Ecriture*, 4 vols. (Paris, 1959–64), IV. The implications of allegorical exegesis of the Scriptures for the history of rhetoric in the earlier Middle Ages has been explored in a very interesting article by A. Strubel, '*Allegoria in factis* et *Allegoria in verbis*', *Poétique*, 23 (1975), pp. 342–57. The present book demonstrates how the Renaissance initiated a reversal of the process analysed by Strubel, robbing allegorical interpretation of the privileged position assigned to it by the theologians and reinstating uses of metaphor and allegory derived from ancient rhetoric.

5. R. Tuve, *Allegorical Imagery: Some Mediaeval Books and their Posterity* (Princeton, 1966)

6. Pierre Fabri, *Le Grand et vrai art de pleine rhétorique*, ed. A. Héron, 3 vols. (Rouen, 1889–90; reprinted Geneva, 1969), I, pp. 12–13

7. *Genealogie deorum gentilium libri*, ed. V. Romano, 2 vols. (Bari, 1951), I, pp. 140–2; Boccaccio's book is independent of the *Ovide moralisé* and of Bersuire, but they have sources in common.

8. Quoted in the very illuminating chapter on neo-Platonic approaches to poetry in C. Trinkaus, *In Our Image and Likeness: Humanity and Divinity in Italian Humanist Thought*, 2 vols. (London, 1970), II, pp. 683–721

9. See the discussion in dialogue form on the rôle of Venus in the *Aeneid*, which forms part of Landino's *Disputationes Camaldulenses*, vol. III; summarised by Trinkaus, *In Our Image and Likeness*, II, pp. 716–21.

10. *Metamorphoses*, with commentaries by Raphael Regius, Petrus Lavinius, and others (Lyons: S. Bivilaqua for J. Huguetan, 1518), fol. lxi v°– lxiii; reproduced in facsimile as the third volume of *The Renaissance and the Gods*, ed. S. Orgel, 44 vols. (New York and London, 1976)

11. For this and other metamorphoses of Venus's shell, see Panofsky, *Renaissance and Renascences*, pp. 80, 86–7.

2. The Three Goddesses: Jean Lemaire de Belges

1. The first book was originally published in 1511 at Lyons (E. Baland), the second in 1512 (Lyons and Paris: E. Baland for G. de Marnef), the third and final volume in 1513 (Paris: G. de Marnef). Unless otherwise indicated, all page references in this chapter refer to the first volume of *Œuvres de Jean Lemaire de Belges*, ed. J. Stecher, 4 vols. (Louvain, 1882–91).

2. Homer, *Iliad*, trans. E. V. Rieu (London, 1950), p. 437 (Book XXIV, lines 25–30)

3. This identification of Mercury with language is made explicit in a text which Lemaire cites at length in his concluding interpretations of the fable, 'Mercure signifie la parole, par laquelle toute doctrine est adressée et insinuée à nostre entendement' (p. 275). It is also found in St Augustine's *The City of God*, Book VII, Chapter 14 (trans. H. Bettenson (London, 1972), p. 271), to which Lemaire would have found a reference

in the commentary by J. B. Pius on Fulgentius's explanation of Mercury (*Enarrationes allegoricae fabularum fulgentii* (Milan, 1498), fol. cii v°). A comparison between Lemaire's references to Mercury and Boccaccio's description of the god shows how consistently Lemaire has stressed Mercury's identification with the arts of speech, as opposed to his other associations (see Boccaccio, *Genealogia*, I, 77–9; I, 137–40; II, 615–16).

4. This interesting little book is reproduced and examined by P. Jodogne, 'Un recueil poétique de J. Lemaire en 1498', in F. Simone, ed., *Miscellanea di studi et ricerche sul Quattrocento francese* (Turin, 1967), pp. 179–210.

5. See P. Jodogne, *Jean Lemaire de Belges, écrivain franco-bourguignon* (Brussels, 1971), p. 256.

6. Lemaire's account has the following features in common with Lucian and no one else: both mention Ganymede at some length; Mercury tells the goddesses to undress (but this is also in Guido de Columnis); both make a particular point about Venus loosing her girdle.

7. Jodogne, *Jean Lemaire*, pp. 434–5

8. *Epistolae Marsilii Ficini Florentini* (Nuremberg, 1497), fol. CCXIII

9. See Jodogne, *Jean Lemaire*, p. 420. Jodogne's reference to Italian painting seems very conjectural. My own equally subjective impression is that she looks every inch a Cranach minx. There are several versions of a woodcut by the elder Cranach, executed in the first decade of the century and showing three naked goddesses appearing to Paris, as described by Guido de Columnis (Plate 3).

10. *C Julii Hygini Augusti Liberti Fabularum liber* (Basel, 1549), p. 23 (fable no. 92)

11. See E. Faral, *Les Arts poétiques du XIIe et du XIIIe siècle* (Paris, 1924), pp. 86–9; the definitive account of the three levels of style in medieval Latin is F. Quadlbauer, *Die antike Theorie der Genera Dicendi im lateinischen Mittelalter* (Vienna, 1962).

12. Faral, in his synthesis of medieval poetic theory (*Arts poétiques*, pp. 89–97), concludes that the grand style was characterised by metaphor and other tropes, the lower styles by verbal figures or schemes, i.e. patterns involving the sound or placing of words. Pierre Fabri, a contemporary of Lemaire, makes the terminology of pastoral a feature of low style, together with diminutives (*Le Grand et vrai art de pleine rhétorique*, I, pp. 27–31).

13. Lemaire would have been highly gratified by the addition of a harp to the version made for Fontainebleau of Raphael's much imitated design for a Judgement of Paris, as well as by the 'accuracy' of the whole composition (Plate 4).

14. The sources of many of Lemaire's allegorical interpretations have been investigated by U. Bergweiler, *Die Allegorie im Werk von Jean Lemaire de Belges* (Geneva, 1976), pp. 70–104.

15. The *Bible des poetes* reproduces the *Ovide moralisé* very closely at this point, but although the *Bible des poetes* had been printed several times before Lemaire wrote the *Illustrations*, it seems likely that it was a

manuscript of some version of the *Ovide moralisé* itself which he had to hand. He elaborates a conceit about Saturn's absence from the feast, the germ of which is clearly in the *Ovide moralisé*, Book XI, lines 1254–5:

> Ni fu pas li vieulz Saturnus:
> Malades iert, si n'i vint mie.

In Lemaire this becomes 'Excepté le vieillard Saturne, triste, melancolique, et tardif, selon la nature de sa planette: Lequel s'excusa de venir, pource qu'il estoit malade. Et aussi que sa sphere et region est trop loingtaine de la terre habitable' (pp. 204–5). The *Bible des poetes* is incomprehensible at this point. The 1484 text reads 'mais point n'y fut samonus pource qu'il malade estoit'; the 1493 text ends a list of gods attending the feast with 'et le dieu Neptunus mais point n'y fut semonus pour ce qu'il malade estoit', which in the later editions becomes 'et le dieu Neptunus: mais point n'y fut semondz pource qu'il malade estoit'. There is no evidence that Lemaire used the *Bible des poetes* in preference to the *Ovide moralisé*, but there are traces of the *Ovide moralisé*, for example the equation of the apple with Paris's own head (p. 272), a rather extravagant amplification of the *Ovide moralisé*, XI, 2498–9, which has no counterpart in the *Bible des poetes*. For its allegorisations of our fable the *Bible des poetes* follows Bersuire (1515 edn, fol. lxxxviii–lxxxix), not the *Ovide moralisé*; there are echoes of the *Ovide moralisé* in Lemaire's interpretations, but no similarities at all with the *Bible des poetes*.

16. Fulgentius, *Enarrationes*, fol. c iiii v°–c iiii+2
17. Boccaccio's main description of Venus is in *Genealogia*, Book III, Chapters 22–3 (ed. Romano, I, pp. 142–52).
18. All three speeches are consummate models of the technicalities of the art of persuasion, both demonstrative and deliberative, as formulated in contemporary handbooks of rhetoric, for example, Fabri's *Grand et vrai art de pleine rhétorique*. The rhetorical aspects of Lemaire's prose are sympathetically analysed in M. F. O. Jenkins, *Artful Eloquence: Jean Lemaire de Belges and the Rhetorical Tradition*, North Carolina Studies in the Romance Languages and Literatures, 217 (Chapel Hill, 1980).
19. Boccaccio, *Genealogia*, Book III, Chapter 23 (ed. Romano, I, p. 151)
20. Would such a simile have been recognisable as Italian in style? It seems to me to be peculiarly Dantesque.
21. Ficino, *Epistolae*, fol. CCXIII. Ficino's sophisticated hedonism is even clearer in the explanation of the Judgement of Paris in his commentary on the *Philebus*, but this particular passage was not in any printed version of this work available to Lemaire; see Ficino, *The 'Philebus' Commentary*, ed. M. J. B. Allen (Berkeley, Los Angeles and London, 1975), pp. 447–53.
22. See Panofsky, *Renaissance and Renascences*, pp. 184–5.
23. Compare Fulgentius, *Enarrationes*, fol. c. iiii v°, and Boccaccio, *Genealogia*, Book VI, Chapter 22 and Book XII, Chapter 50 (ed. Romano, I, p. 304, and II, p. 607).
24. *Ovide moralisé*, Book XI, lines 2401–20 (ed. de Boer, IV, pp. 175–6)

25. Lemaire was unlikely to doubt the authenticity of the *Recognitiones*, when Lefèvre d'Etaples, in the preface to his edition, had followed the example of Pico della Mirandola in accepting it.

26. A commentary on Ovid's *Metamorphoses* was begun at Lyons in 1510, containing precisely this creative mixture of inventiveness and a sense that profoundly significant truths are veiled in Ovid's language. It also relies much on Boccaccio. The author was Petrus Lavinius, who wrote a prefatory letter and poem for the first edition of Book I of the *Illustrations*.

27. Boccaccio distinguishes thus between rhetoric and poetry:"'Habet enim suas inventiones rhetorica, verum apud integumenta fictionum nulle sunt rethorice partes; mera poesis est, quicquid sub velamento componitur et exponitur exquisite' (*Genealogia*, Book XIV, Chapter 7 (ed. Romano, II, p. 701)). The late medieval French context for Lemaire's concept of poetry is illustrated in pertinent detail by M. R. Jung, 'Poetria: Zur Dichtungstheorie des ausgehenden Mittelalters in Frankreich', *Vox Romanica*, 30 (1971), pp. 43–64; see also F. Rigolot, *Poétique et onomastique: L'exemple de la Renaissance* (Geneva, 1977), pp. 50–3.

3. Allegorical Interpretation in a Time of Change: from the Bible to Olympus

1. My references are to the 1539 edition published by D. Janot at Paris with a notable series of woodcuts. Most editions of the *Olympe* were illustrated profusely, doubtless both a cause and a symptom of its popularity.

2. Terence Cave, in *The Cornucopian Text*, approaches the *Grand Olympe* from a rather different direction and finds that its prefaces corroborate his analysis of the sixteenth-century idea of plenitude in expression (pp. 78–101).

3. Erasmus, *De duplici copia verborum ac rerum*, trans. B. I. Knott (*Collected Works of Erasmus* (Toronto, Buffalo and London, 1974–   ); XXIV, Literary and Educational Writings, ed. C. R. Thompson, 2, p. 611)

4. Rabelais, *Gargantua*, ed. R. Calder and M. A. Screech (Geneva, 1970), pp. 64–78; see also M. A. Screech, *Rabelais* (London, 1979), pp. 137–43.

5. Antoine Héroët, *Œuvres poétiques*, ed. F. Gohin (Paris, 1909), pp. 52–5. The most glaring exception to the general trend is, of course, Scève. But it is perhaps interesting to note that he is working within the one area of metaphorical expression which Rabelais presents as truly fulfilling the requirements of humanistic criteria: the emblem (see *Gargantua*, pp. 67–8). Poetry closely related to the religious language of the Bible or the liturgy also tends to retain the allegorical modes, which remain a recognised characteristic of such language. It is from the point of view of the insight given by divine grace (and from that alone) that Marguerite de Navarre can see in Ovid's *Metamorphoses* a series of allegorical variations on the theme of God's love for man (Marguerite de Navarre, *Les Prisons*, ed. S. Glasson (Geneva, 1978), pp. 162–6).

6. There was at least one intermediate adaptation of Lemaire's Judgement of Paris in the period between the original and its transmogrification in the *Grand Olympe*. In 1527 Jean Bouchet inserted a scene into his *Panegyric du Chevallier sans reproche*, which describes how Venus, attended by a retinue of gods and nymphs, visited the young Louis de la Tremoille as he slept in a glade. Parts of Bouchet's account of the goddess consist of whole phrases taken from Lemaire. Some go to form elements in Bouchet's physical description (parts of her body, the jewels in her hair, her posy of roses white and red); some are used to add a few selected allegorisations (the girdle of chastity given by Nature to curb her lasciviousness within the bonds of marriage, the explanation of the Graces). Bouchet seems to go halfway towards the developments we have noted in the *Grand Olympe*. In his treatment of Venus it is purely visual detail that predominates, but there are residual allegorical extensions, and the overall context of the passage is traditional physical interpretation: this Venus is explicitly the planet, visiting a favourite child to tell him that all women will love him because he was born under her star. (The text may be found in *Choix de chroniques et mémoires de l'histoire de la France*, ed. J. A. C. Buchon (Paris, 1856), pp. 738–40.)

4. The Three Goddesses: François Habert

1. There is a detailed bibliography of Habert's works in the edition by H. Franchet of *Le Philosophe Parfaict et le Temple de Vertu* (Paris, 1923); I know of very little critical work on Habert, except for J. C. Margolin's rather destructive analysis of a single poem in his article, 'Erasme, prince des bergers', *Bibliothèque d'Humanisme et Renaissance*, 29 (1967), pp. 407–42.

2. In the case of these two fables there is very little significant difference between the text of the narrative in the *Bible des poetes* and that of the *Grand Olympe*, but Habert's lines at the end of the Narcissus fable, 'Tousjours il veoit sa face claire et blonde/En l'eaue de Stix fort obscure et profonde' point to the *Grand Olympe*, 'il se mire toujours sa face', rather than the 'hideuse face' of the *Bible des poetes*.

3. The history and function of allegorical abstractions in the drama of this period have been thoroughly investigated by W. Helmich, *Die Allegorie im französischen Theater des 15. und 16. Jahrhunderts* (Tübingen, 1976).

4. The best general account of this aspect of humanist educational practice is in Bolgar, *The Classical Heritage and its Beneficiaries*; it is also described very clearly in W. J. Ong, *Rhetoric, Romance and Technology: Studies in the Interaction of Expression and Culture* (New York, 1971), and very comprehensively in J. M. Lechner, *Renaissance Concepts of the Commonplaces* (New York, 1962). Much more ambitious and more speculative, but intriguing in the use it makes of typographical developments, is A. Compagnon's general study of the function of quotation, *La Seconde Main, ou le travail de la citation* (Paris, 1979). The advice of the best of the earlier humanists on how to keep notebooks was collected together very

usefully in the year Habert's poem was published, in *De Ratione Studii . . . opuscula diversorum Autorum perquam erudita* (Basel, 1541).

5. The three poems were reprinted in 1546 (Paris: J. de Marnef), in 1547 (Lyons: J. de Tournes), and possibly in 1548. My quotations are from the 1547 edition.

6. Marot, *Œuvres lyriques*, ed. C. A. Mayer (London, 1964), pp. 114–23.

7. An excellent example of Erasmus's rhetorical and digressive mode of commentary is provided by his edition of the pseudo-Ovidian *Nux*, published in 1524 (modern edition by R. A. B. Mynors in Erasmus, *Opera omnia*, ed. J. Waszink and others (Amsterdam, 1969–), I, i, pp. 139–74). In France this ran to nine editions between 1526 and 1555.

8. See F. M. Higman, *Censorship and the Sorbonne: A Bibliographical Study of Books in French censured by the Faculty of Theology of the University of Paris, 1520–1551* (Geneva, 1979), pp. 47–72. Habert's response to the Sorbonne seems to have been to dissociate himself rather carefully from singers of psalms (*Nouvelle Juno*, p. 29), agree to the burning of books 'remplis de malheureuse esclandre' (*Nouvelle Juno*, p. 26) – and transfer his own to a publisher at Lyons (*Nouvelle Juno*, pp. 5–6).

9. *Les quinze livres de la Metamorphose d'Ovide interpretez en rime françoise, selon la phrase latine* (Paris: M. Fezandat and E. Groulleau). There is a detailed analysis of this translation by A. Leykauff, *François Habert und seine Übersetzung der Metamorphosen Ovids* (Munich, 1904). Contrary to Leykauff's opinion, Habert is scrupulously faithful to Ovid's text, although his expression is often awkward.

Transition: Lection and Election

1. See, for example, St Augustine, *De Doctrina christiana*, Book III, Chapter V: 'You must be very careful lest you take figurative expressions literally. What the Apostle says pertains to this problem: "For the letter killeth, but the spirit quickeneth." That is, when that which is said figuratively is taken as though it were literal, it is understood carnally. Nor can anything more appropriately be called the death of the soul . . . He who follows the letter takes figurative expressions as though they were literal and does not refer the things signified to anything else . . . There is a miserable servitude of the spirit in this habit of taking signs for things, so that one is not able to raise the eye of the mind above things that are corporal and created to drink in eternal light.' (*On Christian Doctrine*, trans. D. W. Robertson (New York, 1958), p. 84)

2. Rabelais, *Le Tiers Livre*, ed. M. A. Screech (Geneva, 1964), p. 54 (Chapter V)

3. *Le Songe de Poliphile*, ed. A.-M. Schmidt (Paris, 1963, facsimile of the first French edition of 1546), fol. 127

5. A Preparation for Reading

1. *Trois premiers livres de la Metamorphose d'Ovide, Traduictz en vers François, Le premier et second par Cl. Marot, Le tiers par B. Aneau.*

Mythologizez par Allegories Historiales, Naturelles et Moralles, re-cueillies des bons Autheurs Grecz, et Latins, sur toutes les fables et sentences. Illustrez de figures et images convenantes. Avec une preparation de voie à la lecture et intelligence des Poetes fabuleux (Lyons: G. Rouillé and M. Bonhomme). There is a short account of the book in G. Demerson, *La Mythologie classique dans l'œuvre lyrique de la 'Pléiade'* (Geneva, 1972), pp. 499–501.

2. See, for example, *Ode à Caliope* (1550); *A son Luc* (1550); *Ode à Michel de l'Hospital* (1552); and later formulations in the *Abbregé de l'Art poëtique françois* (1565) and *Hymne de l'Autonne* (1563). The theories of the antecedents of Ronsard and Aneau among the Italian neo-Platonists are discussed by Trinkaus, *In Our Image and Likeness*, II, pp. 683–721 (the section entitled 'From *Theologia Poetica* to *Theologia Platonica*'). The same ideas were worked into sixteenth-century handbooks on mythology which became standard reference works, for example Giraldi, *De deis gentium* (1548) and Conti's *Mythologia* (?1551).

3. Either *De Deorum imaginibus libellus* (i.e. the descriptions of the gods at the beginning of Bersuire's *Ovidius Moralizatus*, without the interpretations), often attributed to Albericus and printed at Basel in 1549 in one volume with the Greek mythographers cited by Aneau and extracts from Giraldi; or Albericus (Mythographus III), *Allegoriae Poeticae seu de veritate ac expositione poeticarum fabularum libri IV* (Paris, 1520)

4. For subsequent developments in the historical criticism of ancient thought and literature, see J. Jehasse, *La Renaissance de la critique: l'essor de l'Humanisme érudit de 1540 à 1614* (Saint-Etienne, 1976).

5. See P. Kuntze, *Le Grand Olympe, eine alchimistische Deutung von Ovids Metamorphosen* (Halle, 1912).

6. Aneau at this point, as elsewhere in his essay, refers to the authority of Melanchthon, *Enarratio operum et dierum Hesiodi*: 'Porro, ut hoc quoque obiter admoneam, non est semper in fabulis ratio quaerenda; sed satis sit aliquousque deprehendisse, quid significare poeta voluerit . . . nec in expositionibus fabularum ad amussim omnia sunt rimanda' (Melanchthon, *Opera*, ed. C. G. Bretschneider and H. E. Binseil, 28 vols. (Brunswick, etc., 1834–60), XVIII, col. 200).

7. See I. D. McFarlane, 'Reflections on Ravisius Textor's *Specimen Epithetorum*', in R. R. Bolgar, ed., *Classical Influences on European Culture AD 1500–1700* (Oxford, 1976), pp. 81–90.

8. Du Bellay, *La Deffence et Illustration de la langue francoyse*, ed. H. Chamard (Paris, 1904), pp. 86–7

9. The technical history of these editions is to be found in M. D. Henkel, 'Illustrierte Ausgaben von Ovids *Metamorphosen* im XV., XVI., und XVII. Jahrhundert', *Vorträge der Bibliothek Warburg*, 6 (1926–7), pp. 58–144.

10. Jean de Tournes, who published this work and reprinted it in 1564 and 1583, and also brought out versions in Dutch and Italian, had already used the first twenty-one of his illustrations for his 1549 edition of Marot's translation. Marot's literal version was thus at the genesis of

both important sets of French sixteenth-century engravings for the *Metamorphoses*, the Rouillé set used for Aneau's translation, and the de Tournes set which was reproduced and copied in many different types of edition of the work up to the end of the century. Despite the literal accuracy of both sets of pictures, it is part of this curious and complicated history that Bernard Salomon, to whom the de Tournes engravings are generally attributed, seems to have drawn his information from the *Grand Olympe*, rather than from the Latin text. His illustration of the metamorphosis of Cephalus's hound has dogs changing into trees instead of statues, reflecting the misprint common in editions of the *Grand Olympe*, whereby 'marbres' became 'arbres'.

6. Jean-Antoine de Baïf

1. The clearest account of Pléiade ideas on imitation is probably to be found in G. Castor, *Pléiade Poetics: A Study in Sixteenth-Century Thought and Terminology* (Cambridge, 1964); its implications for French writing of the period are studied in a very illuminating way by D. G. Coleman, in *The Gallo-Roman Muse: Aspects of Roman Literary Tradition in Sixteenth-Century France* (Cambridge, 1979).

2. The most recent edition of all nine books of *Poèmes* is the second volume of the *Euvres en rime de Jan Antoine de Baïf*, ed. C. Marty-Laveaux, 5 vols. (Paris, 1881–90; reprinted Geneva, n.d.). My page references are to the second volume of this edition.

3. See M. Augé-Chiquet, *La Vie, les idées et l'oeuvre de Jean-Antoine de Baïf* (Paris, 1909; reprinted Geneva, 1969), pp. 208–36.

4. Ronsard, *Au Lecteur*, in *Œuvres complètes*, ed. P. Laumonier, 20 vols. (Paris, 1914–75), XVIII, pp. 283–4. All references to Ronsard are to this edition unless otherwise stated.

5. In his Medea poem Baïf talks neither of gardens, of pleasure, nor of gifts, but of a commission undertaken with reluctance. It is not a narrative like the other five Ovidian poems, but an extract solely concerning Medea's internal debate about her love for Jason, and it is the only one to be called a translation. Baïf seems to separate it from the others, and indeed its very difference tends to throw into relief the similarities which link the remaining five.

6. Jean-Antoine de Baïf, *Le premier livre des poèmes*, ed. G. Demerson (Grenoble, 1975), p. 13

7. *Picta Poesis*, pp. 14 and 32; *Imagination poétique*, pp. 19 and 44

8. *De Deis gentium*, p. 244

9. Pontus de Tyard, *Œuvres poétiques complètes*, ed. J. C. Lapp (Paris, 1966), pp. 271–2

10. It is difficult to decide conclusively which Latin text Baïf used for his imitations. The choice lies between the edition annotated by the Italian humanist scholar, Raphael Regius (last printed in France in 1528), and the text of the second Aldine edition, which was the standard text for editions of the *Metamorphoses* published in France between 1534 and the

end of the century. In the passages relevant to Baïf the variants are fairly slight and would be unlikely to show up in translation. On balance, the evidence seems to me to favour the Aldine text, but see n. 11 below.

11. They are in one of the explanatory notes to the Regius edition of the *Metamorphoses* (fol. lxii v°), and the slightly confused sense of Baïf's 'ennemy' could be evidence that he has consulted that edition and conflated its two separate notes on polyps.

12. Probably the most familiar quotation to illustrate this commonplace was Ovid's 'Nitimur in vetitum semper, cupimusque negata' (*Amores*, III, iv, line 17).

13. 'Seque vocat bustum miserabile nati' – on Tereus, after eating his own son. In an interesting article on the Pyramus and Thisbe legend, W. G. van Emden has argued for the dependence of Baïf on the *Grand Olympe* and on the *Ovide moralisé* itself ('Sources de l'histoire de *Pyrame et Thisbe* chez Baïf et Théophile de Viau', in *Mélanges de langue et de littérature médiévales offerts à Pierre Le Gentil* (Paris, 1973), pp. 869–79). I am dubious about this. All Baïf's amplifications can be explained, and better explained, by his imitation of Latin poets and of Ovid in particular. It is not necessary to introduce medieval sources for them.

14. I think it is the disjunctive nature of the commonplace origin of Baïf's moral generalisations which has led two modern critics to quite divergent views on *Le Laurier*, another of Baïf's amplified imitations: for G. Demerson (*Mythologie*, p. 178) it affirms the value of marriage, whereas D. Stone reads it as praise of chastity and related virtues ('The Sixteenth Century and Antiquity: a Case Study', in B. C. Bowen, ed., *The French Renaissance Mind: Studies presented to W. G. Moore, L'Esprit Créateur*, XVI, 4 (Lawrence, Kansas, 1976), pp. 37–47).

7. Pierre de Ronsard

1. There is a vast literature on Ronsard's poetry, but so far the single volume which gives the best idea of his variety and imaginative reach is *Ronsard the Poet*, ed. T. Cave (London, 1973); the studies closest to the issues raised in this chapter are I. Silver, *The Intellectual Evolution of Ronsard*, 2 vols. (St Louis, 1969, 1973), and the essay by T. Cave in T. Cave, ed., *Ronsard the Poet*, entitled 'Ronsard's mythological universe' (pp. 159–208).

2. For a description of the methods of one teacher in the early 1570s, see A. Grafton, 'Teacher, Text and Pupil in the Renaissance Class-room: a Case Study from a Parisian College', *History of Universities*, I (1981), pp. 37–70.

3. See Melanchthon, *De locis communibus ratio*, included in the 1541 collection *De ratione studii*. Perhaps the clearest example of this serious and ambitious view of the commonplace book, largely prevalent in the 1530s, 1540s and 1550s, is the *Pandectae* of Conrad Gesner (Zurich, 1548), which is an encyclopaedia of knowledge based on the formula of the commonplace book. Later in the century pedagogues adopted a

much more restrictive attitude, clearly expressed by the Jesuits, which sees the commonplace book as a means of selecting out of ancient literature only those passages which meet with moral approval. For Melanchthon's own application of the commonplace method to theology, see Q. Breen, 'The Terms "loci communes" and "loci" in Melanchthon', *Church History*, 16 (1947), pp. 197–209.

4. *Illustrium poetarum flores. Per Octavianum Mirandulam collecti, et in locos communes digesti* (Lyons, 1576), fol. a 2v°–3. There are numerous editions of this collection, throughout the sixteenth century.

5. Ronsard uses the word 'horreur' in the full sense of the Latin 'horror', defined in the *Latin Dictionary* of Lewis and Short as: 'bristling', 'shaking with fright', 'trembling with joy', 'dread', 'veneration', 'religious awe'.

6. See A. H. T. Levi, 'The Role of Neoplatonism in Ronsard's Poetic Imagination' in T. Cave, ed., *Ronsard the Poet*, pp. 121–58.

7. That the analogies between Ronsard's *pauses* and the strophic structure of Pindaric odes was self-evident to Ronsard's contemporary readers seems clear from their juxtaposition in Vauquelin de la Fresnaye's discussion of the Ode in his *Art poétique*, I, 663–6 (*Art poétique*, ed. G. Pellissier (Paris, 1885), p. 41):

> Si d'une fiction d'un long discours tu causes,
> Tu pourras diviser cette longueur en pauses.
> Ou par les plis tournez des Odes du Sonneur
> Qui Grec sur les neufs Grecs lyriques eut l'honneur.

8. Erasmus defines *enargeia* as follows: 'We employ this whenever . . . instead of setting out the subject in bare simplicity, we fill in the colours and set it up like a picture to look at, so that we seem to have painted the scene rather than described it, and the reader seems to have seen rather than read.' (*De Copia*, p. 577)

9. The theme of mutability in Ronsard's work has been exhaustively documented by M. Quainton, *Ronsard's Ordered Chaos: Visions of Flux and Stability in the Poetry of Pierre de Ronsard* (Manchester, 1980).

10. VI, pp. 73–83; XV, pp. 178–85; X, pp. 275–90; XV, pp. 234–53; XVII, pp. 155–8. The hermaphrodite theme has been explored with reference to the hymns of the seasons in Cave, *The Cornucopian Text*, pp. 242–56. Ronsard could have seen it illustrated in cruder pictorial form on the walls of Fontainebleau (Plate 10).

11. A more detailed study of nymphs in Ronsard's work would have to expand this point. The landscapes of fifteenth-century Italian neo-Latin writers and of Lemaire and the later Rhétoriqueurs are even more heavily populated with nymphs than those of ancient poets, and perhaps just as familiar to Ronsard. Lemaire's vision of the naked Venus is closely associated with nymphs, and it is as a nymph that Polia first appears to join her lover on their quest for Venus in Colonna's *Songe de Poliphile*. For a full documentation of instances where Ronsard refers to

nymphs as sources of inspiration, see F. Joukovsky-Micha, *Poésie et mythologie au XVIe siècle: Quelques mythes de l'inspiration chez les poètes de la Renaissance* (Paris, 1969).

12. For details of some of the texts in Ronsard's mind, see P. Ford, 'Ronsard and the Theme of Inspiration', in P. Bayley and D. G. Coleman, eds., *The Equilibrium of Wit: Essays for Odette de Mourgues* (Lexington, 1982), pp. 57–69.

13. Some idea of Dorat's teaching has been reached from a combination of different sources: see P. de Nolhac, *Ronsard et l'humanisme* (Paris, 1921), p. 72, *passim*; P. Sharratt, 'Ronsard et Pindare: un écho de la voix de Dorat', *Bibliothèque d'Humanisme et Renaissance*, 39 (1977), pp. 97–114; G. Demerson, 'Dorat, commentateur d'Homère' in R. Aulotte, ed., *Etudes seizièmistes offertes à Monsieur le Professeur V. L. Saulnier* (Geneva, 1980), pp. 223–34. Dorat's possibly old-fashioned views on interpretation differ radically from the critical studies of other classical scholars with whom Ronsard associated, such as Turnèbe, who may have pointed him in other directions, towards a rigorously precise understanding of the Greek and Latin literary language. Despite his close relationship with Dorat and his undoubted admiration for his inspiring teaching, Ronsard's own critical sense must have inhibited him from writing poetry like his master's, much of which represents the nadir of sixteenth-century taste.

14. The attitude to mythological interpretation shared by Aneau and Ronsard was by no means exclusive to them. Both the flexible approach and the general limitation of allegorical reading to the traditional areas, historical, physical and moral, are to be found in the commentary *Fabularum Ovidii Interpretatio* by Georgius Sabinus (Wittenberg, 1555; Paris, 1575), as well as in the most important reference work on mythology belonging to the latter half of the sixteenth century, the *Mythologia* of Conti.

15. For Ronsard's attitudes to religion, see A. Py, *Ronsard* (Paris, 1972).

16. The arbitrary nature of neo-Platonic interpretations, which makes them close kin to the fabrications of the contemporary *Bible des poetes*, is well put by E. H. Gombrich: 'The [neo-Platonic] allegory frequently oscillates between the search for the Orphic arcanum, bordering on primitive magic, and the sophisticated conceit, bordering on parlour games.' (*Symbolic Images: Studies in the Art of the Renaissance* (London, 1972), p. 60)

17. The *Bibliotheca selecta* of Antonius Possevinus (Rome, 1593), a massive Counter-Reformation encyclopaedia, tried to reinstate an early sixteenth-century treatise on mythological equivalences and singled out Ronsard's *Hercule chrestien* for special praise.

18. The subject matter of *Hylas*, another mythological narrative in the same collection (xv, pp. 234–53), is not dissimilar. That poem also straddles two modes of poetic experience: the beautiful pool of nymphs where Hylas is gently raped to his easeful death, and the world of harsh reality

where the forlorn Hercules must continue his labours, identified quite specifically at the end of the poem as moral battles. As in the *Hymne de l'Autonne*, the fabulous vision of nymphs is associated with childhood, whilst the language which Ronsard uses for the adult's encounters with the external world is the language of allegorical interpretation.

Epilogue: the Three Goddesses again

1. W. B. Yeats, *Vacillation*
2. What is generally called Baroque poetry, particularly the shorter poems, has been the subject of much recent critical interest. Among many stimulating books, I would single out G. Mathieu-Castellani, *Mythes de l'Eros baroque* (Paris, 1981).
3. My references are to the 1651 edition (Paris, A. Courbé). The *Metamorphoses*, the *Jugement de Pâris* and the *Discours* are paginated separately.
4. *Devis des Dieux, pris de Lucian, Devis premier. Le Jugement des trois deesses* (*Euvres en rime*, ed. Marty-Laveaux, IV, pp. 140–62)
5. La Roque was quite a prolific author of mythological narratives, among them *Les Amours de Pirame et Tisbee*, first published in 1597.
6. La Roque's description of the marriage feast is a loose adaptation of Lemaire in the *Illustrations*, whereas Renouard's much more schematic account recalls the *Grand Olympe*. All the way through, La Roque follows the original Lemaire more closely than Renouard does, but Renouard also adds to the narrative of the *Grand Olympe* episodes in the story which are exclusive to the *Illustrations*. As far as I know, the latest edition of the *Illustrations* belongs to 1549. La Roque and Renouard both vary their sources in quite elaborate and idiosyncratic ways.
7. In the *Illustrations* the passage runs as follows: 'Or nota Paris tout à loisir, la resplendeur de ses tresses dorées longues et espesses, dont les floquons espars sans ordre ça et là, donnoient merveilleuse decoration au chef, et aux espaules eburnines. Considera l'amplitude et spaciosité de son cler front bien arrondy: l'arcure de ses sourciz noirs: la splendeur admirable, et l'attrait amoureux et penetratif de ses yeux vers: la forme de son nez traitiz: la fresche couleur et le beau teint de sa face: la rondeur de ses joues purpurines: la petitesse de la bouche riant, avec l'elevation de ses levres coralines et bien jointisses que d'elles mesmes sembloient semondre un baiser' (pp. 255–6).
8. Dr Cave has reminded me of an additional proof of the survival of our three goddesses, albeit in somewhat reduced circumstances. There is a Judgement of Paris, not at all related to any previous text of the fable, at the beginning of D'Urfé's *Astrée*, Part I, Book IV, pp. 114–17 in the edition by H. Vaganay, 5 vols. (Lyons, 1925–8), vol. I. This part of the work was first published in 1607. In this pastoral re-enactment of the fable, performed in honour of Venus, three shepherdesses are chosen to dispute the apple and a fourth to play the part of Paris. The actual judgement takes place behind closed doors in the Temple of Beauty where the female

Paris scrutinises the three shepherdesses naked 'hormis un foible linge qui les couvre de la ceinture jusques aupres du genouil'. No distinction is made between them. They are just pretty shepherdesses and it is just a beauty contest. There is added erotic interest when Céladon manages to infiltrate the ceremony disguised as a shepherdess disguised as Paris and so see the full measure of the charms of his beloved Astrée (we, of course, do not). Nothing very serious ensues, apart from minor risks to Astrée's maidenly modesty. The sole function of this slightly titillating scene is to set the tone and put in train the action of the rest of the novel. It is the encounter of Astrée and Céladon that interests us, not the judgement of Paris. At no point in the telling does D'Urfé use the potential of the fable to relate his characters to a context of ideas. His goddesses are only human and all that is left of the myth is a sort of residual eroticism, decorously contrived.

BIBLIOGRAPHY OF WORKS
CONSULTED

Primary Sources

Aneau, Barthélemy, *Picta Poesis*, Lyons, 1552

Imagination poétique, Lyons, 1552

Trois premiers livres de la Metamorphose: see Ovid

Apuleius, *Commentarii a Philippo Beroaldo conditi in asinum aureum lucii apuleii*, Venice, 1501

Augustine, St, *On Christian Doctrine*, trans. D. W. Robertson, New York, 1958

The City of God, trans. H. Bettenson, London, 1972

Baïf, Jean-Antoine de, *Euvres en rime de Jan Antoine de Baïf*, ed. C. Marty-Laveaux, 5 vols., Paris, 1881–90, reprinted Geneva, n.d.

Le premier livre des poèmes, ed. Guy Demerson, Grenoble, 1975

Bersuire, Pierre, *Metamorphosis ovidiana moraliter a magistro Thoma Walleys Anglico . . . explanata*, Paris, 1515

De Deorum imaginibus libellus: see Hyginus

Boccaccio, Giovanni, *Genealogie deorum gentilium libri*, ed. V. Romano, 2 vols., Bari, 1951

Bouchet, Jean, *Panegyric du Chevallier sans reproche*, in *Choix de chroniques et mémoires de l'histoire de France*, ed. J. A. C. Buchon, Paris, 1856

Brodeau de Tours, Jean, *Ioannis Brodaei Turonensis Miscellaneorum Libri sex*, Basel, n.d., prefatory letter dated 1555

Catullus, *Carmina*, ed. R. Ellis, Oxford, n.d.

Cicero, *Xysti Betuleii Augustani in M. T. Ciceronis libros III. de Natura deorum, et Paradoxa, Commentarii*, Basel, 1550

Clement of Rome, *Paradysus Heraclidis. Epistola Clementis. Recognitiones Petri Apostoli . . .*, ed. J. Lefèvre d'Etaples, Paris, 1504

Colonna, Francesco, *Le Songe de Poliphile*, preface by A.-M. Schmidt, Paris, 1963, facsimile of the first French edition of 1546

Columnis, Guido de, *Historia destructionis Troiae*, ed. N. E. Griffin, Cambridge, Mass., 1936

Conti, Natale, *Mythologiae sive explicationis fabularum libri X*, Geneva, 1651

Cotgrave, Randle, *A Dictionarie of the French and English Tongues*, London, 1611, reprinted in facsimile, Hildesheim and New York, 1970

Despauterius, Joannes, *De Figuris liber*, Lyons, 1526

Dictys Cretensis, *Ephemeris belli troiani*, Venice, 1499

Du Bellay, Joachim, *La Deffence et Illustration de la langue francoyse*, ed. H. Chamard, Paris, 1904

Œuvres poétiques, ed. H. Chamard, 6 vols., Paris, 1908–31

Erasmus, Desiderius, *Opera omnia*, ed. J. Waszink and others, Amsterdam, 1969, I, i, *Nux*, ed. R. A. B. Mynors

Collected Works, Toronto, Buffalo and London, 1974–, XXIV, *Literary and Educational Writings*, ed. C. R. Thompson, 2, *De duplici copia verborum ac rerum*, trans. B. I. Knott

Estienne, Charles, *Lexicon historicum, geographicum, poeticum*, Paris, 1620

Euripides, *Euripidis tragici poetae nobilissimi Hecuba et Iphigenia latinae factae Erasmo Roterodamo interprete*, Paris, 1506

Fabri, Pierre, *Le Grand et vrai art de pleine rhétorique*, ed. A. Héron, 3 vols., Rouen, 1889–90, reprinted Geneva, 1969

Ficino, Marsilio, *Epistolae Marsilii Ficini Florentini*, Nuremberg, 1497

The 'Philebus' Commentary, ed. M. J. B. Allen, Berkeley, Los Angeles, and London, 1975

Firmicus Maternus, *De nativitatibus* [i.e. *Matheseos liber*], Venice, 1497

Fouquelin, Antoine, *La Rhetorique Francoise*, Paris, 1557

Fulgentius, *Enarrationes allegoricae fabularum fulgentii*, with the commentary of J. B. Pius, Milan, 1498

Gesner, Conrad, *Pandectarum sive Partitionum Universalium libri XXI*, Zurich, 1548

Giraldi, L. G., *De Deis gentium varia et multiplex historia*, Basel, 1548

Habert, François, *La jeunesse du Banny de lyesse, escollier, estudiant à Tholose*, Paris, 1541

La suytte du Banny de Liesse, Paris, 1541

Deploration poetique de feu M. Antoine du Prat, en son vivant Chancellier et Legat de France. Avec l'exposition morale de la Fable des trois Deesses, Venus, Iuno et Pallas, Lyons, 1545

La Nouvelle Pallas, Presentee à Monseigneur le Daulphin, Lyons, 1547

La Nouvelle Iuno, Presentee à ma Dame la Daulphine, Lyons, 1547

La Nouvelle Venus, Par laquelle est entendue pudique Amour, presentee à Madame la Daulphine, Lyons, 1547

Six livres de la Metamorphose d'Ovide: see Ovid

Les quinze livres de la Metamorphose d'Ovide: see Ovid

Le Philosophe Parfaict et le Temple de Vertu, ed. H. Franchet, Paris, 1923

Héroët, Antoine, *Œuvres poétiques*, ed. F. Gohin, Paris, 1909

Homer, *Iliad*, trans. E. V. Rieu, London, 1950

Horace, *Opera*, ed. E. C. Wickham, 2nd edn, Oxford, n.d.

Hyginus, *Fabularum liber . . . Quibus accesserunt similis argumenti: Palaephati de Fabulosis narrationibus liber I. P. Fulgentii Planciadis . . . Mythologiarum libri III . . . Phornuti de Natura deorum, sive poeticarum fabularum allegoriis speculatio. Albrici philosophi de Deorum imaginibus liber*, Basel, 1549

La Roque, Siméon-Guillaume de, *Les Œuvres du sieur de La Roque*, Paris, 1609

Le Fèvre, Raoul, *Le recueil des hystoires troyennes*, Lyons, 1494

Lemaire de Belges, Jean, *Œuvres*, ed. J. Stecher, 4 vols., Louvain, 1882–91, reprinted Hildesheim and New York, 1972

Lucian, *Luciani viri quam disertissimi compluria opuscula longe festivissima ab Erasmo Roterodamo et Thoma Moro interpretibus optimis in latinorum linguam traducta*, Paris, 1506

  Satirical Sketches, trans. P. Turner, London, 1961

Lucretius, *De Rerum natura libri sex*, ed. C. Bailey, 2nd edn, Oxford, 1954

Machaut, Guillaume de, *Œuvres*, ed. E. Hoepffner, 3 vols., Paris, 1908–21

Marot, Clément, *Œuvres lyriques*, ed. C. A. Mayer, London, 1964

  Œuvres complètes, ed. C. A. Mayer, VI, *Les Traductions*, Geneva, 1980

Melanchthon, Philip, *Opera*, ed. C. G. Bretschneider and H. E. Binseil, 28 vols., Brunswick, etc., 1834–60, XVIII, *Enarratio operum et dierum Hesiodi*

Mirandula, Octavianus, *Illustrium poetarum flores. Per Octavianum Mirandulam collecti, et in locos communes digesti*, Lyons, 1576

Molinet, Jean, *Le Roman de la rose moralise en prose*, Paris, 1521

Montaigne, Michel de, *Essais*, ed. A. Thibaudet, Paris, 1950

Mosellanus, Petrus, *Tabulae de Schematibus et Tropis*, Paris, 1542

Navarre, Marguerite de, *Marguerites de la Marguerite des Princesses*, Lyons, 1547, reprinted in facsimile, 2 vols., Wakefield, New York and Paris, 1970

  Les Prisons, ed. S. Glasson, Geneva, 1978

Ovid, *Opera*, 3 vols., Paris, 1762

  Heroidum Epistole . . . Cum triplici explanatione [i.e. with the commentaries of A. Volscus, U. Clericus, J. Badius], Lyons, 1503, a reissue of the first French edition of these commentaries, Lyons, 1500

  Metamorphoseos libri moralizati, with commentaries by R. Regius, P. Lavinius, and others, Lyons, 1518, reproduced in facsimile as the third volume of *The Renaissance and the Gods*, ed. S. Orgel, 44 vols., New York and London, 1976

  La Bible des Poetes de Ovide Methamorphose. Translatee de latin en Francoys, Paris, 1531

  Les XV. livres de la Metamorphose D'ovide . . . contenans L'olympe des Histoires poëtiques traduictz de Latin en Francoys, le tout figuré de nouvelles figures [i.e. *Le Grand Olympe*], Paris, 1539

  Six livres de la Metamorphose d'Ovide, traduictz selon la phrase latine en rime françoise [by François Habert], Paris, 1549

  Trois premiers livres de la Metamorphose d'Ovide, Traduictz en vers François, Le Premier et second par Cl. Marot, Le tiers par B. Aneau. Mythologizez par Allegories Historiales, Naturelles et Moralles, recueillies des bons Autheurs Grecz, et Latins, sur toutes les fables et sentences. Illustrez de figures et images convenantes. Avec une preparation de voie à la lecture et intelligence des Poetes fabuleux, Lyons, 1556

  Les quinze livres de la Metamorphose d'Ovide interpretez en rime françoise, selon la phrase latine [by François Habert], Paris, 1557

Bibliography

Les Metamorphoses d'Ovide Traduites en Prose Françoise, . . . enrichies de figures à chacune Fable. Avec XV. Discours Contenans l'Explication Morale et Historique. De plus outre le Jugement de Paris. [by Nicolas Renouard], Paris, 1651

La Metamorphose d'Ovide figuree, Lyons, 1557

Ovide moralisé: poème du commencement du quatorzième siècle, publié d'après tous les manuscrits connus, ed. C. de Boer and J. T. M. van't Sant, 5 vols., Amsterdam, 1915–38

Peletier du Mans, Jacques, *L'Art Poëtique*, ed. A. Boulanger, Paris, 1930

Pindar, *The Odes of Pindar*, trans. R. Lattimore, Chicago, 1959

Pisan, Christine de, *Le Livre du chemin de long estude*, ed. R. Püschel, Berlin, 1887, reprinted Geneva, 1974

Pontanus Petrus, *Liber figurarum, tam oratoribus quam Poetis vel grammaticis necessarius*, Paris, 1529

Possevinus, Antonius, *Bibliotheca selecta*, Rome, 1593

Puget de la Serre, Jean, *Les amours des Dieux*, Paris, 1640

Rabelais, François, *Gargantua*, ed. R. Calder and M. A. Screech, Geneva, 1970

Le Tiers Livre, ed. M. A. Screech, Geneva, 1964

De Ratione Studii . . . opuscula diversorum Autorum perquam erudita, Basel, 1541

Ravisius Textor, Joannes, *Specimen Epithetorum . . . omnibus artis Poeticae Studiosis maxime utilium*, Paris, 1518

Epithetorum opus absolutissimum . . . Lexicon vere poeticum ad imitationem Graecorum elaboratum, uberem, omnium et verborum copiam complectens, Basel, 1558

Epitome operis epithetorum, Paris, 1562

Renouard, Nicolas, *Les Metamorphoses d'Ovide:* see Ovid

Ronsard, Pierre de, *Œuvres complètes*, ed. P. Laumonier, 20 vols., Paris, 1914–75

Sabinus, Georgius, *Fabularum Ovidii Interpretatio*, Paris, 1575

Sainte-Maur, Benoît de, *Le Roman de Troie*, ed. L. Constans, 6 vols., Paris, 1904

Scève, Maurice, *Saulsaye*, ed. M. Françon, Cambridge, Mass., 1959

Sebillet, Thomas, *Art Poétique Françoys*, ed. F. Gaiffe, Paris, 1932

Susenbrotus, Joannes, *Epitome troporum ac schematum et grammaticorum et Rhetorum, ad Authores tum prophanos tum sacros intelligendos non minus utilis quam necessaria*, Zurich, 1541

Talaeus, Audomarus, *Rhetorica*, Paris, 1552

Tory, Geofroy, *Champ Fleury*, reprinted in facsimile, Wakefield, New York and Paris, 1970

Tyard, Pontus de, *Œuvres poétiques complètes*, ed. J. C. Lapp, Paris, 1966

Urfé, Honoré d', *L'Astrée*, ed. H. Vaganay, 5 vols., Lyons, 1925–8

Vauquelin de La Fresnaye, Jean, *Art Poétique*, ed. G. Pellissier, Paris, 1885

Virgil, *Opera*, Venice, 1480

In Publii Virgilii Maronis Bucolica doctissima atque exactissima Commen-

taria, with the commentary of J. Willichius, Paris, 1547

Georgicorum libri quatuor Pub. Virgilii Maronis Commentariis doctissimis illustrati, with the commentary of J. Willichius, Basel, 1539

Lamberti Hortensii . . . Enarrationes . . . in XII libros P. Virgilii Maronis Aeneidos . . . Adiecimus etiam Christophori Landini allegorias platonicas in XII libros Aeneidos Virgilianae olim conscriptas, Basel, 1577

Secondary Sources

Allen, D. C., *Mysteriously Meant: The Rediscovery of Pagan Symbolism and Allegorical Interpretation in the Renaissance*, Baltimore and London, 1970

Allen, J. B., *The Friar as Critic: Literary Attitudes in the Later Middle Ages*, Nashville, 1971

Augé-Chiquet, M., *La Vie, les idées et l'œuvre de Jean-Antoine de Baïf*, Paris, 1909, reprinted Geneva, 1969

Bergweiler, U., *Die Allegorie im Werk von Jean Lemaire de Belges*, Geneva, 1976

Bolgar, R. R., *The Classical Heritage and its Beneficiaries: from the Carolingian Age to the End of the Renaissance*, Cambridge, 1954; reprinted New York, 1964

Breen, Q., 'The Terms "loci communes" and "loci" in Melanchthon', *Church History*, 16, 1947, pp. 197–209

Castor, G., *Pléiade Poetics: A Study in Sixteenth-Century Thought and Terminology*, Cambridge, 1964

Cave, T., *The Cornucopian Text: Problems of Writing in the French Renaissance*, Oxford, 1979

ed., *Ronsard the Poet*, London, 1973

Coleman, D. G., *The Gallo-Roman Muse: Aspects of Roman Literary Tradition in Sixteenth-Century France*, Cambridge, 1979

Compagnon, A., *La Seconde Main, ou le travail de la citation*, Paris, 1979

Cottrell, R. D., *Sexuality/Textuality: A Study of the Fabric of Montaigne's 'Essais'*, Columbus, 1981

Curtius, E. R., *European Literature and the Latin Middle Ages*, trans. W. R. Trask, London, 1953

Demerson, Geneviève, 'Dorat, commentateur d'Homère', in R. Aulotte, ed., *Etudes seizièmistes offertes à Monsieur le Professeur V. L. Saulnier*, Geneva, 1980, pp. 223–34

Demerson, Guy, *La Mythologie classique dans l'œuvre lyrique de la 'Pléiade'*, Geneva, 1972

Eisenstein, E. L., *The Printing Press as an Agent of Change: Communications and Cultural Transformations in Early Modern Europe*, 2 vols., Cambridge, 1979

Emden, W. G. van, 'L'Histoire de *Pyrame et Thisbé* dans la mise en prose de l'*Ovide moralisé*: Texte du manuscrit Paris, B.N., f.fr. 137, avec variantes et commentaires', *Romania*, 94, 1973, pp. 29–56

'Sources de l'histoire de *Pyrame et Thisbe*, chez Baïf et Théophile de Viau', in *Mélanges de langue et de littérature médiévales offerts à Pierre Le Gentil*, Paris, 1973, pp. 869–79

Faral, E., *Les Arts poétiques du XIIᵉ et du XIIIᵉ siècle*, Paris, 1924

Ford, P., 'Ronsard and the Theme of Inspiration', in P. Bayley and D. G. Coleman, eds., *The Equilibrium of Wit: Essays for Odette de Mourgues*, Lexington, 1982, pp. 57–69

Gombrich, E. H., *Symbolic Images: Studies in the Art of the Renaissance*, London, 1972

Grafton, A., 'Teacher, Text and Pupil in the Renaissance Class-room: a Case Study from a Parisian College', *History of Universities*, 1, 1981, pp. 37–70

Helmich, W., *Die Allegorie im französischen Theater des 15. und 16. Jahrhunderts*, Tübingen, 1976

Henkel, M. D., 'Illustrierte Ausgaben von Ovids *Metamorphosen* im XV., XVI., und XVII. Jahrhundert', *Vorträge der Bibliothek Warburg*, 6, 1926–7, pp. 58–144

Higman, F. M., *Censorship and the Sorbonne: A Bibliographical Study of Books in French censured by the Faculty of Theology of the University of Paris, 1520–1551*, Geneva, 1979

Jehasse, J., *La Renaissance de la critique: l'essor de l'Humanisme érudit de 1560 à 1614*, Saint-Etienne, 1976

Jenkins, M. F. O., *Artful Eloquence: Jean Lemaire de Belges and the Rhetorical Tradition*, North Carolina Studies in the Romance Languages and Literatures, 217, Chapel Hill, 1980

Jodogne, P., 'Un recueil poétique de J. Lemaire en 1498', in F. Simone, ed., *Miscellanea di studi e ricerche sul Quattrocento francese*, Turin, 1967
Jean Lemaire de Belges, écrivain franco-bourguignon, Brussels, 1971

Joukovsky-Micha, F., *Poésie et mythologie au XVIᵉ siècle: Quelques mythes de l'inspiration chez les poètes de la Renaissance*, Paris, 1969

Jung, M. R., 'Poetria: Zur Dichtungstheorie des ausgehenden Mittelalters in Frankreich', *Vox Romanica*, 30, 1971, pp. 43–64

Kuntze, P., *Le Grand Olympe, eine alchimistische Deutung von Ovids Metamorphosen*, Halle, 1912

Lechner, J. M., *Renaissance Concepts of the Commonplaces*, New York, 1962

Lewis, C. T. and Short, C., *A Latin Dictionary*, Oxford, 1951

Leykauff, A., *François Habert und seine Übersetzung der Metamorphosen Ovids*, Munich, 1904

Lubac, H. de, *Exégèse médiévale: les quatre sens de l'Ecriture*, 4 vols., Paris, 1959–64

McFarlane, I. D., 'Reflections on Ravisius Textor's *Specimen Epithetorum*', in R. R. Bolgar, ed., *Classical Influences on European Culture AD 1500–1700*, Oxford, 1976, pp. 81–90

McKinley, M. B., *Words in a Corner: Studies in Montaigne's Latin Quotations*, Lexington, 1981

Margolin, J. C., 'Erasme, prince des bergers', *Bibliothèque d'Humanisme et Renaissance*, 29, 1967, pp. 407–42

Bibliography

Mathieu-Castellani, G., *Mythes de l'Eros baroque*, Paris, 1981

Moss, A., *Ovid in Renaissance France: A Survey of the Latin Editions of Ovid and Commentaries printed in France before 1600*, London, 1982

Nolhac, P. de, *Ronsard et l'humanisme*, Paris, 1921

Ong, W. J., *Rhetoric, Romance and Technology: Studies in the Interaction of Expression and Culture*, New York, 1971

Panofsky, E., *Renaissance and Renascences in Western Art*, 2nd edn, Stockholm, 1965

Pinget, R., *L'Apocryphe*, Paris, 1980

Py, A., *Ronsard*, Paris, 1972

Quadlbauer, F., *Die antike Theorie der Genera Dicendi im lateinischen Mittelalter*, Vienna, 1962

Quainton, M., *Ronsard's Ordered Chaos: Visions of Flux and Stability in the Poetry of Pierre de Ronsard*, Manchester, 1980

Rigolot, F., *Poétique et onomastique: L'exemple de la Renaissance*, Geneva, 1977

Screech, M. A., *Rabelais*, London, 1979

Seznec, J., *La Survivance des dieux antiques*, Studies of the Warburg Institute, 11, London, 1940, 2nd edn, Paris, 1981, trans. B. F. Sessions, New York, 1961

Sharratt, P., 'Ronsard et Pindare: un écho de la voix de Dorat', *Bibliothèque d'Humanisme et Renaissance*, 39, 1977, pp. 97–114

Silver, I., *The Intellectual Evolution of Ronsard*, 2 vols., St Louis, 1969, 1973

Sonnino, L. A., *A Handbook to Sixteenth-Century Rhetoric*, London, 1968

Stone, D., 'The Sixteenth Century and Antiquity: a Case Study', in B. C. Bowen, ed., *The French Renaissance Mind: Studies presented to W. G. Moore, L'Esprit Créateur*, xvi, 4, Lawrence, Kansas, 1976, pp. 37–47

Strubel, A., '*Allegoria in factis* et *Allegoria in verbis*', *Poétique*, 23, 1975, pp. 342–57

Trinkaus, C., *In Our Image and Likeness: Humanity and Divinity in Italian Humanist Thought*, 2 vols., London, 1970

Trousson, R., *Thèmes et mythes: Questions de méthode*, Brussels, 1981

Tuve, R., *Allegorical Imagery: Some Mediaeval Books and their Posterity*, Princeton, 1966

Valéry, P., *Poésies*, Paris, 1956

Yeats, W. B., *Collected Poems*, London, 1955

Zerner, H., *Ecole de Fontainebleau: Gravures*, Paris, 1969

INDEX